FOUNDATIONS OF INDIAN CULTURE

VOLUME II

FOUNDATIONS OF
INDIAN CULTURE

VOLUME II

Dimensions of Ancient Indian
Social History

G. C. PANDE

MOTILAL BANARSIDASS PUBLISHERS
PRIVATE LIMITED • DELHI

Reprint : Delhi; 1995, 2005, 2007
Second Edition : Delhi, 1990
First Edition : Delhi, 1984

ISBN: 978-81-208-0711-2 (Vol. II)
ISBN: 978-81-208-0712-9 (Set)

MOTILAL BANARSIDASS
41 U.A. Bungalow Road, Jawahar Nagar, Delhi 110 007
8 Mahalaxmi Chamber, 22 Bhulabhai Desai Road, Mumbai 400 026
203 Royapettah High Road, Mylapore, Chennai 600 004
236, 9th Main III Block, Jayanagar, Bangalore 560 011
Sanas Plaza, 1302 Baji Rao Road, Pune 411 002
8 Camac Street, Kolkata 700 017
Ashok Rajpath, Patna 800 004
Chowk, Varanasi 221 001

Printed in India

BY JAINENDRA PRAKASH JAIN AT SHRI JAINENDRA PRESS,
A-45 NARAINA, PHASE-I, NEW DELHI 110 028
AND PUBLISHED BY NARENDRA PRAKASH JAIN FOR
MOTILAL BANARSIDASS PUBLISHERS PRIVATE LIMITED,
BUNGALOW ROAD, DELHI 110 007

Preface

The search for the historical explanation of human life and thought has led historians to the attempt to go beyond the surface happenings of short duration to analyse the deeper structures of longer duration. These have been sought to be identified as economic or social or even geographical. Many of these formulations are vitiated by conscious or unconscious assumptions of a positivistic character. Social formations are not like natural formations given independently of the subject. They are in fact subjective-objective in character. As a consequence social formations and idea formations can not really be separated. Being and thought are two inevitably co-present dimensions. Despite this undeniable quality of cultural factors it is common now-a-days to find many historians emphasizing their social origins exclusively. It may be said that ideas do not simply spring from the head like 'Minerva in panoply' but that they derive from a historically given state of social being. But this social being itself is discernible only through reflection over experience and, as such, is related to the self-awareness of the subject. In particular the historian can not discover social formations except as revealed in a historical record which is directly expressive of some consciousness. Thus, despite the radical significance of social being, it has to be reached and understood in terms of a tradition of social experience and awareness. In a profound sense, thus, while social structures underlie surface events, they are themselves inwardly constituted by a historical world of ideas. '*Manopubbaṅgamā dhammā*', all phenomena presuppose the mind.

The present work attempts to analyse the social and idealional foundations of Indian culture. This second part of the work concentrates on the analysis of the social world which is presupposed by the intellectual and symbolic formulations of the Indian tradition. The analysis of the social world, however, involves not merely the appraisal of such objective factors as geography and economy but the delineation of the awareness within which the apperception of such factors took place. In dealing with the social tradition its historicity is sought in the present work to be placed by the side of that perennial ideality which constitutes its constant inspiration. Indian society is not sought to be reconstructed here merely as a museum-model from the scrap-heap of time but as forms expressive of ideas and values, as a dialectically developing theme for commentary. The notions of *deśa-kāla*, *samyagājīva* and *svadharma* may be said to have constituted the basic matrix of social action presupposed by the life of contemplation and symbolic expression in Indian culture.

Apart from the publishers and printers I am thankful to Dr. S.P. Gupta, Dr. S.K. Gupta, Dr. Umesh Chattopadhyaya, Dr. L.M. Dubey and Sri A.P. Ojha for the help they have rendered me in the publication of this book.

Allahabad G. C. Pande
August 17, 1983

Contents

Introduction

The Conception of Social History

SOCIAL history has been "defined negatively as the history of a people with the politics left out." It concentrates on the daily life of the inhabitants of the land in past ages. The appeal of such history is basically imaginative and lies in the "desire to feel the reality of life in the past, to be familiar with 'the chronicle of wasted time' for the sake of 'ladies dead and lovely knights'.[1]"

There is much to commend such a romantic conception of social history but the deeper question of what determines the social process and constitutes its relationship to human nature as a whole cannot be avoided by the historian. It has been justly said that "the social or societal aspects of man's being cannot be separated from the other aspects of his being, except at the cost of tautology or extreme trivialization."[2] But this concept of the history of society as a whole corresponding to the whole being of man suffers from a philosophically 'sociocentric' assumption about man. Whether man is a transcendent spirit or the product of material forces, whether human nature is perennial or historical, are disputed questions and they have fateful consequences for the conception of society and social history.

Ideational Foundations of Society and their Historicity

It is difficult to think of the analytical categories of the social historian in abstraction from the 'real' categories in terms of which human consciousness *historically* articulates itself.[3] It would be perilous for the historian to disregard the conceptual framework implicit or explicit in any historically given social consciousness. Whether its assumptions were right or wrong, would be undecidable except in the light of social science theory which unfortunately has not yet reached agreement on the important issues. With respect to ancient India, thus, what is important is not whether the social historian is an idealist or a materialist, but whether he is able to represent the historical articulations of ancient Indian social self-consciousness.[4] The task of analysing this consciousness and tracing it to its causal roots is undoubtedly important though difficult. While the role of external factors and accidents cannot be gainsaid, it is the inner dialectic of ideas that gives rational intelligibility to social changes. Insofar as human society is a moral order, it cannot but be rooted in ideas and its essential history must be constituted by the dialectic of ideas. The dialectic, however, does not have to be conceived as a purely logical process. It appears to be rather a psychological process where instinctive seeking and practical experience, rational reflection and spiritual understanding mingle and clash. *Praxis* (*Vyavahāra*) and constructs (*Vikalpa*) are interdependent dimensions of the social process.[4a] And behind these, one may descry the seeking for self-knowledge and the self-expressiveness of consciousness.

The Analysis of Social Consciousness in the Indian Tradition

It is a cardinal principle of the Indian tradition that although man's true identity is spiritual and transcendental and can be realized only inwardly in terms of his relationship to God or the Absolute, for practical purposes he acquires an identity in psycho-physical and social terms. Since such an empirical identity rests on the mis-identification of the self with empirical objects like the body, mind and social position, it is universally believed to rest on *Avidyā*, i.e. instinctive ignorance.[5] The empirical objects with which man identifies himself and which, serving as his inner and outer possessions, give him the character of a distinctive natural, social and psychic being are called his adjuncts or *Upādhi* in *Vedanta*. If the soul or transcendental consciousness is the essential part of man's being, *Upadhi* is its 'accidental' part. Self-identification with internal and external *Upadhis* produces the sense of 'I' and 'mine', which is called *abhimāna.* Endowed with *abhimana*, man becomes a socio-spiritual being, at once subjective and objective. The character of his *abhimana* becomes the basis of his social and ritual eligibility or *adhikāra.*[6] *Upādhi*, *abhimāna* and *adhikāra* together determine the social identity of man.[7]

Subjective-Objective Character of Social Consciousness

Race and kinship, geographical, historical and social location, the sense of ethos and ideals may be mentioned as some of the subjective-objective constituents which thus determine social identity. They function in and through subjectivity as apparently given objects of its sense of being, owning and belonging. The empirical self-consciousness, on the one hand, locates itself in a world of space, time and social relations; on the other, it projects an ideal image of itself beyond its actual constraints, into the future or eternity. In its involvement in action or history, humanity is thus guided by a double image of itself, one of its actuality and another of its ideality.[8] Action is oriented towards the *Purusarthas* and carried on within the constraints of situation and eligibility. The way in which a people identify the stable conditions of their actual life and their permanent ideals, also serves to identify their historical being. In seeking to discover what constitutes the identity of a people, thus, it is necessary for a historian to consider their own articulation of their being. Actual geographical conditions may function as causal factors, but what the people think of their geography enters into their image of themselves. The same is true of historical conditions. As to society and ethos, it would be hard to draw any ultimately significant distinction between their being and consciousness since they subsist within the empirical self-consciousness which is subjective-objective.

Ancient Indian Historical Reality and the Non-racial Basis of Indian Society

Although the distinction between Indians and foreigners was clearly recognised from ancient times by Indians as well as foreigners, the basis of this distinction was not racial awareness but rather the distinctive character of the Indian ethos. Race consciousness in the modern sense attaching itself to colour or physical type was never a part of the Indian tradition. It is true that modern European writers advanced the supposition that the Aryan race entered India with a strong race and colour consciousness, that the *Ṛgveda* records the struggle between the Aryans and the native *dasas* who were snub-nosed and black-skinned and that the *Varṇa* system arose out of this colour consciousness.[9] This hypothesis has been uncritically accepted and repeated by modern Indian authors also. The fact is that in the *Ṛgveda-Samhita* 'Arya' is used in the sense of a pious householder.[10] *Dasa* and *dasyu* have been shown by Professor Chattopadhyaya to refer to demons rather than to native Indians.[11] When it is said in the *Ṛgveda*, "I bestowed land on the *Arya*, I gave rain to the munificent mortal,"[12] it is clear that the *Arya* is equated to the mortal who gives. The ancient commentators do not see any ethnic sense in either *Arya* or *Dasa*. In later times, *Arya* clearly came to mean noble. *Arya* was now contrasted with *mleccha* and the sense was of a contrast between the cultured and the barbarian. In the *Dharma Sutras* and Manu, we meet with the term *Aryavarta*, the homeland of the Aryans, in an attempt to indicate a reference group in terms of location. But it is clearly understood that what makes the people of *Aryavarta Arya* is their ethos, not their location.

Tribe and Clan replaced by Varṇa and Jāti as Social Constituents

The fact is that the Pan-Indian *Varṇa* system effectively obliterated the primitive identities of race and tribe. The people of India came to realize their social identity in terms of *Varṇa* and *Jāti*, not in terms of races and tribes. Tribes like the Niṣādas or Kirātas, Cāṇḍālas or Paulkasas, Śabaras or Pulindas, Kaivartas or Khasas all found a place within the *Jātis*. If Kiratas or Nisadas found a low place in the *Varṇa* hierarchy, that was because their mode of life was regarded as ritually unclean, principally because of its connection with hunting or its by-products, trapping or fishing or similar occupations dependent on the killing of life or the products of such killing. The hierarchy was socio-ethical and ritual, not ethnic. Belonging or not belonging to the *Varṇa* system distinguished the Indian from the foreigner in ancient times. In fact, the assimilation of invading foreigners like the Greeks was accomplished by assigning to them a place in the *Jati* system.

The word *jana* has been translated as clan or tribe.[13] Similarly the word *gotra* too has been interpreted as clan or tribe. Here again these interpretations are far from being definitive. *Jana* came to have quite early the sense of people. 'Bhārata jana' thus would mean the people ruled by the family of the Bharatas. This is how the Puranic tradition and commentators would interpret them. Even if *Jana* meant a clan at one time, there is no doubt that the clans became transformed into settlements or *Janapadas.* We might recall how out of the 360 clans or *gentes* of ancient Attica, Cleisthenes created the ten territorial tribes of Athens. In India too, it was only in the republican *Janapadas* that the clan element survived longest. Imperialistic monarchy as well as the *Varna* system both served to suppress clan identities. And this process was already far advanced in the later Vedic age. Even in the early Vedic age, Indra, Mitra and Varuna, the divine prototypes of earthly kings, do not present the image of popular clan leaders. They are rather exalted sovereigns whose sway extends over all the people. This conception could not but correspond to actually held ideals and aspirations. Even in the context of elective kingship, it is the people or *Viśah* who are mentioned rather than the clan or *Jana.*

As for *gotra* which had to be compulsorily mentioned in the performance of ritual or marriage, whatever its original meaning,[14] it became increasingly far removed from any real kinship. Even originally, the *gotra* was relevant primarily for the Brahmanas. Latterly, the other castes claimed the *gotras* of their priest.[15] The *gotra* was a reminder of one's supposed descent from an ancient seer and served to exclude one's marriage within the same *gotra.* As an identifier, it functioned wholly within the *varṇa.*

Traditional Formulation of Social Identity

The attempt to think of the Indian people in terms of a superimposition of races with different physical types is not only modern but palpably unsatisfactory. The mixture of physical types in the Indus civilization has been established to have been similar to what obtains in the Punjab now.[16] Thus it is not possible to attribute the Indus civilization to any particular race conceived as a distinctive physical type. Nor can the people of the Indus civilization be linguistically defined on present evidence. Nor indeed is anything definitely known about the so-called Aryan migration to India. Thus the hypothetical reconstruction of pre-classical history in terms of superimposed ethnic ways has little to recommend it. On the other hand, from classical times the traditional sense of social identity was clearly tied up with a distinctive socio-cultural ethos. This ethos or dharma was then connected with geography through the location of holy places and regions where religious ritual could be practised to special advantage. Thus in recalling one's identity in *Sankalpa-mantras*, one has to think of the *gotra* as also the region within India where the rite is to be performed. In the *Upanisads*, we find kings like Janaka and Ajatasatru identified by their *Janapadas* while sages and students are qualified by their *gotras*. Asoka speaks of himself as belonging to Magadha and ruling over Jambudvipa. In the *Divyavadana*, he is made to refer to himself as *Ksattriya* Śāba, the minister of Gupta emperor Candragupta II, refers to himself as *Kautsa* and *Pāṭaliputraka*.

The traditional sense of social identity (*abhimāna*), thus, although associated primarily with Varnasrama dharma (*Varṇāśramādyabhimāna*) was secondarily associated with supposed kinship groups like the *gotra* and with territorial regions or *Jana-padas*. It is the *Varṇādyabhimāna* which primarily underlay social and ritual rights and obligations, *adhikāra*. It was never connected with race nor even with language, even though the primacy and ritual privilege of Sanskrit were taken for granted and the diversity of spoken tongues noted as a fact.

References

1. Trevelyan, *Illustrated English Social History*, Vol. I, pp. 9-13.
2. Hobsbaum in *Historical Studies Today* (ed. by Felix Gilbert and Stephen R. Graubard), p. 6.
3. Cf. 'The Nature of Social Categories', paper presented by the author at the International Symposium on Philosophical Theory and Social Reality held at the Nehru Memorial Museum, New Delhi, 18th Jan. 22nd Jan. 1982,
4. Cf. R. S. Sharma, 'Historiography of Ancient Indian Social Order' in *Historians of India, Pākistan and Ceylon*, p. 113.

4a. Cf. Kalakowski, *Main Currents of Marxism*, Vol. III, pp. 237-38, 271.

5. See e.g. Śaṅkara's celebrated *adhyāsa-bhāṣya* on the *Vedāntasūtras*.
6. The concept is specially explained in *Mīmāṁsā*.
7. Cf. *Pañcadaśī*, 9.100-01. Three 'selves' are distinguished—social, psycho-physical and real—*Ib.* 12-39.
8. Cf. "The Nature of Social Categories' referred to above.
9. Muir, *Original Sanskrit Texts*, Vol. II, pp. 359 ff.
10. e.g. Sayana on R. 6.22.10; 7.8.3.1 etc.
11. *Studies*, Vol. I, pp. 206 ff.
12. *R.* 4.26.2
13. See *Vedic Index*.
14. Some have surmised a totemic origin for the *Gotras*. Traditionally while eighty thousand were seers who were celebate, eight produced children. *Gotra* refers to their lineage, *Mahabhasya* ad Panini 4.1.79. Cf. Kosambi, *JBBRAS*, 1946.
15. Medhatithi ad *Manu* 3.5 cf. Tod, *Annals*, Vol. I, p. 99
16. See below.

1

Geographical Identity

Expansion of the Geographical Horizon

The geomorphic evolution of India as a separate entity was initiated and completed with the Tertiary through the newly formed seas and the rising mountains. The great plains of north India were formed more recently and gradually by the alluvial deposits of rivers. It is interesting to notice that Arrian[1] and Alberuni[2] express a similar opinion and anticipate the conclusions of modern science. The peninsula and the Himalayas are the other two main geomorphic divisions in India. Of these, the oldest is the peninsula with its topography rendered open and senile by the repetition of numberless geological cycles. The Himalayas present a contrasted relief, 'youthful and highly differentiated'. The Indo-Gangetic Plain is more recent than both, stretching with vast monotony and a surface formed gradually through aggradational processes.[3] It has undergone considerable climatic changes, even in historical times. The tendency towards the drying up of the soil and deforestation made this region habitable only during the past few thousand years.

It is in the Indus Valley in the 3rd millennium B.C. that civilized habitation is first definitely noticeable in India. The climate of Sind and Baluchistan could not be as dry then as now.[4] There must have been enough forests in Sind to provide fuel for baking millions of bricks and rainfall in Baluchistan to make worthwhile the construction of stone-dams to store it. By the time of Alexander, however, lower Sind[5] and Baluchistan[6] had become arid. It should be noted that even the desert of Rajputana was produced within historical times by the gradual triumph of natural aridity over ancient rivers flowing through the region.[7] The Sarasvatī before its final drying up between the 11th and the 13th centuries flowed to the Rann of Kutch which was a fairly deep gulf till the 9th century A.D., the river drying up partly because of the eastward diversion of the Yamunā and partly because of the westward diversion of the Sutlej.[8]

It is generally believed that civilized habitation spread over the Indo-Gangetic valley as a result of Aryan colonization and expansion during the second millennium B.C. and the first half of the first millennium. The geographical horizon of the early Vedic Age extended from Kabulistan in the west to the Yamunā and the Gaṅgā in the east.[9] The region from Sindh to Sarasvatī has sometimes been identified as Saptasindhu. By the later Vedic age, the eastern horizon had receded as far back as Bihar,[10] bringing the Gangetic region, upper and middle, within the Aryan fold which thus moved beyond the Madhyadeśa into the Prācya. Videgha Māthava was apparently the first to pioneer across the Sadānirā into the land which later came to be known by his name, Videha, and which was thus reclaimed from marsh.[11] Fire, which devastated forests, and the plough driven by oxen proved the most valuable allies in this expansion of civilized habitation; the drying up of the riparian soil of Hindustan must have been another factor.[12] It has also been suggested that the use of iron for axes and ploughs was another factor in the Aryan expansion into the lower Gangetic valley.

Tradition associates the name of Agastya with the crossing of the "thousand-peaked"[13] Vindhyas towards the south where he was hailed as the giver of civilization. Vālmīki's *Rāmāyaṇa* recalls the days when some Aryan sages and brave princes were pioneering into the south. It suggests that Aryan expansion southwards from north-eastern India tended to follow a westerly route across central India, from Prayaga to Chitrakūta and thence to Pañcavaṭī near Nasik in the great Daṇḍaka forest, and then to Kiṣkindhā, now placed near Hampi.[14] The easterly route to the south finds mention in Kālidasa;[15] it goes from Vaṅga to Utkala and then to Kaliṅga and further south. Samudragupta, however, had proceeded across southern Kośala and Mahākāntāra to the eastern coast.

It may be recalled that archaeologically it was through the Malwa gap that the influence of the Post-Harappan chalcolithic phase radiated to the Deccan. By the 4th century B.C., the whole of the South was fully known.[16]

Nevertheless, the forest continued to be more prominent in the Deccan and the South than in the northern plain except possibly for its eastern end. A forest belt extended on the lower side of the Madhyadeśa, from the Sarasvatī to the Yamunā, viz. Kāmyaka, Dvaita, and Khāṇḍava. Further east lay Naimiṣāraṇya and Kālakavana. Another and larger forest belt separated Āryāvarta from Dakṣiṇāpatha viz. Kaliṅgāraṇya, Mahākāntāra, Vindhyāṭavī and Daṇḍakāraṇya. Hsuan Chwang speaks of forests between the Indus and the Saurastra. The forests of the Himalayas were well known and extended deep into the *tarai* at one time. The Sālavana of the Mallas is supposed to have been part of the *tarai*.

Trditional Norm : "*Jambūdvipe bharatakhaṇḍe*"

All Hindu ritual has to be preceded by a resolve (*Saṁkalpa*) in which one recalls one's location in space and time. The formula which has been current for a long time refers to the region to which one belongs as Jambūdvīpa, Bharatakhaṇḍa or Bhāratavarṣa and Kumārikā-khaṇḍa. The first of these, Jambūdvīpa, is of great antiquity. Aśoka uses it to designate the realm over which he ruled.[17] According to Buddhist tradition, Jambūdvīpa lay to the south of Meru and the Himalayas are located in it. There are three ranges of three mountains each to the north and beyond them is the situation of Himavan.[18] Beyond it is the lake Anavatapta and beyond that the Gandhamādana mountain. From the lake emerge the four rivers---Gaṅgā, Sindhu, Sītā and Vakṣu.[19] The Jambu tree also grows there. The shape of Jambūdvīpa is like that of a cart (*Śakaṭākṛti*). Its three sides are of two thousand *yojanas* while the fourth, southern side, gets shortened to a mere three and a half yojanas.[20] The significance of Jambūdvīpa lay in the fact that Buddhas and Cakkavattīs could be born only there. Buddha held that the people of Jambūdvīpa excelled in "courage, mindfulness and religious life."[21]

In the *Dīgha*, we find the Brāhmaṇa minister Mahāgovinda dividing the earth into seven equal parts viz. Kaliṅga, Asmaka, Avanti, Sovīra, Videha, Aṅga and Kāsi.[22] This list obviously takes into account only the north-east and the Deccan. The *Aṅguttara* list of sixteen *mahājanapadas* is well-known and shows a much wider horizon of the early sixth century B.C.

The Jain conception of Jambūdvīpa is a wider one. It includes Bhārata as one of its seven regions. The other six are Hemavata, Hari, Videha, Rāmyaka, Hiraṇyavata and Erāvata. They are separated by six mountain ranges—Himavat, Mahahimavat, Nisadha, Nīla, Rukmin and Śikharin. Bhārata is divided into six regions. Similiarly, the Aryan *janapadas* where alone the *Tīrthaṅkaras* and *Cakravartins* are born are listed as twentyfive and half, the half being of Kekaya[23].

The *Purāṇas* divide the earth into seven *dvīpas*, Jambūdvīpa being the central one[24] Jambūdvīpa, again, is divided into nine *Varṣas* and Bhārata is one of them, stretching from the Himalayas to the sea[25] Bhāratavarṣa was again divided into nine *dvīpas* and Kumārīdvīpa was one of them[26]. Of the seven *dvīpas* and nine *Varṣas*, it is difficult to identify any with certainty except Jambūdvīpa and Bhāratavarṣa. As for the nine *dvīpas* among which Kumārīdvīpa is included, the identification of some at least does not seem improbable but many divergent identifications have been proposed[27]. Jambūdvīpa, Bhāratavarṣa and Kumārīdvīpa represent three different conceptions of India in diminishing areas as it were. Jambūdvīpa includes lands to the north of the Himalayas and calls them *Varṣas*. One is tempted to think that this awareness of Central Asia may belong to the days of the Mauryan and Kuṣāna empires. India certainly was called Jambūdvīpa in Mauryan times and the Kuṣāṇa empire had a fair Central Asian component. Nevertheless if we examine the *Varṣas* from Kiṁpuruṣa to Uttara Kuru, we can only be disappointed. The Purāṇic *Varṣas* do not evince any real knowledge of Central Asian lands.[28] Perhaps it is not surprising if we recall that it is the Buddhists rather than the Brāhmaṇas who undertook journeys in Central Asia. The Brahmanical redactors of the *Purāṇas* appear to rely more on imagination than observation as far as lands beyond the Himalayas are concerned.

Bhāratavarsa owed its name to the legendary name of Bharata and was defined as the land north of the ocean and south of the Himalayas—"*Uttaram yat samudrasya himādreś-caiva dakṣiṇam. Varṣam tad Bhāratam nāma Bhāratī yatra santatiḥ.*[29]" The Himalayas were recognised to have a number of ranges. The *Mahābhārata* speaks of three ranges of the Himalayas—Bahirgiri, Upagiri and Antargiri.[30] Described as Devatātma[31], the multiple Himalayan ranges constituted the northern frontier. Bindusara was the northern-most point and it was believed that it was here that the celestial Gaṅgā reached the earth first and divided itself into seven streams. Three of these streams flowed to the east, viz. Nalinī, Hrādinī and Pāvanī. Three flowed to the west viz. Sītā, Vakṣu and Sindhu. The seventh stream or Bhāgīrathī flowed to the south.[32]

The shape of Bhārata was often described as being similar to that of a tortoise lying outspread and facing eastwards, sometimes as being like that of a bow, and very rarely triangular.[33] Bhārata is further described as consisting of nine islands[34]. Even if these islands are difficult to locate, it is in any case clear that the commercial and colonising activities of the Indians towards the south-east helped to give the Puranas some conception of 'Greater India'. If Jambūdvīpa included Central Asian territories, Bhāratavarṣa seems to include south and south-east Asian territories. Perhaps this image of India reflects the conditions of the Gupta period.

Kumārīdvīpa is the ninth of the *dvīpas* included in Bhāratavarṣa. It is said to extend from Kumārī or Cape Comorin to the source of the Gaṅgā and is said to have an extent of one thousand *yojanas*[35]. The meanings of the words *varṣa* and *dvīpa* are not clear and have been debated. They have the sense of well-demarcated geographical regions rather than of "continent" or island' in the usual sense[36].

At the same time Bhāratavarṣa and Kumārīdvīpa were conceived as cultural areas with religious significance; even the Buddhists had noted that beyond India, one did not find the system of four *Varṇas*[37], and that the *Buddhas* and *Cakravartins* could be born only in India. The Jainas agreed with this. The *Purāṇas* hold the same opinion. India is distinguished by the *Cāturvarnya* and is the only place where the proper practice of religion is possible. The prevalence of *Varṇāśramadharma* makes the performance of *svadharma* possible. Hence Bhārata alone is *karmabhumi.* In other countries *bhoga* is possible, but not *karman,* for without *adhikāra, karman* is not possible.[38] Nor can the path of emancipation be trodden without treading that of *karman.* The *saṁkalpa-mantra* only reminds one of the obligations to which one is heir by virtue of being located in Bhāratvarṣa or Kumārīdvīpa and also of the eligibility conferred upon him by that location in the context of moral and religious life. Bhārata being *karmabhūmi,* it is only fitting that in the performance of *karman,* one should remember the privilege of belonging to it and the obligation which that implies.

If we reflect over this situation, we would perceive that as 'geocultural' regions Bhārata or Kumārīdvīpa are bounded by natural and cultural frontiers in a complementary manner. The Himalayas and the sea were natural frontiers but in the north-west and the north-east, especially in the north-west, the frontiers were not so clear as far as natural frontiers went. Culturally, the north-west of India merged into the land of the Yavanas, the north-east into that of the Kirātas. Both of these regions were of the Mlecchas, i.e. of those who did not use Sanskrit or follow the fourfold order.

Boundaries and Divisions : Geopolitical and Geocultural

Traditionally, India was virtually conceived as the South Asian subcontinent. Described as *devatātmā,* the Himalayas with their three ranges constituted the northern frontier which was continued in the north-west by the Hindukush, though sometimes the Oxus was regarded as the limit of 'imperial' conquest[39]. The trans-Indus region, however, was one of dispute between Iranian and Indian cultures in older days. The Indian cultural region was held in classical times to be characterized by the four castes which did not obtain among the peoples who dwelt on the frontiers. The *tīrthas* distributed all over hallowed the Indian territories.

Politically, the whole of India was regarded as the sphere of 'universal monarchy' – *cakravarti ksetra*[40]. This 'Empire' was not held to be opposed to regional autonomy, i.e. to the continuance of subordinate governments in the principal regions or *janapadas*. This notion of Indian unity articulated into the diversity of *janapadas* tended to produce an unstable equilibrium with the result that there was a constant alternation between unity and disunity. The growth of modern nationalism hopefully should alter this situation permanently, though the forces of sub-national parochialism and of trans-national ideologies naturally stand as challenges.

The *janapadas* were originally 'tribal settlements' which came to have a purely territorial significance in course of time[41]. The *janapada* lists in the Puranas are traditional in character and were apparently finalised in early classical times.[42] The growth of regional dynasties and dialects became pronounced after the 9th century and the modern linguistic regions emerged in the mediaeval period. It is, however, only in the recent past that linguistic areas have been considered as a proper basis for the organisation of states. Parochial self-interest and ideology have also tended to project themselves as a plea for 'federalism'. Tradition, however, upholds the primacy of an all India state and *koine*.

Professor Toynbee has distinguished between a conductive 'cultural threshold' (*limen*) and an insulating 'military frontier, (*limes*).[43] In the ancient period, the expansion of Indian culture into Central Asia took place along the routes which led from Kasmira and Gandhara northwards. Although the Iranians had earlier pushed up to the Indus, the Mauryas succeeded in realizing the ideal of the *Cakravarti-ksetra* and including the trans-Indus Indian cultural regions within an Indian empire. In the post-Mauryan age, however, there was a manifest failure to hold the line of the Hindukush and waves of military incursion from Central Asia swept over the Uttarapatha, the Madhyadesa and part of Aparanta. Nevertheless, the Yavanas, Śakas and Kusanas were culturally assimilated so that the vast Kusana empire straddling across the Hindukush helped the expansion of Indian culture in Central Asia. The expansion of Islamic and Chinese influences in Central Asia in the 8th and 9th centuries put an end to Indian influences in that region. From the 11th century, the trans-Indus region was effectively lost culturally as well as politically, though at the political level the Moghals regained the frontier of the Hindukush. It was still a conductive cultural threshold but India was wholly at the receiving end. The last phase of Indian cultural influence crossing into Central Asia ceased with the Turkish conquest of Bihar when the ties with Tibet snapped.

British conquest fixed a military frontier in the northwest in the region of ancient Gandhara and defined a frontier in the north. The rise of Afghan nationalism, the destruction of nomadism in Central Asia, the political and military dominance of communism throughout Central Asia including Sinkiang and Tibet, and the creation of Pakistan, have brought back a geopolitical situation which is partly reminiscent of the days when the Shahi kingdom stood between Aryavarta and the forces of Islam, though in another sense a wholly unprecedented situation has been created where even the Himalayas have ceased to be a wholly dependable line of defence.

Spate has proposed to divide India from the standpoint of historical geography into three regions[44]—Indus valley, Hindustan, and the Peninsula south of the Narbada; and then to further sub-divide these regions into several nuclear and refuge areas. The former represents the major agricultural areas, for the most part alluvial, while the latter are marginal to them and provide cover by desert or forest. Among the nuclear areas are Gandhara, Sapta-Sindhu, Kuruksetra, Pancala, Saurastra, Malwa, Audh, Magadha, Kalinga, Andhra, Cola, Pandya land and Kerala. Refuge areas are Rajputana, Gondwana, Bastar and Rajmahal hills. The main passage from the north to the south is provided by Malwa. Just as in the North, foreign influence entering from the north-west proceeds in diminishing ripples southeastwards, so a similar pattern is repeated in the south where

Maharastra has assimilated more easily while resistance has stiffened further south and east. Both in the North and South, invading influences have tended to follow the highways and to be attracted to nuclear areas, setting up cultural back-washes in the marginal refuge areas which were less accessible.

In fact, the distinction between 'nuclear' and 'refuge' areas is paralleled by the ancient distinction between '*madhyadeśa*' and '*pratyanta*', 'central region' and 'marginal region'. But Spate thinks too exclusively of invasions whereas expansions from the central areas towards marginal areas have also been an equally significant tendency. Besides, with the development of sea power, the pattern of foreign conquest altered completely in modern times, just as the development of air-power and tele-communication has altered the problem of military as well as cultural frontiers. Neverthless Spate has succeeded in bringing out some permanent geopolitical factors underlying the historical geography of India.

Ancient Divisions and Janapadas :

Already in the *Atharva Veda* (XIX, 17.1-9) and the *Aitareya Brāhmaṇa* (VIII. 14) India is divided into five regions—the four quarters and the middle. Asoka's empire has also been supposed to have been similarly divided into five main regions. The *Vāyu Purāṇa* and Rajasekhara follow a similar fivefold division. It is also implicit in the *Raghuvaṁśa*. The *Mbh.* describes *digvijaya* in the four quarters, the *Rāmāyana* similarly the search for Sita. Samudragupta has a virtual threefold divison—the Aryavarta, the Daksinapatha, and the Pratyantas. The *Mārkandeya Purāna* has a sevenfold division, adding the *Vindhyanivāsinah* and the *Parvatāśrayiṇaḥ* to the usual five. The same Purana as well as Varāhamihira have another ninefold division which adds to the four quarters, the four intermediate quarters too. The mistaken notion that the shape of India resembles that of a tortoise vitiates the actual assignment of several regions to their correct direction in this ninefold division. Apart from this, despite its formal character, the fivefold division has a ready application in reality.

In these ancient descriptions, the Indus Valley is generally divided into two, the Punjab along with eastern Afghanistan and Kasmira forming the Northern Route 'or North' (*Uttarāpatha or Udīcya*) while Sindh and Baluchistan are assigned to 'Western India'. This has some historical justification too. As Alberuni says, to reach Sindh "We start from the country of Nimroz, i.e. the country of Sijistan, whilst marching to Hind or India proper we start from the side of Kabul[45]". Sindh lies between two deserts and looks out to the sea while Punjab lies on the great Northern Highway which ran from Vahlika and Gandhara to Madhyadesa and Magadha. From protohistoric days, a commercial and maritime destiny has called to Sindh while the Punjabi is naturally a farmer and a soldier.

'Hindustan' corresponds more or less to the Aryavarta of the ancients. Manu defined Aryavarta virtually as northern India—the area from sea to sea between the two mountains.[46]

This represents the later extended definition with which may be contrasted the earlier one of Bodhāyaṇa—*Prāgadarśanāt pratyak kālakavanād dakṣiṇena himavantam udak pāriyātrum etad āryāvartaṁ tasmin ya ācārah sa pramāṇam. Gaṅgāyamunayor antaram ityeke.*[47] Patañjali restricted Āryāvarta to the west of Kālakavana.[48] Āryāvarta or Hindustan as conceived by Manu was generally divided into three, viz. Madhyadeśa or the region which extended from Vinaśana to Prayaga where the river Sarasvati was lost, Pracya or eastern India which extended up to the sea and Aparanta or western India which included Malwa and Gujarat.

India south of the Vindhyas, called Daksinapatha, was sometimes divided into the eastern Deccan, the south, and the western Deccan, as in the *Brhatsamhita* of Varahamihira.[49] Usually, however, the Daksinapatha was taken as a unity e.g. in the Digvijayas of Raghu and Samudragupta.

The Uttarapatha, Madhyadeśa, Pracya, Daksinapatha and Praticya or Aparanta, thus, represent the five principal divisions of India as recognised in ancient times. In these, the river valleys and the sea-coasts represented the nuclear areas where economic prosperity born of agriculture and trade, political power, and civilized urban life teemed and progressed. Mountain ranges especially the Himalayas and the Vindhyas, and the great desert to the west of the Aravali provided the main refuge areas. Adding an eighth to the seven divisions of the *Mārkandeya Purāna*, we may regard the Parvatāśrayiṇaḥ, the Vindhyavāsinaḥ and the Maruvāsinaḥ as the three main divisions marginal or *pratyanta* to the remaining five nuclear areas. The Maru separated the Uttarapatha from western India and on many occasions, tribes and peoples worsted in the Punjab saved themselves by migrating into the desert or crossing it to western Inḍia or merely skirting it on the north-east. The Vindhyas separated the Aryavarta from Daksinapatha and were from times immemorial the refuge of wild and primitive tribes. While large empires tended to rise and expand in the Uttarapatha, Aryavarta and Daksinapatha, the above mentioned mountains, forests and desert tended to act as their frontier areas (Pratyantas) and tribal states flourished in them. Modern India has had a NWFP and a NEFA; parts of central India functioned as such in ancient times.

Beyond Uttarapatha lay in ancient times the Śakas, Pahlavas Yavanas, Bāhlikas, Kambojas, Tuṣāras, Uttaramadras, and Uttarakurus in a giant semicircle extending northwards and eastwards from the desert of Seistan to Bactria, and beyond the Oxus towards the Pamirs and Central Asia. According to Herodotus,[50] the Sacae who were Scythians wore pointed caps, loose trousers, bows peculiar to their country, daggers and *sagaris* or battle axes. Saka prisoners seem to be similarly represented on the tomb of Darius. The Behistun, Persepolis and the Hamadan inscriptions speak of the Sakas as included in the empire of Darius. They are placed beyond Sogdiana in the Hamadan inscription. Strabo states : "The Sacae and the Sogdiani are separated from one another by the Jaxartes river, and the Sogdiani and Bactrians by the Oxus river."[51] According to Ptolemy the Sakai were bounded on the west by the Sogdianoi.[52] In the second century B.C. if not earlier, the Sakas had also occupied Sakastana or Seistan to the south-east of Drangiana where they were located by Isidor of

Charax in the 1st century A.D. Katyayana and Patanjali mention the Sakas (ad. Panini, IV. 1. 75, and ad. Panini 2.4.10; *Śūdrāṇāmaniravasitānām*), so also Manu, the *Ramayana* and the *Mahabharata*. From the first century B.C., Saka political power expanded over northern and western India.

The Pahlavas were the Parthians who revolted against the Seleucids in 249/48 B.C. under the leadership of Arsakes. The Yonas were the Greeks who as a result of the conquests of Alexander and his successors came to be an important political and cultural force in Iran, Afghanistan and India for several centuries. The *Majjhimanikāya* refers to them along with the Kambojas and mentions that they have only two classes, viz. free men and slaves. Panini too refers to the Yavana script. It is likely that there were Yavana colonies in the Uttarapatha even before Alexander. Arrian refers to one such colony at Nysa. Asoka not only refers to the Yavana rulers Antiyoka and others but also to the Yonas who lived within his own borders and for whom he had his spiritual message inscribed in Greek at Sharrekun near Kandhar. It was the Bactrian Greeks who established principalities in the Uttarapatha after the fall of the Mauryan empire.

In the *Atharvaveda* fever (*takman*) is asked to go to the Mujavanta, the Mahāvṛṣas and the Bahlikas.[53] Ptolemy places Bactriane between Margiane, Sogdiane, Oxus and Areia.[54] According to Curtius, part of Bactria was well-wooded and well-watered and rich in corn as well as pasturage for cattle; but the more extensive part is desert.[55] The city of Bactria was the commercial *entrepot* of Eastern Asia.[56] Hsüan Chwang stated that the extent of Bactria was about 160 miles east to west and 80 miles north to south and it bordered on the Oxus towards the north. Its capital was known as Little Rajagrha and the products of its soil were extremely varied.[57] Bactria rose to political importance when Diodotus "governor of the thousand cities of Bactria". assumed independence and the royal title about the middle of the third century B.C.

The location of the Kambojas has been much debated. They have been placed in the Badakshan and the Pamir regions[58] in the north-west of the Indus and also south of Punch.[59] They are mentioned in association with Bahlikas, Yonas, Gandharas and Daradas.[60] It is true that the Buddhist list of sixteen Janapadas would make them Indian, nevertheless they do not find mention in the campaign of Alexander, nor in Ptolemy or Hsuan Chwang. In this connection, it is significant that Arjuna in his *digvijaya* conquers the Kambojas after conquering the Bahlikas.[61] Similarly, Raghu conquers them after defeating the Hunas on the Oxus. The Kambojas, thus, appear to have been situated in the north-east of Bactria towards the Pamirs. At the same time, the mention of the Parama Kambojas in the *Mbh.* suggests that like the Madras, there may have been Kamboja settlements to the east of the Hindukush and these may have extended from the north-west of the Indus to Rajapura, below Punch. Like the Huns, the Madras and the Rsikas, or the Sakas, Yavanas, Tukharas and the Hunas, a section of the Kambojas too, originally a trans-Indian tribe, apparently crossed into India but did not maintain their identity or importance. The Kambojas were well-known for their horses, gold, and blankets.[62] They had only two classes among them, viz. free men and slaves.[63] They spoke a peculiar dialect, using 'savati' when they meant to speak of 'going.'[64] They lived by agriculture, industry, trade and war.[65]

Stein places the Tusaras on the banks of the Oxus in Balkh and Badakshan.[66] According to Strabo, the Greeks were deprived of Bactriana by the Asii, Pasiani, Tochari, Sacarauli and the Saca. According to Marcellinus, the Tocharii obeyed the Bactrians.[67] Ptolemy places the Tokharoi in Sogdiana in the most northern section of the Jaxartes.[68] They are placed in the far north in the Epics, the Puranas and *Brhatsamhita*. The *Rajatarangini* mentions them repeatedly. The Yue Chi have sometimes been supposed to be included in the Tukharas. The Asiai have been sought to be identified with the Rsikas. Param or Uttara Rsikas might have been even further north.[69]

The Uttarakurus and the Uttaramadras have become mythical although the *Aitareya Brahmana* simply places them beyond the Himalayas in the north.[70] The *Ramayana* places the Uttarakurus on the banks of the river Sailoda where bamboo forests abound.[71] In the *Sabhaparvan*, the Sailoda is placed between the Meru and the Mandara while the Uttarakurus are placed beyond the Mansarovar. They are usually described fantastically especially as a land beyond the reach of men.[72] Originally, Uttarakuru might have stood for Tibet and eastern Turkestan.

The principal route from the west to central Asia passed through Bactria and to proceed to India from here, one came across the Paropanisus either passing Bamian or descending from the Khawak pass into the waters of the Panjshir and then crossing Arachosia along the Kabul river. Arachosia lay between the Hindukush and the Indus, north of Gedrosia.[73] According to Isidor of Charax, the Parthians called it "White India."[74] It represented the land watered by the Vedic rivers Kubha, Kruma, Gomati, and the Suvastu. The two major Janapadas comprised in it were those of Kapisa, and Gandhara, although several other principalities and tribes find mention in this region in different ages. Although the region was included wholly in the Mughal empire and partly in British India, it was subsequently lost completely and became twice removed from Bharata.

Here on the threshold of India proper, we may pause to remember Hsuan Chwang's summary of its physical geography.

"The seasons are particularly hot, the land is well watered and humid. The north is a continuation of mountains and hills, the ground being dry and soft. On the east there are valleys and plains, which being well watered and cultivated are fruitful and productive. The southern district is wooded and herbaceous; the western parts are stony and barren."[75] Much later Abul Fazl praised it for its arable and productive soil, flora and fauna, and mineral resources, but complained that it lacked cool water, grapes, melons, carpets, and camels, and had excessive heat.[76]

Kāpiśī situated near the junction of the Ghorband and the Panjashir rivers was at the meeting place of highways from Kandahar, Bactria and Nagarahara or Jalalabad. Hsuan Chwang states that Kia-Pi-Shi was bounded by the snowy mountains on the north and on three sides by the Black Ridge.[77] It seems to have included Kafiristan and the valleys of the Ghorband and the Panjshir.[78] According to Hsuan Chwang, it had a cold and windy climate and bred *shen* horses. Merchandise from all parts was available here. The people, however, were fierce and coarse and wore clothes of wool and fur.[79]

Kāpiśī occupied in more ancient times the later position of Kabul. Pliny says that Cyrus destroyed the city.[80] but it must have revived, for the Behistun Inscription of Darius speaks of the fortress of Kapisavanti.[81] Panini mentions Kāpiśī (IV, 2.99) and Katyayana speaks of "*Kāpiśāyanaṁ madhu Kāpiśāyanīdrākṣā.*" Kautilya mentions and Kalidasa too sings glories of its vineyards and grape wine.[82] On Indo-Greek coins we read of the 'Kavisiya Visaya" and of the 'Kavisiya nagaradevata'.

From Kapisā, the northern highway passed through Nagarahara (near Jalalabad) and Puskalavati (near Charsadda) to Udabhanda or Und where it crossed the Indus and then extended to Taksasila (near Rawalpindi).[83] Puskalavati or Puskaravati (Greek Peukelaotis) was the ancient capital of Gandhara. In the *Ṛgveda*, we hear of the good wool and sheep of the Gandhari.[84] According to Ptolemy, the Ganderai lay between the Soastas (Swat) and the Indus and had the cities of Proklais and Naulibi. Strabo places Gandarities between the Khoaspes and the Indus, and along the river Kophes.[85] Hsuan Chwang also mentions the Indus as the eastern limit of Gandhara, although in his days its capital was Purusapura, not Puskaravati. Coming from further north-west, he felt its climate warm and moist, without ice or snow. It was rich in cereals and sugar-cane from which 'solid sugar' was produced.[86] From the *Ramayana* and the *Jatakas*, it seems that Taksasila was also included in Gandhara which thus lay on both sides of the Indus.[87] Ptolemy and Hsuan Chwang, however, mention Taxila separately.[88] In Alexander's days too, Peukeloatis and Taxila were separate kingdoms.[89]

Ptolemy places the Lambatai or Lampakas below the sources of the Koa (Kubha) and says that their mountainous region extended upwards to that of Kawedia (Gomeda, Kumuda).[90] According to Hsuan Chwang, the country of Lan-po had a circuit of 1000li. It was backed by the Black-ridge mountains. It was a tributary to Kapisa in his times. The climate had plenty of hoar-frost though not much snow. The soil produced rice and sugar-cane. The people were small in stature, wore garments of white linen, were fond of music, "pusillanimous, deceitful and ugly."[91] Hemacandra in his *Abhidhānacintāmaṇi* says "*Lampākāsta muruṇḍāḥ syuh*". Samudragupta mentioned the Murundas with the Sakas in his Allahabad pillar Inscription. The country has been generally identified with Lamghan, north of the Kabul river and bounded by the Alinagar and Kunar rivers.

Twenty miles south-east on the junction of the Surkhab and Kabul rivers lay the town of Nagarahara near Jalalabad. Ptolemy refers to it as Nagara or Dionysopolis.[92] He places Souastene below the source of the Souastos (Hsuan Chwang's U-Chang-Na). It lay north of Peshawar on the Swat river.[93] It was a succession of valleys, marshes and high plateaus and had thick forests. It produced grapes and turmeric (Ib.). Kasika states, "*Suvāstor adūrabhavaṁ nagaraṁ sauvāstavam*" (ad Panini 4.2.77). There is also a mention of Udyana in the Paladyādigaṇa (Ib. 4,2.110).

Ptolemy places the Goryaia below the Lambatai and Sovastini.[94] Alexander had to cross their territory on the river Gouraias to attack the Assakenoi.[95] The Gauraias has been suggested to have been the ancient Gauri, modern Ghor river. The territory of the Gauraeans apparently lay between the Aspesians and the Asakenoi in Alexander's time. These two tribes suggest by their names that they were the western and the eastern branches of the same tribe. Their capital Massaga might have been the same as Panini's Maśakāvatī.[96] To the west of Arakhosia lay Drangiana and Aria, which refer to the regions of Seistan and Herat.[97]

Varahmihira places Jrnga along with the Sakas in the west.[98] His Hārahūra may refer to Herat.[99] The country of Qatagus or Sattagydia inherited by Darius probably had the Indian name of Sataga and was on the river Gomti or Gomal.[100]

Ptolemy places the Daradrai below the sources of the Indus and says that the mountains in their country are of surpassing height.[101] We may place the Daradrai or the Daradas in modern Dardistan. They were famous for their gold and gold-digging ants.[102]

In the Vedic period, a number of tribes existed to the east of Bahlika: Kamboja, Bhalanasa, Viṣānin, Alina, Mahāvṛṣas, Paktha, Gandhāri, Kekaya, Madra, Śiva, Anu, Druhyu, Turvaśa, Yadu, Puru, Bāhlīka and Kamboja and perhaps the Mahāvṛṣas lay outside Sapta Sindhu. The Pakthas were apparently the ancient Pakhtuns. As mentioned above, Gandhara came to comprise two parts, of which the eastern or Cis-Indus part had its capital at Takṣaśilā. Alexander found the principality of Taxila extending from the Indus to the Jhelum. Hsuan Chwang praised its fertility and rich produce.[103] He found the state of Simhapura 140 miles south-east of Taxila, apparently between the Indus and the Salt Range.[104] The *Mbh* also mentions Simhapura in the north.[105] Ptolemy as well as Hsuan Chwang notice the Kingdom of Uraśa in the Hazara region between the upper waters of the Indus and the Jhelum.[106] The Kingdom of Abhisāra referred to in the *Mbh* and met by Alexander lay above that of Taxila and probably included that of Punch to which Hsuan Chwang refers.[107] Kasmira is mentioned in the *Mbh* and tradition includes it in Asoka's realm. Ptolemy places Kaspeiria below the sources of the Jhelum and the Chenab.[108] The *Lokaprakāśa* mentions the 27 *viṣayas* of Kasmira.[109]

From the *Ramayana*,[110] it appears that Kekaya lay to the west of Vipāśā and not far from Gandhara. The *Bṛhatsamhita*[111] associates Kekaya with Traigarta.[112] In fact Kekaya would appear to have lain between Traigarta[113] to the east and Gandhara to the west.

The Madras, divided into several branches according to Panini (4.2.108), had their ancient capital at Śākala.[114] The Sabhaparvan mentions the conquest of Śākaladvīpa. From

Kasika on Panini[115] Sakala appears a Vahika 'village'.[116] It may be noted that the Madrakāras were among the several branches of the Śālvas.[117]

The coins of the Udumbaras who claimed descent from Viśvāmitra have been found in the Gurdaspur district of the Punjab.[118] The Bolingai have been mentioned by Ptolemy and Pliny.[119] The Śaradaṇḍā river lay between Kurujāṅgala and Vāhika.[120] To Varahamihira just as Madra represents the North so Kuninda represents the north-east. From their coins the Kunindas appear to have inhabited the country of the Sutlej in the Simla Hill states.[121] Ptolemy places them below the sources of the Beas, Sutlej, Yamuna and Ganga.[122] Between them and the Udumbaras lay the Kulutas in the Kulu Valley of the Kangra district.[123] Hsuan Chwang also mentions the principalities of Kululā and Satadru.[124] In his times, the land of the Madras and the Kekayas formed the Kingdom of Takka which stretched from the Beas to the Indus. "The soil is suitable for rice and produces much late sown corn. It also produces gold, silver, the stone called 'teou', copper and iron. The climate is very warm and the land is subject to hurricanes. The people are quick and violent, their language coarse and uncultivated."[125] Near the capital of the Takkas lay the old ruined town of Sakala with a circuit of 4 miles, once the capital of the Madras and Kathioi, Menander and Mihirakula.[126]

Hsuan Chwang also speaks of a separate Kingdom of Jalandhar which had thick forests and produced much rice.[127]

Kasika speaks of Śaivapura as a northern town.[128] It is probably the same as a Śibipura mentioned in an inscription from Sharkot edited by Vogel.[129] The *Mbh.* as well as the *Jatakas* mention the Sibis. According to the *Matsya Purana*, quoted by Alberuni,[130] the Indus passes through the countries of Sindhu, Darada, Zindutunda, Gandhara, Rurasa Krura, Sivapura, Indrameru, Sabati, Saindhava, Kubata, Bahimarvara, Marr, Mruna and Sukurda.[131] The Greeks with Alexander found the Siboi settled below the junction of the Jhelum and the Chenab. "They dressed themselves with the skins of wild beasts, and had clubs for their weapons."[132] Near them lived the Oxydrukoi, Mailoi, Abaotanoi, Xathroi and Ossadioi.

Parāśara as quoted by Utpala mentions[133] "*Madra-paurava-Yaudheya-mālava-śūrasena-rājanyā-rjunāyanatraigarta-Kaika-ya-Kṣudrāh*". The heart of early Vedic civilisation lay in Brahmāvarta which stood for the doab between the 'divine' rivers Sarasvatī and Dṛṣadvatī. The Sarasvatī lay midway between the Sutlej and the Jamuna while the Drsadvati has been indentified with the Chitranga (CHI I). This was the land of the Bharatas. The next in holiness and time was *Brahmarṣideśa* which included Kuruksetra, the Matsyas, Pancalas and Surasenas. In the *Aitareya Brahmana*, the Vasas and the Usinaras are placed along with the Kuru-Pancalas in the middle region. Kuruksetra 'was bounded by the Khandava on the south, Tūrghna on the north, Parīnah on the west.'[134] To the West of it lay the wild tract of Kuru-jangala extending from the Kamyaka Vana on the Sarasvati to the Khandava Vana near the Jamuna.[135] The capital of the Kurus was Hastinapura, near Meerut, till it was washed away by the Ganga in the time of Nicaksu. The Matsya country has been placed to the south of Delhi and to the west of Mathura.[136] *The Satapatha Brahmana* mentions a Matsya rulcr Dhvasan Dvaitavana who performed Asvamedha and gave his name to the Dvaitavana lake.[137] About the Dvaitavana the *Mbh*, states[138]. "*tataśca yātvā marudhanvapārśvam sadā dhanurvedaratipradhānāh/Sarasvatīmetya nivāsakāmāḥ Saras-tato dvaitavanam pratīyuḥ*". Heading towards Viratanagara, the capital of the Matsyas (Med. Bairat), the Pandavas proceeded along the Yamuna on its southern bank and passing through hills and woods, south of the Pancalas and north of Daśārṇa and between Yakrllomas and Surasenas, reached the Matsya realm.[139] Bharata proceeding to Ayodhya from Kekaya passed the Bharunda forest north of the Vīramastsyas on the Sarasvati and the Ganga.[140]

The Pañcālas comprised the five clans of the Krivis, the Turvaśas, the Keśins, the Sṛñjayas and the Somakas in the Vedic Age.[141] The *Mbh.* knows of the northern and the southern Pancalas, divided by the Ganga. Kampilya and Paricakra in the Vedic period and later Ahicchatra were its capital towns. It included the "Bareilly, Budaun, Farrukha-bad and the adjoining districts of Rohilkhand and the central

Doab in the modern Uttar Pradesh.'[142] The Surasenas lay between the Pancala and Matsya territories, Kalidasa mentions Mathura as their capital.[143] From Panini (4.2.118) it seems that the Usinaras and the Vahikas overlapped.

The Buddhist list of sixteen Mahajanapadas adds Vamsa or Vatsa to Kuru, Pancala, Surasena and Matsya. Oldenberg has sought to identify the Vatsas with the Vaśas. The capital of the principality was at Kausambi. The account of Bhimasena's *digvijaya* in the *Mbh.* associates the Vatsa country with the Bhaggas and the Nisadas. The *Dhonasakha Jat.* too makes out the Bhaggas at Sumsumaragiri dependent on the Vatsas[144] for it speaks of the palatial dwelling of prince Bhadda, son of Udayana, at Sumsumaragiri.

Hsuan Chwang came across the following principalities in the Madhyadesa, viz. Mathura (-anct. Surasena), Sthanesvara (-Kuruksetra), Srughna (*Kasika* mentions Srughna many times along with Mathura or Kanyakubja, e.g. 4.3.85, 86, 89 etc. Hsuan Chwang places it between the Ganga and the Yamuna near the monutains, 80 miles north-east of Sthanesvara II. 217), Matipura (east of Srughna across the Ganga, Haridwara lay on its north-western frontier, II, p. 226), Brahmapura (Garhwal and Kumaon, beyond it in the Himalaya lay the country of Suvarnagotra, II, 227), Govisana (near Kasipur), Ahicchattra (capital of north Pancala), Pi-lo-shan-na (about 50 miles south of Ahicchattra and then south-west across the Ganga), Kapitha of Sankasya (40 miles south east of Pi-lo-shan-na-Sankisa. Kasika speaks of the Ayudhajivis of Sankasya), Kanyakubja, Ayodhya, Hayamukha (about 140 miles north-west of Prayag), Prayaga, Kausambi and Visakha (Pi-so-kia).

The *Brahatsamhita*[145] mentions the following principalities in Madhyadesa---Bhadra,[146] Arimeda (probably one of the Med. tribes on borders of Sind and Rajputana whom the Arabs mention, cf. Medapata or Mewar), Mandavya (Kasika has Mandavyapura by the side of Sivapura; the Mands may be connected with the Meds; cf. Mandu), Sālva, Nīpa Ujjihāna (Bharata reached it after crossing the Ganga at Pragvata and proceeding to the villages of Jambūprastha and Varūtha), Sankhyāta, Marubhumi, Vatsa, Ghosa,[147] and Jamuna.

V.S. Agrawal identifies with Yamuna the region of Upper Jamuna near Dehradun and Kalsi,[148] Sārasvata, Matsya, Mādhyamika (near Chittor), Māthuraka, Upajyotisa, Dharmâranya (Naimisa? which is not mentioned here, but mentioned in the verses quoted by Utpala, I. 294), Surasena (not Mathuraka) Gauragriva, Uddehika (Alberuni : Bazzna), Panduguda (Thanesar, Alberuni) Aśvattha, Pancala (Parasara: Uttaradaksina), Saketa, Kanka,[149] Kuru, Kalakoti,[150] Yamuna Kukura (cf. Nasik of Gautami Balasri, the Junagarh Rock of Rudradaman), Pariyatra, Audumbara, Kapisthala,[151] and Gajahvaya.

Manu seems to imply that eastern India began from Prayaga while Rajasekhara makes it east of Varanasi. Vedic literature mentions Kasi, Kosala, Videha, Magadha, Anga. Buddhist literature adds a number of non-monarchical clans—Vajji, Mallas (2), Sakya, Buli, Kālāma, Bhagga, Koliya, Moriya, Videha, Licchavi. Jaina literature adds Vanga and Ladha. Among other states in the east *Mbh.* mentions the Suhma and Tāmralipta. Samudragupta mentions as border states Samataṭa, Ḍavāka and Kamarupa. The *Markandeya Purana* mentions the older Kasi, Kosala, Magadha, Maithila, Vardhamāna, Tāmralipta, Samudra, Lauhitya, and Pragjyotisa and also semi-fabulous tribes like Surpakarna, Vyaghraramukha, Vadanadantura, Purusadaka and Ekapada. Varahamihira mentions Kasi, Kosala, Mithila, Magadha, Suhma, Gauda, Paundra, Vardhamana, Tamraliptaka, Samatata; Pragjyotisa, Lauhitya, Karvata, Candrapura, Udra, Utkala, Mekala and the tribes Vyagramukha, Asvavadana, Danturaka Purusada, Ekapada, Khasa and Ambastha. Parasara, quoted by Utpala, adds Kirata and Vivasana. Rajasekhara mentions among others Mudgara, Malada (mentioned also in the *Mbh*) and Brahmottara.

Kasi, which ceased to be poltically independent in the sixth century B.C., Kosala (between the Gomatī and the Sadānīrā) and the Mallas of Kusinara and Pava are well known to have belonged to eastern Uttar Pradesh. Magadha lay in south Bihar while Videha with Mithila lay in north Bihar. Anga was to the east of Magadha and had its capital at Campa of which the site adjoined Bhagalpur. Suhma, Pundra, Vanga and Samatata lay in west, north, south and east Bengal respectively; *Skanda Purana* says of Gauda that it adjoins Vanga and the *Śaktisaṅgama* places it next to the sea[152]. Kalidasa places Suhma east of Vanga which is described as situated in *Gaṅgāsrotontareṣu*'. Dandin places Damalipta in Suhma. An early Maurya inscription from Mahasthangarh mentions Pundrangara while the Damodar copper-plates speak of Pundravardhanabhukti. Davaka, Kamarupa, Pragjyotisa and Lauhitya belonged to Assam. The reference to cannibals (Purusades) among the wild tribes of this region is noticeable.

Of the Daksinapatha, Vedic literature refers to Andhra and Vidarbha and a number of wild tribes. In the Buddhist literature, we hear of Kalinga and Asmaka. Asoka mentions the Tamil states of the far south which lay on the border of his empire. The *Periplus* distinguishes Dachinabades from Damerika. The *Periplus* as well as Ptolemy survey the ports and emporia of the south in some detail. A succession of powerful dynasties in the post-Mauryan age from the Satavahanas to the Colas lent political importance to the Deccan and the South.

On the east coast, south of river Kapisa lay Utkala or Orissa. Hsuan Chwang places Udra 140 miles south-west of Karnasuvarna. There was a great mountain on its south-west frontier and the sea on the south-east, where lay the important port of Caritra. Almost 240 miles south-west across great forests lay Kongodha which has been identified with the Ganjam district. It bordered on the sea and had high mountain ranges. According to Hsuan Chwang, Kalinga lay further south across a vast forest.[153] Traditionally, Kalinga extended from the Kulaparvata Mahendra of the Eastern Ghats to the sea and from the Vaitarini in the north to the Godavari in the south. It was populous and powerful in the Nanda-Maurya period and became an imperial power under Kharavela. It was famous for its elephants and its people took a leading part in the maritime and colonial expansion of India in south-eastern Asia. North-west of Kalinga across forests and mountains lay Kosala (i.e. Daksinakosala) which Cunningham identifies with Berar or Gondwana. According to Hsuan Chwang, its "frontiers consist of encircling mountain crag; forests and jungles are found together in succession." Nevertheless, he describes the region as fertile and populous. South of it, across a great forest, lay Andhrāpatha, traditionally between the Godavari and the Krsna. The *Aitareya Brahmana* referred to the Andhras as a robber tribe but Megasthenes described them as possessing numerous villages, thirty walled towns and a large army of 100,000 foot, 2000 cavalry and 1000 elephants. Their capital was earlier at Dhanyakataka near Amaravati and later at Vengi. Hsuan Chwang mentions the countries of Andhra and Dhanakataka separately.[154]

Further south lay the Tamil state called Damirika by the Greeks which produced pepper, pearls and beryls and imported much Roman gold in classical times and engaged in maritime and colonial enterprise. The three principal states were the Cola, the Pandya and the Cera or Kerala. The Cola territory traditionally "extended along the eastern, or Coromandel coast from Nellore to Pudukottai, where it abutted on the Pandya territory. On the west it extended to the borders of Coorg." The Pandya territory extended southwards to Cape Comorin including parts of Travancore. Kerala was "the rugged region of the Western Ghats south of the Chandragiri river."

In western Deccan lay Aparanta (north Konkana) and Maharastra; in central and upper Deccan lay Anupa with its capital at Mahismati, Asmaka and Vidarbha. From Central India westwards lay Dasarna with its capital at Videsa, Avanti, and Surastra with Lata to its south and Anarta to its north. Upwards and westwards were the Maru, Sauvira and Sindhu.

The 'divine' Himalayas, as the greatest poet of India described them, gave refuge to many tribes and principalities viz. the Daradas, Hamsamargas, Kunindas, Kartṛpura, Brahmapura, Nepala and Kairatas. The central mountain ranges of the Vindhyas, Pāriyātra and Śuktimān harboured the numerous Āṭavya tribes of the Pulindas, Niṣādas and Sabaras. Mahendra was the upper part of Eastern Ghats, Sahya and Malaya the upper and lower parts of the Western Ghats. while the position of Suktiman remained undecided.

Ancient Routes and Travel

As generally believed, Vedic Aryans gradually advanced from the north-west to the north-east. Thus the east came to be called the 'frontal' direction (*prāñc, pūrva*) and the south the direction to the right (*dakṣina*). This pioneering Aryan trail from the north-west to the north-east came to be followed by trading caravans and invading armies and in course of time Indian literature came to speak of a 'great northern route'. Panini calls it *Uttarāpatha,*[155] while Kautilya speaks of the Haimavata, the Himalayan path, contrasting it with *Daksina-patha* (7.12.30). The *Rgveda-saṁhitā* mentions a banished person turning to the south.[156] It is possible to read in the *Ramayana* of Valmiki an imaginative saga of the southward adventure of an Aryan prince of Kosala who was banished and who moved on foot through forests and hermitages from Citrakuta through Central India in a south-westerly direction to Pancavati in Nasik and thence in a south-easterly direction to Kiskindha near Hampi and further south. In course of time, the southern way came to mean the territories encountered on it. Thus in the *Baudhāyana dharma sūtras* 'daksina-patha' is mentioned along with Avanti, Aṅga, Magadha, Surastra, Upavrt, Sindhu and Sauvira as a marginal territory of 'mixed races'.[157] It may be noted that other routes connecting the north with the Deccan are attested from more ancient times by the archaeological evidence of the spread of Neolithic and Chalcolithic cultures.[158]

Travellers in the Vedic age had to contend with the ubiquitous forest. 'Mārga', in fact, meant a 'track' and the migrating tribes moved and settled by burning down forests, so that Fire was regarded as the leader and pioneer (Pathikṛt).[159] Towards the end of the Vedic Age, the gradual growth of population, technology and trade led to the beginning of a second Urban Revolution and we find the *Atharva-veda-samhita*[160] speaking of the many paths along which clans move and on which chariots (*rathas*) roll and bullock-carts (*anas*) slowly make their way.

The north-western section of the great northern highway was its most ancient part and lay across the regions of Gandhara and Kapisa.[161] The emergence of the Akhaemenian empire which came to include Gandhara and Sindh implied an added importance of the westward and northward extensions of this route. Conquering the Bakhtris, Cyrus moved south-eastwards across the Hindukush barrier and campaigned in the Kabul valley and Darius advanced to the Indus and is reported to have attempted to return through the land-route across Baluchistan, a route which Alexander actually followed although he had entered the Kabul valley from the south-east, proceeding from Seistan to Kandhar and thence northward, along what is now the Kandhar, Ghazni-Kabul route. Ancient Kapisa near the confluence of the Ghorband and Panjshir rivers was the great junction whence three different routes went to Bactra.[162] The north-eastern route followed the Panjshir and used the Khawak pass and then turned westward following the Andarab to reach Balkh. Alexander had used this route to conquer Bactria. A shorter and more central route used the Kaoshan or Kushan pass but was difficult to negotiate. Alexander possibly returned along it after conquering Bactria. The third route lay westward to Bamiyan and thence ascended to Bactra. Hsuan Chwang had followed this route in entering India. From Kapisa, the route proceeded to the Kabul river, the ancient Kubha, and moved eastwards through Nagarahara or Jalalabad which lay on the junction of the Kunar and the Kabul rivers. Further east lay Puskaravati where the joint streams of Panjkora and Swat met the Kabul river. The river Indus was thus crossed at Udabhanda or Ohind, a short distance from Attock, and one proceeded to Taxila, the gateway to the plains of the Punjab. Puskaravati and Taksasila were the twin capitals of ancient Gandhara and the fame of Taksasila as a centre of learning spread far and wide. The route between them did not lie through the Khybar pass which became important only after the rise of the city of Purusapura or Peshawar in Kushan times.

The Kushan empire, straddling the Hindukush, included not only the greater part of northern India but also extensive regions in Central Asia. The almost simultaneous advance of the Han empire to Sin-Kiang opened the caravan routes between China and the west and India. The north Indian highway now joined the great Asian highway spanning the east and the west. Bactria occupied the central position and here caravans met from all sides. From Bactria the route proceeded westwards to Merv, eastwards either through Sogdiana passing Tashkand whence it joined the northern loop of the Silk route at Kucha, or "up the Surkh Ab or Qizilsu, crossing the saddle to the headwaters of the rivers of Kashgar", or up the main Oxus valley, through Sarikol to Kashgar whence one could skirt the Taklamakan desert along its northern or southern margin. There were more direct routes also leading from Gandhara and Kasmira to Kashgar. One of these went upto Udyana through Darel, Gilgit, Hunza and through the Kilik and Wakzish passes to Tashkurgan and thus crossing the Tagdumbash Pamirs to Kashgar. Another proceeded through Skardu and Baltistan and through the Karakoram passes. This was the route along which Fa-Hsien had come to India, for he says that crossing the Bolar Tagh where snow lay 'in winter and summer alike' and then travelling south-west for fifteen days "over a difficult, precipitous, and dangerous road" one reached the Indus.

From Taxila to Mathura, there were apparently several different routes. Alexander is supposed to have crossed the Jhelum either near the town of that name or near Jalalpur and the Chenab near Sialkot; crossing the Ravi somewhere north of Amritsar, he is supposed to have reached the Beas near Gurdaspur. Hsuan Chwang who had proceeded from Taxila to Kashmir, had then travelled eastwards through Sakala and Jalandhara and after crossing the Sutlej proceeded to Mathura in a zigzag manner, first going to Pāriyātra. According to a story in the Mulasarvastivada Vinaya Jivaka proceeded from Taxila to Mathura via Bhadraṁkara, Udumbarikā and Rohētaka. Przyluski has sought to identify Bhadraṁkara with Sakala. Udumbarika must have been a town in the Udumbara settlement which numismatic evidence would place in the Pathankot region.[163] Rohitaka suggests an obvious identification with Rohtak. In the *Ramayana*, the journey to Kekaya lies through Kurujangala and across the Iksumati and the Beas. Alberuni mentions a westward route from Kanyakubja to Ghazna passing through Diyamau, Kuti, Anar, Mirat, Panipat, Kawital, Sunnam, Adittahaur, Jajjanir,

Mandahukur (capital of Lauhavur, east of river Irawa), the river Candraha, the river Jailum, Waihind, Purshawur, Dunpur, Kabul and Ghazna. He mentions another route following a north-north-west direction from Kannauj to Kashmir, passing Shirsharaha, Pinjour, Dahmala, the capital of Jalandhara, Ballawar, Ladda and Rajagiri.

As Taxila was for the Uttarapatha, Mathura was the key town for the Madhyadesa. Here the great northern highway was met by the principal route to the western sea ports, passing through Ujjayini to Bhrgukaccha. Under the Sakas and the Kusanas, Mathura rose to the pinnacle of its glory as a great centre of commerce and administration, diverse religions and art. It was from Mathura that Buddhism was carried by Mahakatyayana to Avanti and Jainism proceeded on its migration to Rajasthan and Gujarat. Mathura continued to flourish in the Gupta period as is evident from the account of the Chinese travellers. In the post-Gupta period, however, Mathura gave place to Kanyakubja as the more prominent place.

From Mathura, the route went to Veranja, Soreyya, Saṅkassa, Kannakujja and crossing the Ganga and Prayaga to Varanasi. Buddhaghosa calls it the shortest path from Veranja to Varanasi.[164] According to Alberuni the way from Kanyakubja to Prayag was as follows—Jajjamau, Abhapuri, Kuroha, Brahmashil, Prayaga. Eastwards lay Banaras, Sharwar, Pataliputra, Mungiri, Jampa, Dugumpur and Gangasagara.

With Varanasi began the eastern part of the northern highway. From here also, a route through Kausambi and Bundelkhand led to Vidisa and Ujjain and the west coast. From Central India, this route also branched eastwards, from southern Kosala towards the east coast, a route which Samudragupta followed in his southern campaign. Other routes led from Banaras to Śrāvastī, Vaisali and Gaya.[165] Eastward from Vaisali and Gaya lay the important river port of Campa whence boats plied to Tamralipti. With the rise of Pataliputra, both Vaisali and Gaya became relatively unimportant. We are told that it took a week by boat to reach Tamralipti from Pataliputra.[166] The northern highway thus ran from Vahlika to Tamralipti and its principal junctions were Kāpiśī, Taksasila, Mathurā, Varanasi, Pataliputra and Campa.

Ujjayini was the key town on the southern route. The routes from Mathura and Kausambi in the north, from Bhrgukaccha and Surparaka in the west and from Mahismati and Pratisthana to the south, all met here. It may be noted that Mahismati has been called the capital of Daksinavanti, Vidisa of eastern Avanti, while Ujjain was the capital of the western or northern Avanti.[167] The principal southern highway passed through Malwa whence it turned either west to the sea-coast or south to Maharastra. The disciples of Bavari in the *Suttanipata* proceed to Śrāvastī from Aśmaka on the Godavari through Pratisthana, Mahismati, Ujjayini, Vidisa and Kausambi. The expansion of Satavahana power to Vidisa must have followed this very route which also led the Sakas to Maharastra from Malwa. The route which Samudragupta took to the south could only be exceptional. In the *Raghuvansa*, the route taken by Raghu for the conquest of the south lies from Vanga to Utkala and further south almost along the sea coast, a route which Hsuan Chwang also followed. Coastal sea-routes to the south were, however, commonly used from Tamralipti in the east and Patala and Bhrgukaccha in the west. Even Mahendra and Sanghamitra take the sea-route to Ceylon from Tamralipti.

The *Mahabhasya* on the basis of Panini and Katyayana speaks of six types of paths—*Vāripatha* or waterway, *Jāṅgala-patha* or desert path, *Sthalapatha* or land route, *Kāntāra patha* or forest track, *Ajapatha* or a steep and narrow mountainous track, *Śaṅkupatha* or 'spike path', i.e. a steep path up a cliff to be ascended with the help of spikes or pegs. The *Mahaniddesa*, as first pointed out by Sylvain Levi, mentions a number of paths—*Jaṇṇupatha*, *Ajapatha*, *Mendapatha*, *Sankupatha*, *Chattapatha*, *Vamsapatha*, *Sakunapatha*, *Musikapatha*, *Daripatha* and *Vettacara*.[168] Of these, Jaṇṇupatha remains doubtful while Ajapatha and Mendapatha appear the same. Of Sankupatha, an excellent description occurs in the *Saddhammapajjotikā*. Chattrapatha might have meant the use of umbrellas like parachutes to descend from heights. Vamsapatha or Vettacara probably meant the use of bamboos for spanning chasms after the manner of rope bridges.

The *Arthasastra* specially stresses the military importance of roads and states "The roads of traffic are a means to overreach an enemy; for it is through the roads of traffic that armies and spies are led . . . . . that weapons, armours, chariots, and draught animals are purchased; and that entrance and exit are facilitated."[169] The king is consequently advised to "not only clear roads of traffic from the molestation of courtiers (*vallabhas*), of work-men (*Karuka*), of robbers, and of boundary-guards, but also keep them from being destroyed by herds of cattle[170]." For the obstruction of traffic, heavy fines are laid down.[171] Kautilya classifies the roads from the point of view of their administrative, military and economic use and prescribes for each a regulation width. It is obvious that the vast Maurya empire depended on the unceasing use of these arteries of information and action which were used constantly by royal courtiers, officials and troops, no less than by merchants, mendicants and adventurers.

Megasthenes tells us that the elephant was counted the highest conveyance, next came chariot and four horses, and then camel and finally vehicles drawn by a single horse. Apart from these conveyances of distinction, there were humbler and slower but commoner means in the asses, mules and bullock-carts. It is curious that Megasthenes does not mention the palanquin. Nor is there any explicit reference in the *Arthasastra* unless its '*laghuyana*' meant a palanquin. Megasthenes refers to the custom of setting up pillars at every ten stadia and to the officers in charge of roads. According to Kautilya, the roads were ultimately the charge of the Samāhartā. Asoka tells us of the care he took of the amenities of travellers by having shady trees planted by the wayside and by making provision of drinking water for men and beasts. The *Jatakas* mention inns or rest-houses, generally inside the city-gates. The Chinese travellers attest to the existence of *Puṇyaśālās* at regular intervals in the Madhyadesa.

References

1. McCrindle : *Alexander*, pp. 88-89.
2. Alberuni, op. cit. I. 198.
3. Spate, *India and Pakistan*, p. 3.
4. This is the older view,which has been challenged.
5. McCrindle, *Alexander*, p. 162.
6. Ibid 173-75.
7. Wadia, *Geology of India* p. 396, Krishnan, p. 533.
8. Krishnan, p. 39.
9. *C.H.I.* Vol. I, but contra Raychaudhari, *Studies in Indian Antiquities* pp. 51-52.
10. For Janapadas known, see *Vedic Index*.
11. *PHAI*, p. 55.
12. As late as the 7th century, Hsuan Chwang states that the land in Magadha is low and damp and the inhabited towns built on the high uplands. Of the land in Samataṭa, Tāmralipti, Karṇasuvarṇa and Kāmarūpa too, he says that it is low-lying. It seems, in fact, that many cities of Bengal become established "as the ground became desiccated enough to be habitable only about 1000 years ago." (Wadia, p.3.92)
13. *Rāmāyana*: 'Kiṣkindhā Kāṇḍa'.
14. Cf. Levi, *Pour. l 'histoire du Rāmāyaṇa.*
15. *Raghuvaṁṣa*, 4. : Raghu's *digvijaya*.
16. The Deccan was clearly known in Buddha's times. By the 4th century B.C., we have celebrated *dākṣinātya* authors like Bodhayana, Āpastamba and Kātyāyana. Kautilya and Aśoka clearly know of the Far South.
17. Minor Rock Edict I.
18. *Koṣa*. Vol. II, p. 513. These mountain ranges have been called ant-like, *Kīṭādri* which has been explained as referring to their ridges—vide Poussin, op. cit. Vol. III, p. 147, fn. 3.
19. Sītā has been identified with the river of Yarkand and Vakṣu with Oxus—Ibid. p. 148, fn.
20. *Kośa*, Vol. II, pp. 511-12. *Dīgha*. 'Mahāgovinda Sutta' already speaks of 'this great earth', (*mahāpṛthvī*) as being broad in the north and narrow in the south like a cart, which shows how ancient this tradition was.
21. *DPPN*. Vol. I. p. 942. The reference is in *Aṅguttara*.
22. *Dīgha*, Vol. II.
23. Cf. J.C. Jain. *Ancient India as Described in the Jaina Canon.*
24. e.g. *Mārkaṇḍeya*. 51.5.7; cf. Alberuni, op. cit. Vol. I. pp. 233 ff., 251 ff Dr. V.S. Agrawal. *Matsya Purāṇa*, diagram facing page 184 seeks to represent the four continents as subsumed under the seven continents. This diagram apparently works out what Alberuni quotes of the commentator of Patañjali, op. cit. Vol. I, pp 248-249.

25. e.g. *Vāyu*, I. 34. 9-34.
26. *Mārkaṇḍeya*: *Indrandvipaḥ Kaserumānstāmraparṇī gabhastiman / Nāgadvīpastathā saumyo gandharvo varuṇastathā// Ayam to navamsteṣām dvipaḥ sāgarasamvrtah / Yojanānāṁ sahasram vai dvipoyam dakṣiṇottarat. //*
27. Cf. M.R. Singh, op. cit., pp. 8-10.
28. This is not to say that no knowledge of central Asian lands is to be found anywhere in the *Purāṇas*. Sakadvīpa, the rivers Sītā and Vakṣu and several *Janapadas* mentioned in connection with them seem to derive from real information.
29. *Viṣṇupurāṇa*, 2.3.1.
30. *Mbh*. 'Sabhā' 27.3 :
Antargiriṁ ca Kaunteya tathaiva ca bahirgirim / Tathaivopagiriṁcaiva vijigye puruṣarṣabha / /
31. *Kumārasambhava* 1.1. Here the Himalayas extend from the western to the eastern ocean as a measuring rod (*Mānadaṇḍa*). Kālidāsa makes Raghu's *digvijaya* extend upto the Oxus—*Raghu* 4.
32. e.g., *Vāyu*, 47.37-41.
33. *Mārkaṇḍeya*, 57.58-59; Nilakaṇṭha ed *Mbh*. VI 6.3-5; cf. Alberuni, op. cit. Vol. I, pp. 296 ff.
34. *Vāyu* 45. 80-81 :
Ayam tu navamasteṣām dvīpaḥ sāgarasaṁvṛtaḥ Yojanānāṁ sahasram tui dvipoyam daksinottaram // Āyato hyākumārikyād āgaṁgāprabhavāccavai.
Matsya, 114. 9-10. The first verse is the same as above, the next has slight variation—Āyatastu *Kumārīto gariġāyāḥ pravahāvadhih.* Rājaśekhara, *Kāvyamīmāṁsā*, p. 223 *Kumārīpurāt prabhrti Bindusaro vadhi yojanānāṁ sahasraparimāṇam atiryak cakrarartikṣetram.*
35. See supra.
36. Dr. S.M. Ali's work *The Geography of the Puranas* (New Delhi, 1966) is the most serious attempt to interpret Geography as a scientific discipline. He explains 'dvipa' as a 'human region' and seeks to identify the seven *dvīpas* on the basis of their cilmatic and vegetational data—Ibid pp. 39 ff. He follows Alberuni and Abul Fazl in identifying the 'nine divisions' of Kumaridvipa within India and explains *Mārkaṇḍeya Puranas—Samudrāntritā jñeyāstetvagamyāḥ parasparam*" as merely referring to inaccessibility generally—S.M. Ali op. cit. pp. 128 ff.
37. *Kośa*, 3rd chap.
38. *Vāyu*, 45. 82-86.
Dvīpo hyupaniviṣṭoyam mlecchai rantesu nityaśāh Purve Kirātā hyasyānte paścime yavanāh smrtāḥ // Brāhmaṇāḥ Kṣattriyāḥ Vaiśyāḥ madhye Sudrās cabhāgaśaḥ / Ijyāyuddhavanijyābhir vartayanto vyavasthiāḥ...Iha svargāpavargartham pravrttiry eṣumānuṣī//Mārkaṇḍeya 55.21-22 *Tat Karmabhumir nāptiḥ punyapāpayoh /*
Mārkaṇḍeya, 56, 1-2 *Krtaṁtretā dvāparam ca tatha tiṣyam catuṣṭayam // Atraivaitad yugānam tu cāturvarṇyam ca vai dvija //*

Matsya, 114.5-7 *Bharaṇāt tarjanāccaiva manur bharata ucyate Nirukta-vacanaiścaiva Varṣam Bhāratam smṛtam | | Yatah svargaśca mokṣaśca madhyamaścāpi hi smṛtaḥ |*
Na Khalvanyatra maṛtyānāṁ bhūmau karmavidhiḥ smṛtaḥ |. Pṛthivyāṁ bhāratam varṣam karmabhūmir udāḥrtā | Bhāgavata, 5.7.11 *Tatrāpi bhāratameva varṣam karmakṣetramanyaṣṭavarṣāṇi svargiṇām puṇyaśeṣopabhogasthānāni bhaumāni svargapadāni vyapadiśanti*·
cf. V. S. Agrawal, *Matsya-Purāṇa* pp. 190-91, where several of these passages have been quoted.

39. *Raghu*, 4.
40. *Arthaśāstra*, 9.1.
41. Cf. S. B. Chaudhuri, *Ethnic Settlements in Ancient India* (1955); V. S. Agrawal compares the *Janapads* to Greek city States—*IHQ*
42. Cf. D. C. Sircar, I.H.Q., XXI., *pp*. 297 ff.
43. *Study of History*, Vol. VIII, p. 2.
44. Spate, *India and Pakistan*, p. 148, Subbarao in his *Personality of India* has sought to consider the relevance of Spate's ideas for the prehistoric period.
45. Alberuni, *India*, I. p. 198.
46. *Manusmrti*, 2.22.
Āsamudrāt tu vai pūrvāt āsamadrāt tu paścimāt |
Tayor evāntaraṁ giryor āryāvartaṁ vidur budhāḥ ||
47. Bodhayana, *Dharma Sūtra*, 1.1.10-11.
48. *Mahabhasya*, (Kielhorn's ed.) i.475.
49. Cf. *Brhatsamhita*, Vol. I, p. 62.
50. Herodotus, *Historles*, p. 439.
51. Strabo, XI. 8.2.
52. McCrindle's *Ancient India as described by Ptolemy*, p. 283.
53. *AV*. V. 22.5
54. Op. cit.,p. 267.
55. Ibid. pp. 270-271.
56. Heeren, *Asiatic Nations*, quoted ibid. p. 873.
57. Watters, I. pp. 108-09.
58. *Achaemenids*, pp. 8-9; *Sārthavāha* p. 67.
59. *PHAI*, pp. 48-49.
60. Asoka RE, *V*, MN, loc. cit; *Mbh*., 27. 22-25, *Ramayana, Kiskindha*, 43. 11-12, *Raghu*, 4.68-73
61. loc.cit.
62. *Raghu*, loc. cit. DPPN. I. 625; *Mbh*.
63. *Majjhima*, see *infra*.
64. Yaska, *Nirukta*, Naigamakāṇda, 2.1.
65. *Arthasastra—Vārtāśastropajīvinah*.
66. *Raja-Tara* I. p. 136.
67. Ptolemy, p. 324.
68. Ibid. p. 276.
69. *Sarthavāha*, p. 8.
70. *Aitareya Brāhmaṇa*, 8.14, 23.

71. *Kishkindha*, 43.39.
72. *Mbh.* I. pp. 323-24.
73. Ptolemy, p. 317.
74. Ibid. p. 319.
75. Op. cit., II. pp. 129-30.
76. *Ain-e-Akbari*, III, p. 10.
77. Op. cit., I. p. 116.
78. *PHAI*, p. 287, S. Chattopadhyaya, *The Achaemenids*. p. 18.
79. Ibid. pp. 116-17.
80. *PHAI*, p. 239.
81. *The Achaemenids*, p. 7.
82. *Raghu*. 4.65.
83. *Sarthavaha*, pp. 7 ff.
84. *R.* I. 126.7.
85. McCrindle, Ptolemy, p. 115.
86. Op. cit , II. p. 150.
87. *PHAI*, pp. 59. cf. *Rāma "Sindhor ubhayataḥ pārśve deśaḥ paramaśobhanaḥ"* (7.100.11)
88. Cf. Cunningham, *Ancient Geography*, p. 48.
89. Cf. *C.H.I.*, Vol. I, p. 355.
90. Op. cit., p. 104.
91. Watters, Vol. I, p. 181.
92. Op. cit., p. 113.
93. Watters, op. cit., II. 166-67.
94. Op. cit., p. 105.
95. Ibid. p. 111.
96. McCrindle, Alexander, pp. 334-35.
97. Ibid. pp. 306 ff; 313 ff.
98. *Bṛhatsaṁhita*, XIV.
99. Ibid. pp. 3,11.
100. Cf. Chattopadhyaya, *The Achaemenids*, p. 6.
101. Ptolemy, op. cit., p. 105. Cf. Kāśikā ad Panini 4.2.83; *Dāradi sindhuḥ*.
102. Ptolemy, op. cit., p. 107.
103. Beal, ii. pp. 179.
104. Ibid. p. 1.
105. *Mbh.* Sabha.
106. Cunningham, *Ancient Geography*, p. 103.
107. *PHAI*, p. 248; Beal, II, 199.
108. Ptolemy, p. 108.
109. p. 60.
110. *Rāmayana*, II, 68 & VII. 100-101.
111. *Bṛhatsaṁhita*, I. p. 295
112. Ibid. p. 293.
113. Cf. "*Āhustrigartaṣaṣṭhāṁstu Kauṇḍoparathadāṇḍakī Krauṣṭakir jālamānisca Brahmagupto tha Jānakiḥ* | *Kasika* ad Pa. 5.3. 116.

114. See. *PHAI* p. 65, fn. 7.
115. *Kasikā*, ad Panini, 4.2.117.
116. Alexander found the land between the Jhelum and the Beas in the hands of the two Poruses, Adraistai, Kathioi, Siboi and Phegelas. (*PHAI* pp. 249-52) Porus was apparently a Puru or Paurava who is placed in the *Ram. Mbh.* and the *Brhatsamhita* in the north. Varahamihira associates Pauravas with the Madrakas and Malavas.
117. "*Udumbarās tilakhalā madrakārā Yugandharāḥ | Bhuliṅgah śaradaṇḍāsca śālvāvayavasam jnitaḥ ||* (*Kasika* ad Pa. 4.1.173).
118. *C.H.I.* I. pp. 528-29.
119. McCrindle : Ptolemy, p. 163.
120. *Ramayana*, II. 68.15.
121. *C.H.I.* I. p. 529.
122. Ptolemy; op. cit., p. 105.
123. Ibid.
124. Beal, II. pp. 210-11.
125. Ibid. II. p. 201
126. Ibid. p. 202.
127. Ibid. II. p. 209.
128. *Kāśikā* ad Panini, 4.2.109.
129. E.I. 1921. p. 16.
130. Sachau, Alberuni, I. p. 261.
131. Cf. *Vāyu*—"*Daradāñśca sakāśmerān Gandhārān Varapān dvayān Sivapurān induhāsānsca Visarjayan | Saindhavān andhra-Karakān bhramarābhika— rohakān ||* (47.45.46).
132. McCrindle, Alexander, p. 232.
133. Utpala's Comy on *Brhatsamhita*, Vol. I, p. 265.
134. *C.H.I.* I. p. 116, *Taitt. Aran.*, quoted.
135. Cf. *Ram.* II. 68-13 : "*To hāstinapure gaṅgām tīrtvā pratyan mukhā yayuch | Pāñcāladesamamāsadya madhyena Kurnjangalam ||*"
136. *PHAI*, p. 67.
137. *Śatapatha*, xiii, 5, 4, 9.
138. *Vanaparvan*, 177, 21.
139. *Virataparvan*, 5.1.4.
140. *Mbh.* II. 71.5.
141. *PHAI*, p. 71.
142. *PHAI*, p. 70.
143. *Raghu*, 6.48.
144. *Jat*, 353.
145. *Brhatsaṁhitā*. 14-2-4.
146. Cf. "*Bhadrān rohitakāñścaiva āgreyān mālvānapi, Gaṇānsarvān Vinirjityā nitikrt prahasanniva*" *Mbh.* III. 254 19-20.
147. "*Ghosā dvaitavanesarve tvat pratīksā narādhipa Mbh.* II. 238. 23 Also cf. Ghosundi, Ghosa."
148. *Panini-Kalīn Bharata*, pp. 69-70.
149. Cf. Kakas near Sanchi.

150. Kuru, Kalakuta cf. *Sabhāparvan* 26. 3-4: *Ānartān Kālakūrāñśca Kulikāñśca vijitya*; cf. 16. 20. 26 : *Kurubhyah prasthitāste tu madhyena Kurujāṅgalam* | *ramaym padmasaro gatvā Kālakūtamatītya ca* || *Gaṇḍakim ca. Mahạsonam sadānīrāṁ tathaiva ca* ||

151. Cf. Hsuan Chwang's Kapitha.

152. Quoted by Raychaudhuri, *Antiquities.*

153. Cf. Kalingaranya in the Pali texts.

154. Cf. IA XV. p, 172.

155. '*Uttarāpathenāhrtahrtān ca*' 5.1.77).

156. '*Sarat Padā tu dakṣinā parāvṛn*' (10.61.8).

157. '*Avantayọ rga-magadhāh surāstrā daksināpathah* | *upāvrt sindhu-sauvirāh ete sankīrnayony an* || (3.1.14).

158. Cf. Subbarao, *Personality of India.*

159. Cf. R. 6.2.12 : *sugeśūta durgeṣu pathikrd vidānah*'; Cf. SB.'s well known story of Videgha Mathava following Agni Vaisvanera towards the east.

160. 12.1.47 : '*Ye te panthāno bahavo janāyanā rathasya vartmānasaśca yātave*'.

161. Foucher suggested that the Aryans followed the grand route' from Bactria to Bamiyan Kapisa, Puskaravati and Taxila in entering India. This is clearly speculative; Foucher, *La Geographieancienne du Gandhara*, *BEFEO* (90).

162. Cf. Tarn, *The Greeks in Bactria and India.* p. 139.

163. Revata proceeds from Kanyakubja to Udumbara, *Cullavagga*, p. 421.

164. Cf. *DPPN*, II p. 930.

165. Cf. Ibid. p. 275.

166, Ibid. II. p. 179.

167. Ibid. II. p. 623.

168. Motichandra, *Sarthavaha* p. 130.

169. Shamasastry, p, 334.

170. Ibid. p. 48.

171. Ibid. p. 194.

2

Growth of Population

Modern Perspective

Malthus argued in 1798 that there is a constant natural tendency to over-population in every society, for men increase at a faster rate than food supplies,[1] the necessary adjustment between the two being effected by preventive and positive checks. Since Malthus published his Essay, world population has increased enormously. The population of Western Europe has passed during the last two centuries through a veritable 'demographic cycle' which has tended from a 'high stationary' to a 'low stationary' phase.[2] This has happened because the adoption of various preventive checks has decreased the birth-rate while the Agrarian and Industrial Revolutions and the improvement in public health measures have decreased the death rate. In India, however, only the earlier stages of the 'demographic cycle' have been operative yet. In the sixteenth century, she is estimated to have had a population of about a 100 millions.[3] By the middle of the 19th century, the population had increased to about 150 millions. It was 203 millions in 1871, 254 millions in 1881, 279 millions in 1891, 353 millions in 1931 and 389 millions in 1941.[4] In a century, thus, the population of India has more than doubled itself while it was practically stationary in the preceding three centuries.

Pre-Industrial Age

Before the Industrial and Scientific Revolutions, human population appears to have remained on the whole in a 'high stationary' phase. Doubtless, the adoption of settled agriculture at the dawn of civilization must have meant a great rise in the level of population equilibrium. It is not certain if the later use of iron meant any significant change in this level On the whole, "in unimproved peasant conditions, birth rates and death rates are both high and the population remains fairly steady, fluctuating up and down according to food-supplies, pestilences, wars etc."[5] An illustration may be obtained from China, which is the only country where a long tradition of census records has come down from ancient times. These records show that in Pre-Manchu times, population tended to rise rapidly but was restrained by periodical destruction. Already in the 9th century B.C., China north of the Yang tze kiang is stated to have had a population of 21.7 millions.[6] Between A.D. 2 and 155 the average of the census gives 63.5 millions. In A.D. 180 it was 23.1 millions, in 606 it doubled, increased rapidly and then declined to 43.2 millions in 733. By A.D. 1097, it had risen to 101.2 millions but in the Mongol and Ming periods, it declined by 40 to 50 per cent.[7] In other words, for nearly 2500 years the population of Pre-Manchu China fluctuated between 20 millions and 100 millions.

It is probable that for India in ancient times, a similar state of affairs held good. Although census records were not unknown then,[8] none have been preserved for the sceptic to doubt. The available evidence is indirect and scanty but it may be eked out with considerations of general probability in the light of the demographic perspective indicated above.

Prehistoric India

Since food supply, security of life, and the social attitude towards the size of the family are the chief determinants of population, it must have been small in the Stone Age but must have increased greatly with the discovery of agriculture and the domestication of animals. Thus north-western India in the third millennium B.C. had at least two large cities—of which the present sites have a circumference of more than three miles and of which at least one probably covered a square mile of well-inhabited area—several smaller towns and numerous villages.[9] This civilized society of chalcolithic India with developed agriculture, commerce and town-life extended over a thousand miles from the foot of Simla Hills to the Arabian Sea. Assuming the urban population to have been 50,000, we may estimate the total population of Harappan India at half a million to a million persons.[10] This would be a fairly conservative estimate. In the second millennium B.C. town life declined in this area but had again recovered by the middle of the next millennium. Although a gradual desiccation of Baluchistan, Sindh and W. Rajputana took place in ancient times, Sindh remained prosperous and populous throughout, as is indicated by later Greek and Arab accounts. The Aryan expansion in the second millennium B.C. brought the greater part of north India from Kābulistān to Bihar under the plough. The Vedic attitude towards the family reflects the need and trend of this period of agricultural expansion. The Vedic Aryans fervently prayed for progeny and larger numbers and would have blessed every mother with ten children.[11] With such a social attitude and fresh cultivable land easily available, population must have tended to increase in geometric progression.

From Bimbisāra to Aśoka

By the fifth century B.C., the whole of northern India execpt for Bengal had been settled and town life was flourishing. Expansion to the south had also clearly begun. Herodotus writing about the middle of the century described the Indians as the most populous nation in the known world and so prosperous that they paid to the Achaemenian Empire the huge revenue of 360 talents of gold dust, which was equivalent to more than a million pounds sterling and was one-third of the total levy on the Asiatic provinces.[12] Since this description relates only to that part of north-western India which formed the twentieth satrapy of Darius, we may turn to Buddhist records for contemporary north-eastern India. We are told that Magadha including Aṅga, had 80,000 villages.[13]

The Śākyas are supposed to have had at least 160,000 families.[14], The population of Vaiśālī has been given as 168,000[15], the assembly of the Licchavis consisting of 7707 rājas.[16] Buddhist records speak of six great cities at the time of Buddha's death—Campā, Rājagṛha, Śrāvastī, Sāketa, Kauśāmbī and Vārāṇasī—all lying between modern Allahabad and Bhagalpur. For Vārāṇasī a circumference of 12 yojanas was claimed ! (*Jātaka* I, 125). According to Hsuan Chwang the circumference of ancient Vaiśālī was 70 li, which would be near that of Alexandria in the first century A.D. as reckoned by Pliny (*Life of Greece*, pp. 592-3). Rhys Davids has estimated the population of northern India as fifteen to twenty millions in this period.[17] This would appear to be a conservative estimate.

In the fourth century B.C., the Greeks who came with Alexander have left behind certain observations regarding the population and armed forces of some Indian states. We are told that the Kingdom of Taxila between the Indus and the Jhelum was very fertile and densely populated.[18] Again, between the Jhelum and the Beas, there were nine nations and 500 cities that were conquered by the Macedonians. None of these cities was less than Cos Meropis.[19] Between the Jhelum and the Chenab lay the Kingdom of Poros and upwards the territories of the Glausai or the Glauganikai. The former contained 300 cities,[20] the latter al least 37 towns, the smallest of which contained over 5,000 inhabitants and many contained more than 10,000.[21] The army of Poros consisted of 50,000 foot, 3,000 horse, about 1,000 chariots 130 elephants.[22] Since even in 1914 France and Germany could only mobilise one in thirty, the population of the Kingdom of Poros could not have been less than 1,680,000. The Glausia with an urban population of at least 2,00,000 could not have been less than a million and a quarter. East of the Ravi lay the Kathaioi. When their stronghold Saṅgala was stormed, 17,000 were killed and 70,000 taken captive.[23] These casualties were much heavier than those suffered by Poros. We would be safe in regarding the Kathaioi as at least a million. The Agelessoi who lived in the lower part of the Chenab-Ravi doab had an army of 40,000 foot and 3,000 horse.[24] The Oxydrakai and the Malloi lived below the confluence of the Chenab and the Jhelum. They had an army of 90,000 foot, 10,000 horse and 900 chariots.[25] This suggests a population of over three millions. The Abastanoi dwelling on the lower Chenab had an army of 60,000 foot, 6,000 cavalry and 500 chariots.[26] This indicates a population of over two millions. We are told that the banks of the river were most thickly studded with their villages.[26]

Thus seven states of the Panjab, viz. that of Poros, the Glausai, the Kathaioi, the Agelessoi, the Oxydrakai, the Malloi and the Abastanoi, occupying some of the territories between the Jhelum and the Beas, had a population of more than ten millions. In this very region, there were several other states like Abisares, Gandaris, Adraistai, the realm of Sophytes, of Phegelus, the Siboi, the Xathroi, and the Ossadioi about whom we do not get any figures. The states in the Sind were fairly populous, for the Greeks in their campaign in these parts killed 80,000 and sold multitudes into slavery.[27] Similarly, the territories west of the Indus contained powerful states like Peukelaotis in the Pesawar district and the Aśvakas on the Swat. The Aśvakas had an army of more than 30,000 foot, 20,000 horse and 30 elephants.[28]

From these accounts, it is clear that to the Greeks, who had come with Alexander and had seen the ancient countries of Egypt and Western Asia, north-western India appeared full of populous states and the numbers they give for these states and the figures they mention for the armies of some of them suggest that an estimate of twenty millions for north-western India extending upto the Hindukush and including Sindh would not be an exaggeration.[29]

Over north-eastern India sprawled the Magadhan Empire. It was reported that the "country was exceedingly fertile, and that the inhabitants were good agriculturists".[30] The empire had an army of 80,000 horse, 2,00,000 foot, 8,000 war chariots, and 6,000 war elephants. When Candragupta mounted the throne, he increased the army to 6,00,000 men and with it "subdued the whole of India".[31] From this, the population of northern and north-eastern India may be estimated to have been at least twenty millions.[32]

In the Deccan and the South, we hear that the Andarai had thirty walled towns and an army of 1,00,000 foot, 2,000 cavalry and 100 elephants.[33] The Calingai had 60,000 foot, 1,000 horse and 2,700 elephants.[34] The Pandae had 300 cities, 1,50,000 foot, and 500 elephants.[35] These large figures get some confirmation from the fact that according to Aśoka (R.E. XIII) in his war against Kaliṅga 1,00,000 persons were killed, 1,50,000 taken captive and many times that number wounded.[36] Later, in the first century B.C. Khāravela declared that in his twelfth year of rule, he led forth an army of 1,00,000 from Kaliṅga to intimidate the rulers of the north.[37] Andhra and Kaliṅga both belonged to eastern Deccan but there were several states in western Deccan for which we have no figures. Similarly, from the grammarian Kātyāyana we know that by the side of the Pāṇḍyās, there were the Colas and the Keralas. The population of the Deccan and the south, thus, must have been at least ten to twelve millions.

We may conclude, then, thet by the end of the fourth century B.C., the population of India was at least fifty millions. It is likely that the Greek figures show exaggeration but this would be offset by the fact that in calculating from them, we have atributed to ancient states in India the efficiency in military organisation possessed by west European states in 1914.[38]

The foregoing account would suggest that from the age of Bimbisāra to that of Candragupta Maurya, the population of India probably doubled itself. This should hardly surprise us if we reflect over the territorial, political and economic development which took place during the period. During the third century B.C., under the peace and welfare activity of the Mauryan state, population must have tended to grow further rapidly. The *Arthaśāstra* even discusses the contingency of over-population in certain areas and suggests that the state should undertake to bring fresh land under cultivation, establish new villages and encourage suitable migration.

After the Mauryas

The fall of the Mauryan Empire was followed by three

centuries of political turmoil when several waves of foreign invaders came in through the north-west. Apart from the positive check to population which such conditions of political insecurity imply, the growth of the ascetic attitude must have acted as a kind of preventive check. Formerly the Brāhmaṇical lawgivers were not favourable to the ascetic doctrines which Buddhism and Jainism preached.[39] The *Arthaśāstra* was definitely hostile to the influence of such heretical mendicants and sought to restrain the tendency of indiscriminately renouncing the world.[40] But now Buddhism was more popular than ever and Manu is fully reconciled to the claims of asceticism. He upholds the ideal of a small rather than a large family.[41] It is of course true that the ideal of continence in marriage must have been largely ineffective in practice and while the gradual lowering of the age of marriage of girls must have added to the birth rate, the disappearance of *Niyoga* and gradually of the remarriage of widows must have acted in a contrary direction.

From about the first century A.D. the Kuṣāṇas, the Western Satraps and the Sātavāhanas established strong states and must have lessened insecurity. At the same time, there was a remarkable growth of maritime trade with the West and Roman gold poured into India.[42] From the east coast proceeded commercial and colonial enterprise towards south-east Asia. Similarly in the north-west under the Kuṣāṇa empire, trade with Central Asia flourished and the northern highway winding from Mathurā to Puruṣapura and beyond was brisk with caravans from far away. If the breakdown of the Kuṣāṇa Empire in the third century inaugurated a long period of political confusion in the north-west, the rise of the Gupta Empire revived the ancient glories of Magadha and established a period of peace and prosperity which included the whole of northern India from sea to sea. Population must have been on the upgrade.

It has even been contended that the increased pressure on land in the Gupta period led to the fragmentation of holdings and the reduction of their size.[43] The account of Fa-Hsien certainly indicates a very prosperous and popular

Madhyadeśa. In the eighty Yojanas before the pilgrim reached Mathurā, he passed monasteries containing in all about 10,000 priests. Mathurā was clearly a large city, for it had twenty monasteries with some 3,000 priests.[44] Magadha had the largest number of towns and cities of all the countries of Middle India.[45]

After the Guptas

The fall of the Gupta Empire and the invasion of the Hūṇas doubtless spelled disorder especially in the north-west. In the seventh century, the account of Hsuan Chwang indicates that many changes had occurred since the days of Fa-Hsien. In north-western India Kashmir, Multan, Sindh and Jalandhara were prosperous and populous, but Gandhara, Udyana, Siṃhapura, Uraśa, Pun-nu-tso, and Rajapura were not so well developed. The towns and districts of the ancient Madhyadeśa continued to prosper. Sthāneśvara, Mathurā, 'Govisana,' Kānyakubja, Kauśāmbī, Vārāṇasī and Chen-Chu (Ghazipur!) are mentioned as especially rich and well populated. Even Brahmapura (Garhwal and Kumayun) is stated to have been prosperous and populous. The Buddhist towns of north-eastern U.P.—Śravastī, Kapilavastu, Rāmagrāma, and Kuśīnagara had, however, become desolate. In Bihar, the picture had altered much since Fa-Hsien. Walled cities like Vaiśālī and Pātaliputra were in ruins and had few inhabitants but the towns or villages were thickly populated. An idea of what Hsüan Chwang means by a town may be gathered from the fact that speaking of the Vṛji capital which was in ruins but still had about 3,000 houses, he expresses the opinion that it might be called a town or a village. The soil of Magadha was rich and fertile but it was low and damp and used to get flooded in rains when boats remained the only means of communication and transport. Bengal certainly had made much progress since its debut in the Gupta period. Puṇḍravardhana, Tāmralipti and Karṇasuvarṇa were prosperous and thickly populated. The Deccan and the south were full of forests. Kalinga which formerly had a very dense population was now sparsely populated. So were the territories of Dhanakaṭaka, Colas and Mala-Kūṭa. Southern Kosala, however, was well populated with towns and villages close together. Kāñcī was a big town and so were the capitals of Koṅkaṇa and Mahārāṣṭra. It appears that the richest and most densely populated parts of India were in the west—Gujarat, Kathiawar and Malwa.

In short, in the seventh century A.D. population had declined in the NWFP, northwestern Punjab, northeastern U.P., Bihar (at least the urban population) and eastern Deccan. Madhyadeśa, Malwa and Gujarat, Sindh and Multan continued to flourish. Kashmir and Bengal had become more important. Big forests were particularly noticeable only in the Deccan and the south. In the territories of Udyāna too, thick forests are mentioned. We may presume the same for the northern mountaneous and the north-eastern frontier areas.

In the Arab accounts of the 9th, 10th and 11th centuries, India appears as one of the four great kingdoms of the world, the other three being the Caliphate, China, and the Eastern Roman Empire.[46] The Arab merchant Sulaiman of the 9th century mentions the realms of Balhara, Jurz and Ruhmi as the most important in India, all three being mutually at war.[47] These are the realms of the Rāṣṭrakuṭas, the Gurjaras and the Pālas. The King of Ruhmi or the Pala ruler had 50,000 elephants and the very number of the washermen in the army amounted to ten or fifteen thousand.[48] Al Masudi in the 10th century stated that Bauura, King of Kanauj, had four armies each of which numbered 7,00,000 or 9,00,000.[49] Multan is stated to have had around it 1,20,000 towns and villages.[50] Debal and Mansura were the other two most important cities in Sind. Mansura was a mile long and a mile broad.[51] The capital of Balhar was Manukir or Mānyakheṭa. Rashidud-Din stated on the basis of Al Biruni that Gujrat comprised 80,000 flourishing cities, villages, and hamlets.[52] Ten thousand villages maintained the temple of Somanātha.[53] The country of Sawalak, i.e. Sapādalakṣa comprised 1,25,000 cities and villages.[54] Malwa had 18,93,000 villages.[55] These same figures occur in the

Tarikhi Wassaf. The *Kāvyaśikṣā* of Vinayacandra also gives 70,000 villages for the Gurjaradeśa and 18,92,000 for Mālava-deśa.[56] The *Prabhāvakacarita* of Hemacandra describes Arṇoraja as the lord of Sapādalakṣa. According to an inscription, a King of Medāpāṭa or Mewar possessed 10,00,000 tracts of land (*Laksa-Kṣitiśa*).[57] According to *Prabandhacintāmaṇi*, Pṛthvīrāja was the lord of 1,25,000 tracts of land (*Sapādalakṣa-Kṣitipati*). Telangana in Alauddin's time had 30,000' tracts of country'.[58]

Like Vinayacandra, *Aparājitapṛcchā* also mentions 18,92,000 as the number of villages in Ujjayinī. It gives 36 lacs of villages for Kānyakubja, 18 lacs for Gauḍa, 66,063 for Kaśmīra and 3½ lacs for Maru. In many inscriptions from the Deccan and the South, exceedingly large figures are similarly associated with certain regions, viz. Vānavāsaka 12,000, Nolamavāḍi 32,000 and Gāṅgavāḍi 96,000. The three Mahārāṣṭras are stated to have had 99,000 villages.[59] The Kavaḍidvipa or northern Koṅkaṇa was called lakh-and-a quarter, while the territories of the Western Calukyas were called seven-and-a lakh country. (Fleet: *Bombay Gazet*, I, pt. II, p. 298 n. 2). These and other similarly large figures have excited much controversy and it has been suggested that they stand not for villages, but for estates or revenue or population.[60] All these interpretations are remedies of despair and appear far-fetched. To reconcile these figures with probability, we have to remember in the first place that the recent increase of population in India should not be supposed to have meant an increase in the total number of villages. On the contrary, the fact that in divided India small villages with population less than 500 number more than 3,80,000 and yet contain only 26.5% of the rural population, suggests that the recent phenomenal growth of population in India has been due to the growth of the medium and large sized villages and towns. In many cases, these bigger villages must have grown by the a malgamation of smaller villages scattered in the neighbourhood, these smaller villages becoming the hamlets or 'purwas' of the bigger village. Thus the actual number of villages instead of increasing would decrease with any marked increase of population. This would be clear if we reflect over the fact that while the number of villages in Central India is nearly 2½ times of that in Western India, its population is hardly 10% more. Besides, we have to remember that the proportion of urban population must have been much less than now. We may thus expect that villages in ancient India were probably more numerous though smaller and more scattered than now.[61]

In the second place, there is probably a great deal of overlapping in the numbers of villages given for states like Kanauja, Gauḍa, Mālava and Gurjara. The numbers probably refer to these states at their maximum extension. It is well-known for instance that the kings of Kanauja and Gauḍa were long rivals and claimed the imperial title and on occasions, the rulers of Gauḍa came up to Kanauja. Besides, it is possible that in estimating these figures, many conventional titles conferred on feudatories or assumed by ambitious rulers may have been taken realistically. Similarly, on occasions, territorial divisions may have been assumed to have had the number of villages required in them by convention.[62] In fact, it is likely that the figures of villages for the different states were reached from counting its major territorial divisions and feudal lords and then assuming that for each their conventional connotation in terms of the number of villages comprised in or ruled by them actually held good. Such assumptions are likely to lead to 'inflated' figures and these would get further 'conflated' on account of the overlapping of empires and imperial claims. This also explains why the figures for definite territorial divisions like Koṅkaṇa are more modest and reasonable than for Imperial states like Kanauja or Gauḍa.

Arab accounts thus confirm the directions of population growth discernible in Hsuan Chwang. Kashmir and Sindh, Kanauja and Gauḍa, Gujarat and Malwa became the leading states in northern India in the 9th, 10th and 11th centuries. From inscriptions it appears that Maru or Rajputana gradually emerges into importance and in the south under the Eastern Cālukyas, the Colas and the Pāṇḍyas there was a remarkable expansion of political activity and accumulation of wealth. We may suppose that the growth of population kept pace *pari passu.* Rashidud-Din calls Malbar or Coromandel coast, 'the Key of Hind', possessing many cities and villages and engaged in a brisk and profitable trade with Chin and Machin, Hind and Sindh.[63] Of the country about Cape Comorin, it was earlier declared that 'no Kingdom has a more dense population'.[64]

Whether we look to the general impression of Arab travellers or to the number of villages in different parts of India reported by them and by literary works and inscriptions, or to the large armies then maintained, it appears probable that while northern and western India under the Gurjara-Pratihāras, Pālas and Rasṭrakūṭas had not declined in population since earlier times, the Deccan and the South were more densely populated under the Rasṭrakūṭas, Cālukyas and Colas than before. If the population of the Deccan and Vijayanagara in the sixteenth century was about 30 millions,[65] it could not have been much less under the Colas and the same equivalence probably held good of India as a whole which in the 12th century could not have been far behind the 100 million mark.

NOTES AND REFERENCES

1. Malthus, *An Essay on Population*, Vol. I. pp. 5ff, (Everyman's Library Ed.).
2. S. Chandrasekhar, *Hungry People and Empty Lands*, pp. 27ff. (Baroda, 1952); E. John Russel, *World Population and World Food Supplies*, pp. 18-19 (London, 1954).
3. Moreland, *India at the Death of Akbar*, p. 22 (London, 1920).
4. S. Chandrasekhar, op. cit., pp. 152ff; Baljit Singh, *Population and Food Planning in India*, p. 3 (Bombay, 1947).
5. E. John Russel, op. cit., p. 18.
6. This is based on Ma-Tvan-Lin's account of the 13th Century A.D. which refers to a census of those times. It has been utilized by several modern writers e.g,, Latourette.
7. Ibid.
8. *Arthaśāstra*, II, XXXVI.
9. Wheeler, *The Indus Civilisation*, pp. 15, 36.
10. Cf. Fairservis in Possehl (ed.), *Ancient Cities of the Indus*, p. 84. The population of ancient Egypt in the 13th century B.C. has been estimated from 3 millions to 4.5 millions.—Will Durant, *Oriental*

Heritage, p. 214; cf. J.A. Wilson *The Culture of Ancient Egypt*, p. 271 (Phoenix Books).

11. Cf. *Ṛgvedasaṁhitā* X, 85.45.
12. Herodotus, *The Histories*, p. 215 (The Penguin Classics); cf. *C.H.I.* I, p. 335. In the 5th century B.C. the population of Attica had been estimated at 315,000 (Will Durant, *Life of Greece*, p. 255); Laconia had 376,0000 (*Ib.* p. 74).
13. Rhys Davids, *Buddhist India*, p. 24. Modern Bihar has 71,378 villages (*Times of India Directory for 57-58*, p. 345.).
14. Ibid. p. 18.
15. *Mahāvastu*, I. p. 214 (tr. J.J. Jones); cf. K.P. Jayaswal, *Hindu Polity*, p. 51, fn., 5; cf. *Mahāvastu* I, p. 216—84,000 Brāhmaṇas of Magadha.
16. Rhys Davids, op. cit., p. 41.
17. Ibid. p. 34.
18. McCrindle, *Ancient India, its Invasion by Alexander the Great*, p. 343, 94. Philostratos described the city of Taxila as being about the size of Nineveh. (A.N. Bose, *Social and Rural Economy of Northern India*, II. p. 169).
19. McCrindle, op. cit., p. 112, fn. I. Plutarch mentions 15 tribes, 5,000 considerable cities, and villages without number (ibid. p. 309) Arrian speaks of 7 nations and 2,000 cities (ibid. p. 133).
20. Ibid. p. 309, fn. I; cf. *CHI*, I. p. 360.
21. McCrindle, op. cit., p. 112.
22. Ibid. p, 274. The figures vary in different accounts.
23. Ibid. p. 119.
24. Ibid. p. 285.
25. Ibid. p. 234.
26. Ibid. p. 252.
27. Ibid. p. 254.
28. Ibid. p. 66.
29. In the 2nd century A.D. Egypt had a population of 8.5 millions, Syria 10 millions and Palestine 2.5 millions. Cities like Alexandria and Antioch each contained over half a million (Will Durant, *Caesar & Christ*, pp. 495-500, 510-11, 535). Jerusalam had 1,00,000, Carthage and Ephesus over 2,00,000 (ibid. pp. 535, 515, 40).
30. McCrindle, op. cit., p. 121.
31. Ibid. p. 310. Candragupta also had 30,000 horse and 9,000 elephants besides the chariots and the infantry of 6,00,000 (Smith, *Early History of India*, 4th Edition, p. 131). This was not a militia but a standing army "drawing liberal and regular pay and supplied by the government with horse, arms, equipment and stores". (ibid.)
32. Pāṭaliputra was 9 miles long and 1.5miles broad (ibid. p. 127). Strabo described Alexandria in the 1st century A.D. as only 3 miles long and 1 mile broad. Its population exceeded half a million (*Life of Greece*, pp. 592-93; *Caesar and Christ*, pp. 295-500). In 189 B.C. the city of Rome had a population of 2,57,000 (*Caesar and Christ*, pp.

81). In 1941 Patna had nearly 2 lacs, but, though at the same site, it is not a continuation of the ancient city.

33. McCrindle : *Ancient India as described by Megasthenes and Arrian*, p. 141.
34. Ibid. p. 138.
35. Ibid. p. 151.
36. R. K. Mukherji estimates the population of Kaliṅga at 25 millions! (*Aśoka Inscriptions : A Commentary*, p. 23. Allahabad, 1942).
37. Barua, *Old Brāhmī Inscriptions*, p. 32.
38. The population of the Roman Empire in its early centuries has been estimated by Beloch as 54 millions, by Gibbon as 120 millions,—Gibbon, *Declinc and Fall of The Roman Empire*, I, pp. 37-38 (Modern Library); *Caesar and Christ*, p. 364. The Han Empire exceeded 60 millions.
39. See the author's *Studies in the Origins of Buddhism* (Allahabad, 1957), Chapter IX.
40. *Arthaśāstra* (tr. Shamasastry), p. 47.
41. Cf. *Kullūka on Manu*, 3.45,
42. Gibbon, op. cit. I, pp. 49-50. Rome's annual loss is estimated at 8,00,000 pounds sterling (ibid.).
43. R.S. Sharma, *The Śūdras in Ancient India*, pp. 230-31, 234.
44. Fa-Hsien, *Travels*, tr. Giles., p. 20.
45. Ibid. p. 47.
46. Elliot and Dowson. *Early Arab Geographers*, p. 3 (Pub. Susil Gupta).
47. Ibid. pp. 4-6.
48. Ibid. p. 6.
49. Ibid. p. 29.
50. Ibid. p. 30.
51. "The estates and villages dependent on Mansura amount to 3,00,000" (Ibid. p. 31.)
52. Ibid. p. 93.
53. Ibid. p. 134.
54. Ibid. p. 95
55. Ibid. p. 96,
56. Pran Nath, *Economic Condition of Ancient India*, pp. 35-36.
57. Ibid. p. 38; *E.I.* II no. XXXII, pp. 415-17.
58. *History of Ghazni*, pt. II, *Elliot & Dowson*, pp. 53-54.
59. Pran Nath op. cit. p. 35; Altekar : *Rāṣṭrakūṭas and their times*, p. 139.
60. Pran Nath, op. cit., pp. 26ff; Rice, *Bhandarkar Comm. Vol.*; Altekar, op. cit. 139ff; V.S. Agrawal, *Journal of the U.P. Historical Society*, 1951-52, pp' 290-91; B.N.S. Yadav, *Aspects of Society in Northern India in the Twelfth century A.D.* Nilkantha Shastri, *JOR.*, 1930.
61. According to *Śukranīti* Grāma of a Krośa; *Agnipurāṇa*, Grāma of six families (vide Yadav, op. cit.); cf. Altekar, size of 30 grāmas

granted by Rājarāja (op. cit. p. 148); Kauṭalya, 100 to 500 families, boundaries of a Krośa or two. (l.c.).

62. Altekar, op. cit., p. 149.
63. *Early Arab Geographers*, p, 96.
64. Ibid. p. 10.
65. Moreland, op. cit., p. 10.

3

Economic Ideas and Attitudes

General Profile

Economic development is a prime value in contemporary society which aims not only at the constant betterment of the standard of living but at a constant acceleration of the rate of betterment. Nothing can present a greater contrast to it than the traditional economy of India of which the most important revolutions were completed before the beginning of historical times and which has been, in a fundamental sense, stable with but minor changes over the historical millennia. It is true that this striking continuity has been questioned by some historians who are assiduously seeking to reconstruct changes in economic life in the different epochs of Indian history and on that basis seeking to illustrate the historical development of India in accordance with Marxian prophesy. This would be, in part at least, a significant historical enterprise but the limits of its success are somewhat narrow. And that is because the advancement of production technology since the Iron Age was only of marginal significance till the Industrial Revolution.[1] Population fluctuated at a high stationary level. Cities remained few and far between, the villages numerous, isolated and largely self-sufficient. Agriculture continued on traditional lines, transport was slow and risky. Trade was confined largely to luxury items except for the needs of the bigger cities. Crafts depended on traditional skill and remained with guilds or hereditary subcastes. Different stages of economic development peacefully coexisted. Tribal settlements or *Pallis*, villages and towns represented such different stages. No one thought of a general economic improvement of the whole society as a realistic goal. The economic order appeared to be perennial, subsisting by its own little-understood laws. No one thought it possible to transform it and tradition preserved no memory of any revolutionary changes in it in the past except that of fall from a primeval golden age when man did not have to labour to produce his food. Nor was wealth regarded as the *summum bonum*.

Vedic View

The Vedic outlook on life may be described as one of integral welfare. It does not formulate itself in terms of that sharp duality between Nature and Spirit, which is so characteristic of the post-Vedic classical phase. It postulates a basic harmony between man and nature. It does not, therefore, see any contradiction between secular welfare and happiness in after life. Since the gods are themselves the creative powers underlying nature, there is no question of any contradiction between the natural and the divine. Gods are both personal and impersonal manifesting themselves in terms of an immutable Law governing the cosmos but also as gracious persons showering their bounty on the righteous and the pious. Man himself is created to fulfil his divinely appointed destiny, to live a full life but to live it through the favour of the gods, in pious obedience to their views. Worshipping the gods, man fulfils himself. The mode of worship consisted in sacrificing to the gods, sacrificial ritual being the symbolic re-enactment of the timeless divine act of creation. Ritual was modelled on the cosmic law or *rta*.

In the Vedic view, man does not seek to fight or conquer nature as such. The only fight man is required to wage is against Darkness. The struggle of Light against Darkness is the basic strife out of which the cosmos is created. Creativity is in fact nothing except the victory of light, the manifestation of the divine law. In human life, the moral struggle provides the parallel to this perennial cosmic struggle. To give freely is the nature of the gods, while to withhold and be niggardly is the hallmark of the enemy. Vedic piety, thus, laid the greatest stress on giving freely, and condemned niggardliness. Man lives by the bounty of the gods. To deserve it, he must practise bounty himself. Nature as such is not niggardly for it is instinct with divine bounty. There is, however, a constraining force of niggardliness and darkness which man must seek to conquer to exemplify his solidarity with the gods. Sacrifice or *yajña* symbolises man's remembrance of the gods, his willingness to give up so that he may be worthy of receiving.

Yajña provided the basic model of social activity.[2] All work must be an act of worship or sacrifice, so that the fruits to which it leads may be regarded as a gift from the gods Work is not a mere egoistic expenditure of energy or an act of calculated causation or production. It is a participation in a spontaneous process in which the creative energies of nature overcome the obstruction of original inertia or Darkness. Right living and ritual living thus coalesce. *Yajña* provides a pervasive symbolism for the whole of life. The *Bhagavad-Gita* succintly summarises it when it says "In the beginning, the Lord of creatures created men along with the sacrifice and said to them. 'Produce and multiply with this which shall fulfil your wants. Think of the gods with this and they would think of you. Thus mutually cultivating you shall reach the highest good. Nourished by the sacrifice, the gods will give you the goods you want. In fact, to appropriate goods given by them without sacrificing to them amounts to theft. The good people who consume what remains over from sacrifice are freed from all sins. Those who cook only for themselves merely consume in sin. All creatures are dependent on food. The production of food depends on rain. Rain comes from the sacrifice, sacrifice is produced from work. Work arises from Adoration, Adoration from the Immutable. Thus the all pervasive force of Adoration is eternally latent in the sacrifice. Those who do not follow the spontaneous cycle live in vain, sinful and sensual,." Gods represent the creative and beneficent powers working in nature. Although they work by an immutable law, they are nevertheless capable of a personal response to man's heart-felt adoration and prayer. Virtue and piety result from man's sense of dependence on the gods, his willingness to sacrifice and participate in the struggle of good against evil. The activities of production and reproduction were not set apart as evil or neutral but as fundamental aspects of an integrated search for fulfilment.

Vedic ethos abhorred the independence of economic life. The concepts of value, welfare and wealth were held in close connection. The most valuable or *varenya* was doubtless Light, the object of the most famous prayer of the Hindus. Welfare was conceived in terms of man's divinely ordained fulfilment. It consisted in living naturally where the meaning of nature was read in terms of ritual symbolism. For such a pious life, peace and happiness, vigour and glory were held to be divinely assured. While the gods Indra and Agni stood for Power and Wisdom, the gods Pūṣan and Bhaga, Ṛbhus, Tvaṣṭā and Viśvakarman presided over the economic activities of the people. The technical and the ritual aspects of productive activity were closely united just as the forms of wealth were conceived in close connection with the favour of the gods. Neither production nor consumption could be right without being viewed rightly. That is, as giving to and receiving from the gods.

Quite a few scholars think of Vedic ritualism as a primitive husk of myth, magic and superstition out of which small kernels of technology developed. They picture the sacrifice as rain-making magic or as the symbolic expression of the social power of the priests. The *yajña* has even been interpreted as symbolising the economic life of the commune. All these interpretations tend to think of the sacrifice apart from its symbolism and wisdom or its pervasive relationship to the whole of life and work. Priestly orthodoxy did tend in later times to give a magical interpretation to ritual occasionally, and the temptation to discover in myth the veiled statement of physical principles was doubtless strong in later times. But these tendencies miss the spontaneity, the integrality and the natural symbolism of the conception of sacrifice in the earlier period. In any case, the Vedic ethos has given some fundamental and lasting attitudes which underlie traditional economic life in India. It stresses harmony between man and nature and evinces care for preserving the balance of man's environment. It welcomes prosperity and fulfilment without turning the gain of material goods into an exclusive end. It discourages economic egoism and competition and lays emphasis on socially ordered co-operation. It favours simplicity and charity, and condemns niggardliness of all kind. It does not draw any sharp distinction between private and public welfare, nor between welfare and wealth. Gaining livelihood, apparently, was not yet a problem. At least, it was not so much of a problem as to shake man's faith in the bounty of the gods.

Post-Vedic attitudes

The Vedic equation of work and worship, wealth and welfare, man and nature was rudely broken in the post-Vedic period. The transition may be noticed in the Upanisads. The Upanisads do not totally condemn the goods of this world, even a sage like Yajnavalkya gladly accepts the prize of cattle and gold at the court of king Janaka. The virtue of food is often exalted. *Anna* is used in the sense of the material sustenance of human life and declared to be *Brahman*. It is said one should not censure food; one should, in fact, praise it (*Taittirīya*, 3. 7.10).

Nevertheless despite the realization of the essential and necessary contribution of food to man's sustenance, it was clearly realized that wealth yields only transitory and limited satisfaction. Wants are never fully satisfied. The principle of want or *Kāma* thus acquires a negative character. In the *Bṛhadāraṇyaka*, Maitreyi does not want wealth when she learns that it has no relevance to immortality. '*amṛtatvasya tu nāśāsti vittena*'. Similarly Naciketas declares "*na vittena tarpaṇīyo manuṣyah*" man cannot be satisfied by wealth. The *Taittirīya*, in fact, gives us an anti-Benthamite felicific calculus or '*ānandasya mīmāṁsā*.' It says that if we regard the full happiness of man to consist in a combination of youth, hope, strength, firmness and having in one's possession the whole world full of wealth, then, hundred such pleasures will constitute the happiness of a Manusya-Gandharva. And that measure of happiness also belongs to a priest who is untouched by want. In fact, however large may be the measure of happiness that we may imagine, it will never exceed the happiness of a wantless priest. Sanatakumāra in the *Chāndōgya* sums up the matter by saying that worldly people define plenty in terms of cattle and horses, elephants and gold, slaves and wife, fields and houses. But these do not really constitute plenty because they are all dependent on something other than themselves. Whatever is dependent, is limited and whatever is limited, cannot give true happiness. True happiness lies in infinity. Infinity is that which depends on itself and not on anything else. Thus the path of true happiness is quite different from the path of worldly goods. The former moves towards freedom, the latter to increasing dependence.

In the 6th century (B.C.), Vedic ritualism co-existed with materialism and asceticism. Ritualism retained its appreciation of wealth but tended to emphasize a supernatural causality in the production of good luck including wealth. Asceticism rejected not so much the necessary role of wealth in society as the pursuit of happiness through the satiation of wants and the instincts of acquisitiveness and possessiveness. It is true that the ideal of *aparigraha* or non-possession for the mendicants meant the vow of poverty. Still, the monasteries did acquire considerable wealth and managed it. Besides, it was admitted that all need not be mendicants. In fact, in the *Cakkavattisīhanādasutta* it is clearly stated that general poverty in society is the source of crime and violence. The righteous king must eradicate poverty. The householders favoured the ideal of *aparigraha* in the sense of *alpaparigraha* i.e. limited possession. The Buddhist and Jaina lay-followers were not unoften wealthy merchants. The emphasis was on earning wealth through right means, restraining the quest for possessions, using wealth appropriately especially in charitable ways, and remaining inwardly unattached and equanimous with respect to the vicissitudes of material fortunes. Although this attitude cannot be called Calvinist, it did imply an economic philosophy which sought to hormonize spiritual and economic life. The key-concept here is a two-fold distinction, viz. between wealth as means and wealth as property and between right and wrong means. What needs to be restrained is the attachment inborn in the acquisitive and proprietary instincts. At the same time, the means of acquiring wealth and the use of wealth as means both need to be purified. The concept of *samyag ājīva* or right livelihood aptly expresses ideals. Wealth is a means to living, not an end nor the means to fulfilment. The productive activity itself is not simply as amoral means to be judged on purely utilitarian criteria. It is also a moral vocation, the ethical quality of which cannot be disregarded.

The Brahmanical lawgivers also accepted the distinction between right and wrong ways of livelihood. Manu says that in normal times, the Brahmana should adopt a livelihood which seeks to avoid violence to living beings.[3] The accumulation of wealth should be limited to the necessities of life[4] and should be only through approved means. Manu thus classifies the various means of livelihood—*ṛta, amṛta, pramṛta, satyā-nṛta* and *śvavṛtti*. These are ordered according to the hierarchy of their value. The last is forbidden to the Brahmana. *Ṛta* is gathering particles and sprays of grains from naturally growing plants. *Amṛta* is what is obtained without asking. *Mṛta* is what is obtained by asking. *Pramṛta* is cultivation, *Satyānṛta* is business. *Śvavṛtti* is service.

It would be clear from this that violence, dependence and falsehood were sought to be avoided in the choice of a proper livelihood. The characterization of trade as 'tiue and false' is as interesting as that of agriculture as involving violence. For Manu, thus, the essence of right livelihood consists in its minimality and purity.

In this traditional scheme, pleasure was a lower objective, the *summum bonum* being conceived as *mokṣa*. Economic and political institutions were regarded as parts of a single public order and given a dual status. They constituted utilities or *artha* in so far as they were means to the advancement of public welfare and happiness. At the same time, they were part of a moral order imposing duties and obligations. Political economy, to use an old word which is showing signs of a come back, was conceived both from a utilitarian as well as ethical point of view in the *Arthaśāstra* as well as *Dharmaśāstra*. The ethical point of view inculcated the virtue of disinterestedness, renunciation, resignation and contentment. It represented work as the fulfilling of an obligation arising from one's station in society. In discouraging the pursuit of gain as such and all ambitions seeking to go beyond one's traditional social situation, it was an essentially conservative point of view for which the politico-economic order was only a necessity arising from man's unregenerate nature.

The utilitarian point of view was upheld specially by the *Lokāyata* thinkers and it is they who seem to have played an important part in the rise of political economy as a science in ancient India. The earlier literature of the science has unfortunately been all lost and the *Arthaśāstra* already shows a swing towards orthodoxy. The *Lokāyata* philosophy managed to survive only as a thin trickle and was for all practical purposes swamped by orthodoxy. Nevertheless, the science of *vārtā* was developed as a practical science of managing the means of livelihood.

Although *vārtā* was regarded as one of the four *vidyās*, it is curious that we do not hear of any comprehensive ancient treatise on *vārtā* as such. There were however, many specialized treatises on the different technical activities which were comprised within *vārtā*. Thus we hear of works on agriculture by Gautama, Śālihotra and Parāśara, Videharāja's treatise on commerce, works on crops, the health of trees, metallurgy, meteorology etc.[5] Perhaps *vārtā* as a science was early incorporated in the Arthaśāstra. Originally, the word *vārtā* had the sense of livelihood or profession. "*Ājīvo jīvikā vārtā vṛttir vartana-jīvane*"[6]. The three major professions were agriculture, cattle-rearing and commerce. To these were gradually added money-lending and manufacture as separate items.[7] These modes of livelihood were well-known from earlier days and were probably included in commerce in the earlier threefold listing on account of their intimate connection with it.

In the beginning, thus, *vārtā* seems to have stood for the systematization of the current technical lore relating to agriculture, veterinary science, forestry, trade, mining and metallurgy etc. in order that the pursuit of the various means of livelihood could be facilitated in an age where the traditional vocations had crossed the stage of primitive simplicity. Scientific and technical studies had already reached the stage of systematization as behoves Śāstraic works generally, even though methodologically they must have been largey empirical. The *arthaśāstrā* refers to the *adhyaksas* or the supervisors who were practically experienced people as authorities in the technical fields included in *vārtā*.[8] The fact that there were experienced people who could teach practical arts in accordance with systematic treatises suggests that a professional class of experts had emerged with reference to *vārtā* as it had with reference to *daṇḍanītī*. Now such a class of experts in agriculture, forestry etc. could not have emerged without a class to patronize them socially. This class could only have been of large land-holders, businessmen, etc., a new aristocracy of wealth which is referred to in early Buddhist and Jaina *sūtras* as the class of *gṛhapatis*.[9] Such a class undoubtedly needed professionally competent assistants in business. Just as *daṇḍanīti* presupposed professional administrators and a new monarchy in place of a merely hereditary aristocracy, *varta* presupposed the growth of a new class of businessmen whose position depended on their enterprise[10] and an economic order which obviously required technical competence for its management. The growth of *vārtā* shows that the gradual development of productive forces and market organisation had reached a stage where technical know-how could be looked upon as a means of deliberately transforming them.

It is in the background of developing technology, an enterprizing business class with liquid resources and professional assistance that the rise of a *vārtā* as a distinct science should be placed. Its rise implies the conceptual emergence of a distinctly abstract economic category. Agriculture, trade, etc. were known and studied from before. Now they are subsumed under the general aspect of means of livelihood, as diverse modes of the primary economic activity of gainful employment. This ancient conception of the primary economic category has a distinctiveness of its own. Aristotle had distinguished Economic and Chrematistic, the former being "the art of gaining a livelihood and limited to procuring these articles that are necessary to existence and useful to a household or the state." Chrematistic, on the other hand, depends on exchange and money and seeks unlimited wealth.[11] The conception of *vārtā* includes both these aspects since it does not limit livelihood to mere necessity or comforts but connects it with the production of goods which can be exchanged gainfully. The end of *vārtā* is to provide 'grains, animals, gold, raw materials from the forest and labour' and these are to be used, apparently as means to secure ends in general.[12]

Vārtā was not conceived either as domestic economy or as a generalized science of wealth. It was above all conceived as political economy, the science of economic policy used by the state. The means of livelihood are socially organized resources for the support and fulfilment of life.[13] They need to be regulated by the state in public interest so that there may be security as well as welfare.[14] *Vārtā* was, thus, integrated with *daṇḍanīti* into the *Arthaśāstra*. It has been compared to European Cameralism but although there is a similarity in the common emphasis on the strength of the state through the husbanding of economic resources, *vārtā* did not suffer from any overemphasis on the accumulation of gold. Its conception of public welfare was also more enlightened. In fact, the conception of *arthaśāstra* towards which *vārṭā* strove in conjunction with *daṇḍanītī* is that of social security and public welfare.

Since *vārtā* was expected to be learnt from the *adhyaksas*, the *adhyakṣa-pracāra* of the *Arthaśāstra* may be relied on to give a brief idea of the themes, principles and policies which constituted *varta*. The first theme which we meet here is the settlement of the countryside (*Janapada-niveśa*). This includes the sketch of a model village as also of the conditions under which land was given to farmers. The various afflictions of agriculture and ways of promoting it were also discussed in this context. The use of non-agricultural land as pastures and forests was another item of discussion. The construction of forts and town planning including the policy to be followed towards foreigners was another subject. The storage of treasures and goods constituted a distinct department. Public finance was perhaps the most important part of *vārtā*. It included a discussion of the sources of revenue, the heads of expenditure and the preparation of the budget. The systematic maintenance of accounts and other statistical and non-statistical records was another important theme for departmental work. Separate attention was devoted to the prevention of corruption by officers. Mining and metallurgy were important subjects and special attention was devoted to precious metals and stones. Coinage and the circulation of coins were matters for careful study and regulation. Separate Directorates specialized in agriculture, trade, forest produce, standardization of weights and measures. measures of space and time, customs and tolls, textiles, spirituous liquors, animal slaughter, regulation of courtesans, shipping, cattle. horses, elephants, chariots and pasture lands. The subject matter of *vārtā*, thus, included whatever was capable of yielding revenue or requiring expenditure and this included all manner of economically significant activities. This comprehensive sphere was sought to be regulated by the state on the basis of detailed knowledge and records. It involved the fixation of prices, wages, rent and interest rates, taxes and fines. It also involved the promotion of production and trade, the maximization of revenue for the state compatibly with the pursuit of public welfare. This task presupposed a close empirical study of economic phenomena. This also led occasionally to the formulation of principles about property, pricing, taxation, the fixation of wages, etc. Although the right of private property was generally admitted, sometimes the right of the state over land was asserted. In any case, the state had the right to levy taxes and regulate business in the interest of justice and public security. Prices were sought to be connected with the cost of production and the scarcity of the product. Taxation was to maximise revenue without hurting the people or their business.

While the bulk of the economic activity of the times must have followed the static lines of custom, traders were apt to seek to maximize their gains and the princes sought to maximize their revenues for the sake of power. The *Arthasastra* sought to regulate these diverse tendencies in order to help the creation of a secure and prosperous social order. The leadership in this process was placed in the hands of the prince assisted by experts. This expertize was provided by *vārtā*.

REFERENCES

1. It is oniy the recent Industrial Revolution which is comparable to the archaic Agrarian Revolution, cf. *The Fontana Economic History of Europe*, Vol. III, pp. 7ff.
2. For Dange *Yajña* represented the productive activity of the primitive commune—*From Primitive Communism to Slavery.*
3. Manu, 4.2ff.
4. For Kullūka this includes the maintenance of the family and the performance of scriptural and ritual obligations.
5. Śaṅkarārya's comy, on *Kāmandakīya Nītisāra*,, II. 14; Bhaṭṭasvāmin's comy. on *Kautiliya*, II. 24, p. 134 (ed. Jayaswal and Banerji Sastri, Patna, 1926); N.N. Law, *Studies in Indian History and Culture*, pp. 384-402; K.V.R. Aiyangar, *Aspects of Ancient Indian Economic Thought*, p. 36; K.T. Shah, *Ancient Foundations of Economics*, p. 2.
6. *Amara*, 2.9.7.
7. *Vayu*, 8.124 describes *Vārtā* as *arthasādhikā*. *Artha* (1.4.) mentions the three-fold *Varta*. *Sukraniti* (1.311) and the *Bhagavata* (X.24.21) mention the four-fold Varta including *Kusida*. Karmanta or manufacture is mentioned in the *Devipurana* quoted by Aiyangar, op. cit., p. 15.
8. *Artha* 1.5.8. *Vārtām adhyaksebhyah*; *Manu* (7843) wants economic enterprises to be learnt from experience-*vārtārambhaṁśca lokataḥ*.
9. The exact meanings of the terms *Grhapati* and *Sresthin* remain to be worked out. They certainly attest to the existence of a wealthy urban class deriving its income from business and/or land. Mendaka and Anathapindika are examples—see Malalasekare DPPN, The Jaina *Uvasagadasao gives a* generalized picture of this class.
10. e.g., *Cullakasetthi jataka* narrates the rise of a clever business man from poverty to riches by initiative, investment and profitable buying and selling.
11. Cf. Marx, *Capital* Vol. I, pp. 150-51, fn.
12. *Artha* 1.4.1. "*dhānya-paśu-hiraṇya-kupya-viṣṭipradānād-aupakārikī.*"
13. Cf. *Kamandaka*, 1.12; *Ramayana*, 2.100.48.
14. *Artha* 1.4.2. "*Tayā svopaksam parapakṣam ca vaśīkaroti Kośadaṇḍābhyām.*"

4

Vedic Pattern of Livelihood

Zimmer and Baden Powell, Mcdonell and Keith have drawn a picture of the Vedic village which has been generally repeated by subsequent writers. The growing mass of archaeological evidence in recent years has not so far been brought to bear upon this picture significantly because of the difficulty of identifying Vedic culture archaeologically. The culture of the Painted Grey Ware sites is sometimes held to be the most important claimant for identification with Vedic culture.[1]

It is a common enough assumption that Vedic society was wholly rural. In fact, a predominance of pastoralism has been imagined for the earlier period. These suppositions do not stem simply from a reading of Vedic literature but are at least equally dependent on a hypothesis about Aryan migrations from days when nothing was known of the Indus civilization. Since the discovery of that civilization, the question of its relationship with the Aryans and Vedic culture has naturally arisen and diverse views have been pronounced upon it. It is unfortunate that the authorship of the Indus civilization is itself unknown and is likely to remain so unless its unique script can be definitely deciphered.[2] Meanwhile, it is generally accepted as a working hypothesis that since the Vedic culture was pastoral or rural, it must have been different from the Harappan which was urban. Turning to the *Ṛgvedasaṁhitā*, it is not surprising to discover that it concerns itself more with natural and ritual phenomena than with human habitations. From the epics, we learn that the seers lived in hermitages. Even in the *sūtras*, we find a view mentioned that the *Vedas* should be studied only outside the village. The seers neither traded nor farmed but lived on the herds of cattle tended by their disciples and the produce of the forest. Despite outward similarities, life in the hermitages ought not to be confused with the life of pastoralists in *ghoṣas* or of tribals in *pallīs*.

When the hymns do move out to mention the settlements of kings and the people, we hear of the *grāma* as well as of the *pur*. In fact, while *grāma* occurs only nine times in the *Rk saṁhitā* with *grāmya* occurring once, *pur* occurs no less than eighty-five times. There are three references to *krs/kṛṣi* and two to *vanij*. This does not at all suggest a wholly rural background. It is, however, argued that while *grāma* meant a village, *pur* did not mean a city but rather a temporary place of refuge which might be constructed with "ramparts of hardened earth with palisades and a ditch". *Pur* has also been interpreted to mean a natural stronghold or mountain fastness. Grassmann says that *pur* is "fester Platz, Burg, ursprünglich der (im Falle der Gefahr mit Menschen und Gütern gefüllte) gefüllte Platz (von *pur*)"[3]. This etymology is convincing enough but the qualification added within brackets is without any warrant. In later usage, *pur* certainly meant a city which was in fact fortified but the word for fort, *durga*, was different. The question is, do we have any firm ground for proposing a different meaning for *pur* for the earlier period? Pischel and Geldner thought that *pur* should be given the meaning of town with fortifications.[4] This has been questioned on the analogy of ancient Germanic and Slav tribes but that really begs the question. This analogy is in fact contradicted by the experience of the ancient Greeks and Hittites who entered areas with ancient urban traditions.

On this latter analogy, some scholars have supposed that the *pur*s referred to the fortified towns of the Harappans whom the 'Aryans' attacked and destroyed. 'Aryans' like their god Indra, thus, became the destroyers of cities and their own culture becomes nomadic and rural with a vengeance[5] ! This, however, again begs the question.

We have argued that the struggle of Indra against the *dāsas* and *dasyus* has nothing whatever to do with any supposed struggle of the 'Aryans' with the non-Aryans. In fact, the *Ṛgveda* does not contain any racial associations in the words *ārya* and *dāsa*. Perhaps the ancient 'Aryan' invaders of India did not suffer from the racial consciousness of modern Westerners. Or perhaps the hymns were composed long after the era of conflict was over. In this situation of uncertainty, it would be rash to conclude on hypothetical grounds that the *pur*s refer to the non-Aryans or that the *paṇis* were non-Aryans.

If we exclude unproved hypotheses, we are left with the references in the *Ṛksaṁhitā* to *araṇya*, *grāma* and *pur*. The *pur* appears to have been a fortified place with defensive ramparts and a surrounding ditch.[6] Vṛtra had hidden the cows in the *pur* which has been compared to the clouds, apparently on account of its towering battlements. Apart from this difference in terms of security and presumably of size and population, we should not presume any great qualitative difference between Vedic villages and towns. The connection with *Pani* probably indicates the greater prominence of trade in the towns.

It may be mentioned here that Dr. Ghurye has recently supported the existence of townships in the Rgvedic period by a number of arguments, the most important of which is the use of horse-drawn vehicles, especially of two or more horses. They pre-suppose fairly wide and good roads. When we are told that it was undignified for one to come to the place of sacrifice in a one-horse carriage, it is implied that the settlement was large enough to require to be covered in a horse carriage.[7]

The society reflected in the *Ṛgveda* shows us at least twenty distinct professions—rower (*aritṛ*), boatman, corn-grinder, priest, poet, smith (*karmāra*), smelter and welder (*dravitṛ*, *dhmātṛ*), ploughman, herdsman, village headman, carpenter, chariot-maker, charioteer, barber, merchant, weaver, writer, physician, *Kāru* and brahman. We can, in fact, presume the existence of several other professions. For example, the potter was certainly a specialist, and so must have been the flint worker. The hunter similarly must be presumed. Later Vedic literature gives a much larger list but some of the items found there were probably present earlier. The division of labour was growing continuously and it is difficult to draw too sharp a line between the earlier and the later periods.

In any case, we must not press the rural-urban dichotomy too far in the Vedic context. The basic pattern of life was one and continuous and is more easily understood in terms of what is generally held to be rural. Despite the variety of crafts and the existence of professional traders, the towns were presumably political and defensive rather than commercial settlements. Many of the townsmen like the villagers would still be working on surrounding fields or tending cattle during the day but retiring behind the shelter of the town defences at night. The villages were small as well as big, for we hear of the 'big village' (*mahāgrāmaḥ*).[8] It has been pointed out that the village consisted of arable fields (*kṣetra*) around habitational dwellings in the middle. Around the fields lay the pasture land (*gavyūti*) and around it the ubiquitous forest. The forest (*araṇya*, *araṇyānī*) was looked upon with apprehension as well as reverence. In a hymn devoted to it, it is described as "balmy, redolent with fragrance, rich in food, uncultivated, the mother of beasts". It is fearful in the evenings with strange sounds but offers a fill of delectable fruits to eat.[9]

Tracks or paths for moving on foot or bullock carts or horse-drawn chariots connected the villages which in the later Vedic age at least were near enough to allow a traveller to reach even distant Gandhara by asking the way from village to village.[10]

As indicated above, agriculture, cattle-rearing and handicrafts constituted the principal occupations of the people in the village. Agriculture was contrasted with such wasteful activities as gambling,[11] although gambling along with racing appears to have been popular. It was implied that agriculture would mean wealth (*vitta*) and a proper home with cattle and wife.[12] Cultivation was carried on with an ox-driven plough. The plough was called *lāṅgala* or *sīra*. *Sīra* has been connected with *sītā* or furrow by Grassman and would thus mean the tool scratching lines or furrows.[13] It may be recalled that *kṛṣi* itself has the etymological sense of 'scratching'. The ancient method of cultivation was probably of scratching the earth with a pointed stick. Although the meaning of *lāṅgala* is not wholly certain, it was probably connected with the later word for stick (*laguda*).[14] The tip or point became the share of the plough when it replaced the digging stick or hoe. This transformation doubtless went back a long time, for although Kosambi had thought that Harappan agriculture had been carried on with a hoe, Lal's discovery of the ploughed field at Kalibangan definitively disproves that suggestion.[15] In later Vedic times, the share appears to have been of metal since the plough has been described as lance-tipped (*pavīravat*) and its handle is distinguished from the point.[16] Similarly, in later Vedic *saṁhitās*, a team of oxen are referred to as drawing the plough which was apparently very heavy.[17]

Agricultural operations were connected with appropriate ritual and the verses of R. IV. 57 were recited in commencing ploughing. The hymn mentions several deities which personify the agricultural operations. *Kṣetrapati* is the lord of the field. *Śunāsīrau* are a pair of deities personifying the plough. *Sītā* is the furrow-goddess. The farmers using the plough are called *Kīnāśa*, a word of uncertain etymology. This hymn occurring in the family-*mandalas* also disproves the suggestion that the occurrence of references to ploughing mainly in the first and tenth *mandalas* indicates that it may have been little known earlier.

The *Ṛgvedasaṁhitā* has in all about thirty-six references to 'agricultural field' (*kṣetra*) and 'arable land' (*urvarā*) occurring separately or in compounds with *pati*, *vid*, *jit*, etc. Most of the references relate to the winning or gaining of *kṣetra*.[18] Such acquisition apparently makes one the master of the field.[19] The arable land is treated at par with one's possessions like cattle or children.[20] It is clearly implied as a personal and private possession.[21] The measuring of the field with a rod is referred to[22] and this strergthens the impression of agricultural land as individual property. *Ksetra* or *urvarā* is contrasted with *khilya* or waste-land as much as with *gavyūti* or pasture as with *aranya* or forest.[23] From a relatively obscure allusion, it has been concluded that *khilya* also had the sense of land in between cultivated fields.[24]

Perhaps it could be land left fallow, rather than unfertile land.

It is, of course, difficult to decide how far this personal ownership of land was individual and how far it was vested in the joint family. Property belonging to the head of the family was to some extent certainly partible. Whether land was so partible is not certain, though, on later analogy, likely. "There was no question of ownership vesting in the king. In fact, in discussing the Viśvajit sacrifice, the *Mīmaṁsāsūtras* explicitly repudiate the view that the king could give away the whole land. Nor is there any clear trace of the ownership of agricultural land by the village community as a whole."[25]

Beyond the fields lay the pasture or *gavyūti.* Long ago, Sir Henry Maine had drawn the analogy of ancient German tribes where the pasture land was the property of the community.[26] The *Rksaṁhitā* has twelve references to *gavyūti.* The seers pray that pastures may be wide,[27] inexhaustible,[28] sprinkled with *ghṛta.*[29] Beyond the pastures lay the woodland, a dark green sea. It was a source of food—roots, fruits, game and honey. Wild grains abounded in it. It could be cleared for cultivation when necessary. Such clearings were called *vṛjana,* although the term has been variously interpreted. Fire rather than the axe appears to have been the principal tool of clearing the forests even in the later Vedic age. Whether any one laid a claim of ownership on forest land at that distant epoch is not known.

Although agriculture depended mainly on the natural fertility of the soil and rain, artificial irrigation as well as the use of manure appears to have been known. We hear of artificial wells as distinguished from natural springs. The well or *avata* is described as "*Iṣkṛtāhāvam avatam suvaratram*" and again as "*droṇāhāvam avatam aṁsacakram aṁsatrakośam siñcata nṛpānam.*[30]" Griffith translates " . . . . from the, well with pails prepared and goodly straps . . . ." and "pour forth the well with stone wheel, wooden buckets, the drink of heroes, with the trough for armour[31]". From this the *Vedic Index* understands "The water was raised by a wheel (*cakra*) of stone, to which was fastened a strap (*varatra*), with a pail (*kosa*) attached to it when raised it was poured (*sinc*) into buckets (*ahava*) of wood".[32] Prof. Ghurye comments that the *Vedic Index* has failed to comprehend the mechanism of buckets on a belt.[33] Apart from wells, artificial water channels appear to be mentioned.[34]

In *R.* 10.101.3-6, the process of sacrifice is compared with that of agriculture. The processes of ploughing, sowing and reaping are here mentioned graphically. *Śatapatha Brāhmaṇa* (1.6.1.3) only elaborates this as "ploughing, sowing, reaping and threshing".[35] The ripe grain was first cut with a sickle (*dātra sṛṇi*).[36] It was then bound into bundles (*parśa*) and threshed on the floor of the granary (*khala*[37]). "The grain was then separated from the straw and refined either by a sieve (*titau*) or a winnowing fan (*śūrpa*). The winnower was called *dhanyakrt* and the grain was measured in a vessel called *urdara*[38]." The art of agriculture was taught to men by the Nāsatyas. They represent the divine archetype of the cultivator. "Wishing to teach man, O Aśvins, you first cultivated grains by a plough in heaven."[39] The plough is here called *Vṛka*. Here ploughing is raised to a cosmic dignity and thus rendered fit for the ritual ceremonies of R. 4.57 and the imagery of R. 10.101. Attuned to divinity, the farmer, singing to his steers, is more than a mere gleaning from perennial folkways.[40]

As for *yava* which the Nāsatyas cultivated first in heaven, it seems correct to hold that it was in this period "a generic term for any sort of 'grain' and not merely 'barley' ".[41] We gather that *yava* was cultivated with oxen,[42] gladdened by rain[43] and filled in the *urdaras*. It was also cooked with milk.[45] In the later *Saṁhitās* and *Brahmaṇas*, we hear of wheat and barley, rice, sesame and various pulses.[46] The cultivation of hemp and sugar-cane was also known at that time. There were various seasons for sowing and reaping different crops and two harvests were mentioned.

The food offered to the gods gives us an idea of what men must have consumed. In a tradition recorded later, we are told that *Yava* is the foremost of the substances fit for oblation and rice comes next. Alternately, one could use milk or curd. Flesh and oil could also be used. The *Grhyasutras* speaking of the morning and evening oblations into the fire mention boiled rice and barley.[47] In the larger sacrifices too, the food offered consisted of *soma*, flesh, milk and milk-products, and preparations of barley and rice. The Br. Up. (6.4) speaks of rice prepared with milk, or curd or sesame or meat. The vessels used were of baked clay or wood or metal such as copper or brass or precious metals.[48]

The houses in the villages were constructed almost entirely of perishable material like wood, bamboo and thatch and divided into several parts like the sitting room (*sadas*) or the women's apartment (*patnisadana*). A hymn in the *Atharva* prays that the house with its horses and kine should "rise up for great felicity and fortune". It is referred to as a spacious store full of corn and high-roofed. It was robed in grass (*tṛṇam vasāna*) with a pillar and bamboos atop (*ṛtena sthūṇām adhiroha vaṁśa*).[49] It is worth noting that in the later Vedic texts, the use of bricks is well attested in connection with the construction of fire altars. And these bricks included burnt bricks. Archaeologically, the beginning of townships goes back to what is generally regarded as the later Vedic period. These early towns were surrounded by ramparts and massive walls.[50] But the houses in the towns continued to use timber largely till much later.

The use of iron clearly began in the later Vedic age.[51] Presumably swords and arrowheads, axes and ploughshares were fashioned from iron. Whether this had any marked effect on the clearance of the forests or the productivity of agricultural land, is a debatable point. As a well-known passage in the *Śatapatha* tells us, the Vedic expansion towards the north-east beyond the *Sadānīrā* used fire for the clearance of forests. *Mbh* tells us of the burning down of the Khandava forest.

The Vedic age was one of "migrations and settlements". While the geographical horizon of the early Vedic age extended from the *Kubhā* to the *Ganga*, the later Vedic age saw the emergence of Kasi, Kosala and Videha as great kingdoms. Anga, Magadha, Vanga, Pundra and Andhra are glimpsed as tribes outside the pale.[52] The expansion of the geographical horizon was thus truly remarkable in those days of dense forests and must have been slow, lasting over a long time.

Although 'Aśvin' itself suggests horse-riding, the horse-chariot and the bullock-carts were the ancient modes of travel and cartage respectively. In the later Vedic age when the Vedic people had reached the 'east', the use of elephants, perhaps, came to be known.[53] The *janas* settled into *janapadas* and powerful monarchies arose.

The basic pattern of social life which came to be established during all these changes was rural-agricultural with forest hermitages and primitive tribes on the one side and a few towns with defensive arrangements and administrative importance on the other. Life was lived under conditions of material simplicity and an unending cycle of ritual regulations which must have been interwoven with a pattern of folk customs and festivals. Three great institutions determined the web of social life—the public authority of the king exercised at the village level through the *grāmaṇī*, the system of kinship wherein the joint family played the most important part, and the agricultural system which was basically one of peasant proprietorship. Although a clear distinction was made between sovereignty and property, the king, it seems, could assign to a private person, generally a learned Brahmana, the use of revenues of a village. It was thus a legitimate ambition for one to 'wish to acquire a village' (*grāmakāma*) and we find ritual prescriptions detailed for its fulfilment.[54] A purely contractual bond of service or commerce was apparently not prominent yet. Political obedience and loyalty, domestic affection and duty, hereditary vocations and immemorial usage governed the even and cyclical tenor of life.

REFRENCES

1. B.B. Lal, 'P.G. Ware Culture' in UNESCO *History of Central Asia*. The article was presented as a paper in Indo-Soviet Joint Seminar, Allahabad p. 82.
2. Cf Gregory L. Possehl (ed). *Ancient Cities of the Indus*, pp. 255ff; cf. N.D. Sethna, *Karpāsa* which argues that Vedic Culture was prior to the Indus Civilization.
3. *Wörterbuch zum Ṛgveda*, under *pur.*
4. Wheeler, *The Indus Civilization* (3rd ed), pp. 131-32.

5. *Vedic Index* under *pur*.
6. Cf. R. 8.92; 10.108; 10.138 etc.
7. Ghurye, *Vedic India*.
8. *V.I.* refers to *Jaiminiyopaniṣad Brāhmaṇa*. It may be mentioned, however, that *R* itself has *mahāgrāma*, *R*. 10.78.6—but it seems to refer to a big 'horde' on the move (*yāman*).
9. R. 10.146.
10. *Chāndogya*; cf. *Atharva*, 12.1.47.
11. R. 10.34—'*akṣair mā dīvyaḥ kṛṣim it kṛṣasva*'.
12. Ibid. '*tatra gāvah kitaya tatra jāyā*.'
13. Grassmann, op. cit.
14. Cf. Mayrhoffer, op. cit.
15. D.D. Kosambi, *Ancient Indian Culture and Civilisation*; B. B. Lal, *Puratattva*.
16. Cf. *Vedic Index*, II, p. 231. Dr. R. S. Sharma would, however, have the Vedic plough as wooden. It may be remarked that the wooden character of ritually used ploughs is not an index of contemporary usage since ritual often tends to reproduce archaic conditions.
17. Cf. *Vedic Index*, II, p. 451.
18. e.g. *R*. 1.112.20; Ibid. 1.33.15; ibid. 10.32.7; *Ib*. 4. 38.1; ibid. 7.19.3; ibid. 9.85.4.
19. Ibid. 4.57.1-3; ibid. 7.35.10; ibid. 10.66.13. These references are apparently to the deity *Kṣetrapati* who like *Vāstoṣpati* is only the divine counterpart of human masters of the field or home. cf. ibid. 8.21.3—*aśvapate gopate urvarāpate*.
20. Ibid. 4 41.6; ibid. 6.25.4.
21. *q. I*8.91.5-6.
22. Ibid. 1.110 5.
23. Ibid. 10.142.3; *Ib*. 6.47.20; ibid. 6.61.14. It may be remembered that '*aranya*' is etymologically derived from *arana* or distant.
24. Ibid. 6.28·2; cf. *V.I.K.* ad *hilya*
25. G. C. Pande in *History of the Panjab*, Vol. I.
26. *Village Communities in the East and the West*.
27. *R*. 974. 3; ibid. 5.66.3; ibid. 7.77.4; ibid. 9.78.5; ibid. 9.85.8.
28. *Ib*. 10.14.2.
29. Ibid. 10.80.6; ibid. 3.62.16; ibid. 7.62.5; ibid. 7.65.4; ibid. 8.5.6.
30. *R*. 10.101.5-7.
31. Griffith, op. cit., Vol. I, p. 541.
32. *Vedic Index*, Vol. I, p. 40.
33. Ghurye, op. cit., p. 227.
34. *R*. 7.49. 2; ibid. 4.58.5; ibid. 7.69.12.
35. "*Kṛṣanto ha smaiva pūrve vapanto yanti lunanto apare mṛṇantah*......"
36. R. 10.131.2. *dāntyanupūrvaṁ viyūya*; *Ib*. 10.101.3 *sṛṇyaḥ pakvam eyat*.
37. Ibid. 10.48.7. *Khale na parṣān*.
38. *Vedic Index*, I, p. 182.
39. *R*. 8.22.6 : "*Daśasyantā mānavampūrvyaṁ diviyavaṁ vrkena Karsathah*." Also Ibld. 1.117.21.
40. Ibid. 8.20.19 : "*Gāya gā iva carkṛṣat*," cf. *Ghurye, op. cit*.
41. *V. I*. Vol. II, p. 187.

42. Cf. *R.* 1.23.15.
43. Ibid. 2.5.6; Ib. 5.85.3.
44. Ibid. 2.14.11.
45. Ibld. 8.2.3.
46. *Vaj. Sam.* 18.22. "*Vrīhayaṣca me yavāśca me māsāśça me tilāśca me mudgāśca me, Khalāśca me priyaṅgavaśca me anavaśca me śyāmākaşca me nīvārāśca me godhūmāśca me masūrāśca me.*" Mahidhara explains that while *śyāmāka* was grown in the villages, *Nīvāra* grew wild in the forests.

    It has been argued with telling effect that there is no definte evidence for the knowledge of cotton in either the earlier or the later Vedic age, which is extraordinary since the Harappans knew cotton—see Sethna / op. cit..
47. Kane, op. cit. Vol. II, Pt. I, p. 681.
48. Cf. *Vedic Index* , I pp. 30, 130, 516.
49. *A. V.* III. 12.
50. Cf. *e.g.* Prof. G.R. Sharma's Excavations at Kausambi.
51. It has been argued that black *ayas* was bronze, not iron—see Sethna, op. cit.
52. *Aitareya Brahmana.* 7.18; *Atharva* 5.22.14; *Aitareya Āranyaka,* 2.1.1.
53. *Ch. Up* I 10.1 refers to *ibhyagrāma.*
54. *Vedic Index*, I, p. 246.

5

Rural Agrarian Pattern in the Post-Vedic Age

The great grammarian Patanjali discusses the meaning of the word *grama* at several places. Commenting on Panini 1.1.7 he says "The word *grama* has many meanings. Sometimes it is used for a collection of houses (*śālāsamudāya*), as for example, when it is said 'the village is burnt'. It is also used for the surrounding hedge (*Vāta-parikṣepa*), as for example, in '(he) has entered the village'. Again it is used for men, as for example in 'the village has gone, the village has come'. It is also used for (a settlement) with its woodland, boundary and the levelled ground, as when it is said 'the village is gained'. This is the meaning when two villages are said to be adjacent, i.e. uninterrupted by any other village in between."[1]

Grama originally had the sense of a collectivity and came to mean a settlement. In Panini 6.2.84: "*grāma anivasantaḥ*", both senses are implied. As a settlement, a village was distinct from a town but the word *gramà* was sometimes used ambiguously. Patanjali has an interesting disquisition on the subject.[2] "A village is different, a town different. How is that known? Thus somebody asks another, 'where do you come from? (Do you come) from a village?' The other replies, 'Not from a village, but from a town.' But, well, is not a village the same as a town? How is that known ? From social usage. The actions which are forbidden for the village are forbidden even more so for the town.[3] Thus the village cock is not to be eaten, nor the village pig." This rule excludes the town cock and the town pig even more. 'The *Vedas* are not to be studied in the village', excludes their study in the town.

Hence what is a village is a town. Then how is it that on one's being asked 'where do you come from ? (Do you come) from a village?' one answers 'Not from a village but from a town' ? What one asserts is a special kind of settlement. There are different kinds of settlements—village, hamlet, township, urban area."[4] Patanjali implies that *grama* could be used in a general sense meaning any settlement and also in the specific sense of a non-urban rural settlement.[5]

The *Samantapasadika*, the commentary on the *Vinaya*, states that the word 'village' is used to exclude the forest or wilderness. As a general term for settlement, it includes the town (*nigama* and *nagara*) also. Here also the context is the same as in the grammatical works alluded to above, viz. the application of rules for settlements in general. In fact, one can trace here a development of usage. The original *sikkhāpada* only distinguished *gāma* from *Arañña*.[6] The ancient *Vibhaṅga* on this defines the villages as consisting of "one hut, or two huts, or three huts or four huts; having human inhabitants or *not having them*; (ranch) consisting of two or three houses where cattle are stationed but without any regular streets etc. or a caravan station for more than four months."[7] Here settlements are viewed as small villages, including 'ghost' villages, scattered ranches and encampments. *Samantapasadika*, written in Ceylon, explains that the boundaries could be ramparts of brick or at the least merely a hedge of thorny branches. The village apparently had an *Indra* post or *Indrakila* in the middle. Large settlements could have two of them, one in the middle, the other on the outskirts. The *Abhidhamma* text *Vibhanga*, in fact, defines the forest as extending between the external *Indrakīlas*.[8]

A Jaina text discusses several criteria for defining the extent of a village, viz. the limits within which the cattle graze, the boundaries whence the grass-cutters or wood-cutters go out or return, or the conventional boundaries in terms of a garden or well. A place of the local deity or worship (*devakula*) and an assembly hall (*sabha*) are mentioned as the centre of the village.[9] From these early references, we may conclude that villages were scattered in diverse shapes and sizes, distinguished from the woodlands which surrounded them and the towns which were met with more sparingly. The centre of the village was a place of festive or ritual significance and its boundaries were marked out. Farming, grazing, woodcutting and handicrafts constituted the economic activities of the village. The round of festivities and ritual constituted the social life of the village. Visiting jugglers, acrobats, actors and mendicants punctuated this rhythm. The *grāmaṇī* ensured that crimes were checked and taxes paid.

On the average size, number and population of the villages, the evidence is naturally diverse. The *Arthasastra* would like the village to consist of one hundred to five hundred families and to extend to one or two *Krosas.* Its boundaries were to be fixed with reference to such features as "a river, a mountain, a forest, a stretch of pebbles, sand etc., a cavern, an embankment, a *Sami* tree, a *Salmali* tree or a milk tree (like Asvattha, Nyagrodha etc.)."[10] One of the commentaries, however, holds that it is the distance between the villages which is to be one or two *krosas.* The village itself is to have a radius of four *krosas.*[11] On the other hand, the *Agnipurana* declares that a village may consist of six families including the village elder.[12] In view of what has been said above, there is really no contradiction here.[13]

As to the number of the villages, the figures appear extravagant and pose a problem. The *Vinaya* speaks of 80,000 villages in Magadha in the times of Bimbisara.[14] *Aparājitapṛcahā* and other texts give the total number of villages as over ninety lacs. Various attempts have been made to explain these figures but it cannot be said that the problem has been solved as yet. Most probably, the figures are conventional and exaggerated referring to the imperial claims of the regional dynasties and are in this sense essentially overlapping.[15]

The population of the village naturally consisted of diverse castes and classes and their proportion must have varied in different regions and ages. But it is interesting to note that while the *Arthasastra* would like the newly settled villages to have a majority of śūdra cultivators (*śūdra-karṣaka-prāyam*),[16] the *Manusmrti* expresses a preference for a place with a majority of the upper castes.[17] The *Markandeya purana* again, thinks of the village as consisting of cultivators and having a majority of the *śūdras*.[18] A Jaina *purana* of a still later date endorses this position of the *śūdras*.[19] Perhaps it may be concluded that in course of time in some areas the actual labouring population in the village came to be recruited more and more from classes of which the status was held to be that of the *śūdras*. This could have resulted partly from the upper castes in the villages tending to become owners rather than actual cultivators of land,[20] and partly from the adoption of agriculture by tribal population living near the margins of the old villages. Śūdra cultivators were recongnised from earlier times and in the system of Mixed Castes, the range of the *śūdras* was considerably extended. Yuan Chwang also speaks of *śūdras* as cultivators.[21] But it would be wrong to take it as a universally valid fact. In any case, it does suggest that the ancient system of peasant proprietorship was being modified by a growing vogue of landlordism in the Gupta and post-Gupta times.

Among the classes of rural population, the *Dharmasutras* mention, 'Cultivators, traders, herdsmen, money-lenders and craftsmen'.[22] Turning to a much later period, we find reference to the householders or *kutumbins* led by the Brahmanas and others.[23] The *kutumbins* apparently were agriculturists and the expression is reminiscent of Pali '*gahapati*'. Thus the occupational and caste divisions in the village did not coincide but overlapped.

The village craftsmen included the carpenter, the blacksmith, the potter and the barber.[24] They appear to have worked for themselves as well as for the villagers generally on the basis of compensation in kind through the assignment of land or its produce.[25] Panini tells us that *grāma-takṣā* meant a common village carpenter as distinguished from *kauṭa-takṣā* who worked independently in his own workshop.[26] Another *sūtra* of Panini defines the accent of compounds beginning with *grama* and ending with the name of a craft. The *Kasika* gives as illustrations, *grāmanāpita* and *grāma-kulāla*.[27] The basic relationship of the village craftsmen to their partners is economic and contractual, not ritual. There is no trace of any *Jajmani* system here.

The use of iron for tools is widely attested in the early

Buddhist literature. We hear of *ayokapāla* (iron pot), *ayokūṭa* (iron hammer), *ayokhīla* (iron stake), *ayogula* (iron ball), *ayoghana* or *ayomuggara* (iron club), *ayosaṅku* (iron spike), and *ayonangala* (iron plough).[28] Axe or *pharasu* is mentioned but apparently not specifically iron axe.[29] This would tend to contradict the assumption of Dr. Kosambi and his followers who attribute the settlement of the middle Ganga basin to the discovery of the iron axe.

The iron ploughshare (*phāla*) is vividly described at several places as heated during the day and then sizzling and steaming when plunged into the water.[30] Perhaps the word '*phāla*' not merely meant the ploughshare but any piercing or cutting tip. The *Kasibharadvajasutta* of the *Suttanipata* describes the plough (*nangala*) as consisting of share and tip or goad (*phalapacana*), pole (*īsā*), tie (*yotta*=Vedic *Yoktra*) and *Yoke* (*Yuga*).

In Pali, the old Vedic word *langala* (=nangala) continued but in Panini it seems replaced by *hala* of which the parts are the same as mentioned above—*īsā*, *potra*, *kuṣī*, *varatra* and *yuga*. *Kuṣī* replaces *phāla* and *potra* is a new word.[31] The measurement of fields is regularly implied. The officer in charge of this may be seen in the *Jatakas* and the *Arthaśāstra* and appears to develop like the modern 'Collector' into the Asokan *Rajuka*.[32]

The cultivation of rice required water-immersed fields which were called *kedāra* and Panini has a special *sūtra* to signify the collection of *kedāras*.[33] Several varieties of rice are mentioned including the famous variety ripening in sixty days.[34] Although Panini belonged to the north-west, it is obvious that the expansion of settlements towards the east in the later Vedic age brought in general changes in the cultivation of crops. The cultivation of sugar-cane was important from a commercial point of view.[35]

Seasonal loans among the cultivators appear to have been important enough to account for several distinct *sūtras* in Panini.[36] Part of the growth of agricultural labour must have come from cultivators with holdings too small to afford even a plough[37] just as indebtedness led to slavery.

The basic features of the rural pattern with its variety of crops and agricultural techniques and the mosaic of professional classes and castes, thus appear to have been well established by the Maurya age. Although no agricultural or horticultural works of the age have survived, the *Arthaśāstra* evidences a developed knowledge of crops and irrigation. *Bṛhatsaṁhitā* of the Gupta age shows the continuation of the scientific knowledge of agriculture. It tells us about how to predict rain and clouds[38] and to estimate rain quantitatively.[39] It also details the varieties of crops and ways of predicting the produce.[40] An apparently much later work, *Kṛṣiparāśara*,, gives a resume of agriculture as it was practised towards the end of the ancient period.[41]

If the Vedic pattern of life was governed by the notion of *Ṛta*, divine ordinance and ritual, the pattern of post-Vedic life was governed by the notion of *Dharma*, immemorial usage and social obligation. Over the centuries, such usage and norms were codified on a national basis. This broad framework of social ethos as laid down in the *Dharmasūtras* over-rode the details of regional and epochal variations which, within measure, it accepted as authoritative. A peculiarity of the Brahmanical law-givers was their distaste for merely economic activity. They looked down upon the villages as they did upon the cities. There was a rule that the *Vedas* were not to be studied in the villages, a rule which was later on interpreted to mean only those villages where the sudras were in a majority.[42] Baudhayana roundly declares that agriculture was destructive of the *Vedas* (*Kṛṣir-Veda-vināśinī*).[43] It is obvious that the centres of Vedic study lay outside the villages, in hermitages. It seems that by the age of the *Dharmasūtras*, traditional Vedic culture was becoming archaic and self-consciously out of tune with the villages as populated by multitudes of ignorant and non-brahmanical classes engaged in economic pursuits, such as farmers, cowherds, craftsmen and labourers. The older Vedic integrity of life and social structure had broken down and the brahmanas sought to maintain their leadership by an elaborate canoncial regulation which deliberately put merely 'economic' values and classes at a low level. In the Brahmanical scheme of life, a person of the upper three classes avoided all productive economic activity in three out of the four stages of life and lived outside the village during the period. At the same time, it is obvious that the brahmanas had ceased to live simply by alms or gifts. Gautama thus permits the brahmana to engage in agriculture, trade and money-lending *through others* i.e. slaves or servants or tenants.[44] Buddhist canonical literature readily confirms this by speaking of brahmanas owning landed estates and managing farms. *Suttanipata* thus speaks of Kasibharadvaja and Sundarika Bharadvaja. Buddha taught them that the true art of cultivation lay not in cultivating fields but in cultivating the moral self, thus annulling the Brahmanical compromise with agriculture.

Although the tradition of sages and mendicants preferred the solitude and silence of sylvan retreats to the 'impure' life of the villages, the latter were ubiquitous, largely self-sufficient and except for persistent famines or misrule, imaged as happy and prosperous in classical literature. Throughout the classical period, the countryside retained its woodland setting and the evils of deforestation were unknown. Valmiki's *Rāmāyaṇa*, Kalidasa's *Raghuvaṁsa* and the *Gāthās* of Hala present a picture in which the village and the woodland are never apart. Ponds and lotuses, bees and elephants are constant motifs. Milk and fruits, curd and butter, flowers and honey are referred to as common products. While large landed estates cultivated by slaves, servants, hired labourers and tenants were not unknown, peasant proprietors cultivating their own fields with the help of their families constituted the bulk of the farmers. Cattle was maintained along with farming although a special caste of cowherds existed and was specially important in certain areas. Slaves and landless labourers available for hire could only be a small class in the village. As already mentioned, a limited class of hereditary craftsmen like the carpenter, the smith, the barber and the potter were part of the village economy.[45] Subsistence farming was the rule and an occasional mart or fair must have supplied the needs of the farmers and cowherds constituting the mainstay of the village population. Wandering mendicants, minstrels, jugglers and acrobats occasionally passed through the village.[46] The seasonal round of agriculture punctuated by festivals woven round its diverse aspects and the domestic round of rearing and marrying children in accordance with prescribed ritual and custom constituted the course of life in the village. The village headman and elders managed its affairs as far as public work and the settling of disputes were concerned. The burden of taxation was light and foreigners were surprised to note that normally even the armies spared the countryside from destruction.[47]

While the villagers mostly dwelt in houses of mud-bricks and thatch and wore little except a cotton *dhoti* and some kind of a wrap on the upper part of the body and a turban on the head, they did not lack food in quantity or quality as milk products and the products of the forest supplemented the produce of the farm. Wheat, barley or rice with pulses, *ghee* and salt constituted the staple diet.[48] Meat and milk products must have formed part of the diet of the more properous section in the village.

The simplicity, plenty and harmony which characterized the rural pattern of life owed its origin to a variety of factors. It presupposed the bounty of nature and broke down if the monsoons failed persistently. But it also rested on the maintenance of ancient Aryan or Vedic institutions. The right of individual ownership of land and cattle tempered with the right of the community over common land, pastures, ponds, etc. made effective through the vitality of the village councils kept in check for a long time those processes which lead to the concentration of land in the hands of a few with the resultant growth of some kind of a servile status for the many. Similarly, the ancient tradition of the king as responsible not only for the security but also the prosperity of the community and the conservatism which limited the right of the king to only a light degree of taxation in accordance with custom, kept in check the exploitation of the villages for the extravagance of the courts and the aristocracy. A final factor in the situation was the Brahmanical system of castes with its duties, which united the different professional and hereditary groups in a harmonious and co-operative social whole and reconciled the individual to his lot, instilling in him the virtues of contentment in happiness and resignation in the face of calamity.

While the basic pattern of rural life—its self-sufficiency, isolation, harmony and unchanging rhythm—as revealed in the Vedic and early post-Vedic times must have continued as a standing keynote, some changes undoubtedly took place in the classical and post-classical times. The pressure of population in some areas necessitated that efforts be made to bring new land under cultivation. The policy of settling new or abandoned areas enunciated by Kautalya is an illustration. Nevertheless, it must be remembered that the growth of population in ancient times was followed by periodic decimation. Large areas continued to be under the forest till late mediaeval times[49] and there is no doubt that no dearth of usable land was faced in ancient times.

The fertility of the soil was proverbial and "The Greek writers burst into exuberant praise of the fertility of the Indian soil and favourable climatic condition and river-system........."[50] "Megasthenes indicates the fertility of India by the fact of the soil producing two crops every year both of fruits and grains. [Eratosthenes writes to the same effect, for he speaks of a winter and a summer sowing, which both have rain.........[51]" According to Eratosthenes, during the summer rains "flax is sown and millet, also sesamum, rice and *bosmorum* and in the winter time wheat, barley, pulse, and other excellent fruits unknown to us."[52] In the third century B.C., Theophrastus mentions a variety of agricultural and horticultural produce from India—cardamum, cassia, cinnamon, nard, pepper, ginger-grass, citron, rice, lentil, cotton, jack fruit, banana, mango and ebony. Other classical sources mention sugar-cane, indigo, gum, aloes, coconut, melon, peach, apricot, millet, etc. (Adhya, *Early Indian Economy*, p. 143). The celebrated Chinese history '*Chien Hen Shu*' speaks of the Indian produce of rice, wheat, pulse, millet, hemp, grape and other fruits, sandal-wood, bamboo etc. (ibid. p. 41).

Brhadarnyaka (VI.3.13) mentions ten varieties of cultivated grains (*grāmya*):

> *Daśa grāmyāṇi dhānyāni bhavanti vrīhiyavāstilamāsā anupriyangavo godhūmāśca masurāśca khalvāśca khalakulāśca*

Apart from these, wild grains, fruits and vegetables grew without cultivation, which is noticed in the epics and astonished the Greeks. The *Arthasastra* mentions three sowings and a large number of crops—"

> *Śālivrīhi kodravatilapriyangudāraka—varakāh pūrvavāpah, mudgamāsaśaimbyā madhyavāpāh, kusumbhamasura-kulathayava-godhūma-kalāyātasī sarṣapāh paścādvāpah*

(2.24.12-14). Apart from these, the *Artha* mentions the cultivation of diverse varieties of vegetables—beans on creepers, roots, greens, long pepper, grapes, sugar-cane, scented and medicinal herbs and grasses. It distinguishes between wet crops (*kaidāra*), winter crops (*haimana*) and summer crops (*graiśmika*). Rice is described as the best crop, sugar-cane the most difficult. Vegetables lie in between. Different methods of irrigation are described and the rainfall for different types of land and areas of the country are measured. It is obvious that by the Maurya age, the science of agriculture was a subject of careful study. *Arthaśāstra* speaks of experts in *kṛṣi-tantra, śulba and vṛksāyaurveda.*

Behind this development in agriculture, one may suppose, lay the force of demand from urban centres, inland marts and ports, riverine and oceanic. In the countryside adjacent to such centres, cultivation from a commercial point of view must have grown up. Cotton and sugar-cane were among the cash crops of the day. The *Periplus* mentions a number of agricultural products which were exported from Ariaca to East Africa, viz. rice, wheat, *ghee* and sesamum oil. Caravans moved with these and other products from different parts of the country to the famous cities, ports and marts. There was a considerable element of risk and adventure involved in this trade and it was more in the nature of the trader's enterprise than a regular or necessary part of the rural pattern. Such commercial cultivation must have been financed or managed by the richer vaiśyas in the countryside and their counterparts in the cities. The stories of the *Bṛhatkathā* illustrate the high adventure of trade, especially of oceanic trade.

As already mentioned, the *Dharmaśutras* do not envisage trade in foodstuffs. The farmers apparently produced their own food, the brahmanas obtained gifts, the ruling classes lived on taxes, the artisans, labourers and slaves were paid in kind. The farmers included the *vaisyas*, some *brahmanas* and *ksattriyas* and some *sudras*. The *Arthaśāstra* prefers the *sudras* as cultivators, while Manu prefers the upper castes in that role. Hsuan Chwang refers to the *sudra* as cultivator—Beal II. p. 138. The assumption that actual farm work must have been done by those who did not own the land (e.g. Adhya, op. cit. p. 44, A.N. Bose, op. cit.,) supposes without ground that the system of large estates cultivated by tenants or labourers accounted for much of the cultivated land. On the contrary, the farmer usually designated as *gahapati* in Buddhist literature or as *kautumbika* in the inscriptions does not appear to be normally a big landlord but only a modest farmer. The *Arthaśāstra* states that in the absence of prior stipulation, the actual cultivator would be entitled to the tenth portion of the produce.[53] Slaves and labourers on farms or vegetable gardens, fruit orchards or flower gardens were to get food for themselves and their families and one and a quarter *paṇas* as wages per month. Tenants who brought their own capital shared the crops, keeping half of the produce. Other tenants who merely constituted their labour obtained one-fourth or one-fifth of the produce. These rates obtained apparently both for crown land and private estate. Only, in the case of private estate, land revenue was payable to the state. This was traditionally one-sixth of the produce. This was called *bhāga*. *Bali* was apparently another cess. There was also a steep water rate called *Udaka-bhāga* where facilities for artificial irrigation existed.

It has been argued that the gifts of land during the pre-Gupta and Gupta times led to the growth of large estates and contributed to the feudalization of the rural pattern.[54] The gifts recorded in epigraphs of the period actually were only to learned brahmanas or monasteries or temples and in the case of the first, as has been pointed out by Dr. Dashrath Sharma, no rule of primogeniture obtained to lead to the growth of large estates.[55] They were purely religious grants with appropriate though varying exemptions (*parihāra*).[56] It is true, however, that the growing practice, especially in post-Gupta times of paying officials by assigning to them the whole or part of revenue recoverable from a village or villages must have tended to create a right which would be virtually hereditary so long the office was inherited. The *Manusmrti* envisages a hierarchy of officials in the countryside who lived on village revenues.[57] The Gupta empire shows hereditary officials but the inscriptions do not record any grants of land to them. Hsuan Chwang mentions the payment of officials through land grants[58] and in the post-Gupta period, we get epigraphic as well as literary evidence to the effect that a series of subordinate rulers[59]-cum-officials of the king existed who laid claims on the revenues from the villages assigned to them.[60] The resultant system displayed some affinities to the 'feudal systems,[60] but there was no serfdom at least as a distinct legal status[61] nor was the ownership of land taken away from the peasant proprietors[62] who were simply subjected to a more rapacious and anarchic system of taxation by a hierarchy of ruling chiefs. At the same time, the organisation and functioning of the village community and its corporate life continued, especially in the south.[63] Finally, there is no reason to assume that there was any substantial class of landless or servile labourers in this period. The village

Kalibangan : Ploughed field of Pre-Harappan period, 2500 B.C

crafts continued though the guilds gradually turned into sub-castes under conditions of static and isolated social existence in the countryside. But the kinship and caste bonds continued without loss of vigour and there is no reason to assume that people sought protection by personal attachment and subordination to chiefs.[64]

Thus towards the end of the ancient period, while peasant proprietorship and the corporate life of the village community continued along with the ancient kin and caste systems, a class of subordinate rulers and officials had been superimposed as virtual landlords, the number of imposts had increased and the structure of castes and sub-castes had become more elaborate. But there were no serfs nor any numerous class of slaves or landless labourers. There was no dearth of land in relation to the population nor any general sense of poverty or scarcity of food in the villages except in times of persistent failure of rain when the condition could be very bad indeed.

REFERENCES

1. Kielhorn (ed) *Mahabhasya* Vol. I (Poona, 1962), p. 59.
2. *Mahabhasya* (Rohtak, 1963), Vol. VIII, p. 325.
3. *Pradipa* : because the town has even greater impurity.
4. *Pradipa* : a village has a majority of brahmanas and farmers, a hamlet has cattle, a town has walls and moat and guild activities, an urban area is the same but is a *deśa* rather than a *saṁsthāna*.
5. Dr. V. S. Agrawal has surmised that the distinction between village and town was clear in the north-east but not in the north-west (*India in the Age of Panini*, Hindi version, p. 77). This is not quite borne out by Patanjali as may be seen above.
6. *Pārājika*, 1.2.68.
7. Ibid. *l.c. Vibhaṅga*, *Parajina*, pp. 56-57.
8. *Samantapāsādikā*, Vol. I, pp. 293-96.
9. Vide, J. C. Jain' *Ancient India as depicted in Jain Canon*, p. 82.
10. Kangle, *Arthaśāstra*, Vol. II, p. 55.
11. Ibid. fn.
12. *Agnipurana*, 165.11.
13. Cf. Dr. Pran Nath, *Economic Condition of Ancient India*, p. 26; Kane, op. cit., Vol. III, p. 140, fn. 182. Both the scholars search an unreal average.

14. *D.P.P.N.* Vol. II, p. 402.
15 Cf. *JBRS,* 1959, p. 389; Dr. BNS Yadava, op. cit., pp. 234 ff; Dr. Pran Nath, op. cit., p. 26; J. V. P. H. S., 1951-52, pp. 290-91. Dr. Kane's critique of Pran Nath (l.c.) misses the problem altogether.
16. *Arthasastra*, 2.1.1.
17. *Manusmrti* 7.69. Similarly *Gautama dh* s. 9.65—*aryajanabhuyistham.*
18. *Markandeya* : *Tathā Śūdrajanaprāyā susamrddha Kṛṣīvalā ksetropayogabhūmadhye vasatirgrāmasaṁjṅikā.*
19. Vide, Yadava, op. cit., p. 96, fn. 448.
20. It may be recalled that Brahmanical social theory looked down upon manual labour and assigned it to the sudras. The brahmanas were allowed farming only in times of distress. According to Gautạma, e.g. even then the brahmana was not to engage in it directly—*Gautama dh. s.* 10.5.6 : *Krsi-vanijye cāsvayaṁkrte*; *Kusīdam Ca.* Although Buddhist literature does show brahmanas engaged in agriculture, the tendency for them to get their work done by tenants or labourers of a lower caste presumably gained ground gradually.
21. Beal, II, p. 138.
22. *Gautama*, 11.23 : '*Karsakavaik-paśupāla-kusīdi-kravaḥ sve svenivarge.*
23. Damodarpur Copper Plate of G.Y. 163 : Baigram Copper Plate of G.Y. 128.
24. The *Arthasastra* refers to the *grāmabhṛtakas* at several places—2.1.11; 3.11.29; 5.2; II; 5.3.23; but does not enumerate them. cf. C.H.I. Vol. I, p. 477.
25. Cf. *Gautama*, 10.30-33.
26. Panini, 5.4.95.
27. Ibid. 6.2.62.
28. Panini attests to the bellows (*bhastrā*), iron hammer (*ayoghana*) and tongs (*Kutilika*) of the Smith-VII. 3.47, III. 3.82, IV. 4.18.
29. Panini's *drughana* signifies an axe-III. 3.82.
30. The variant '*cira-ratta-tatta* for '*divasasantatte*' excludes the possibility of the heating being merely in the sun.
31 Cf. V. S. Agrawal, *op. cit.*, p. 201.
32. Cf. Panini's *Ksetrakara*—3.2.21.
33. Panini, 4.2.40.
34. *Vrīhi*—ibid. 5.2.2., 4.3.146, 2.2.23; *Śāli*, 5.2.2; *mahāvrīhi*, 6.2.38, *Saṣṭhika*, 5.1.90.
35. Cf. ibid. 8.4.5.
36. Ibid. 4.3.47-49.
37 Ibid. 5.4.121.
38. *Brhatsmhita*, Chap. 21-22.
39. Ibid. Chap. 23, 28.
40. Ibid. Chap. 29.
41. *Kṛṣiparāśara*, ed and tr. G. P. Majumdar and S. C. Banerji, Calcutta, 1900. The work has been placed by the editors between A.D.950-

1100 though it has been placed by J. C. Roy between the 6th and the 8th century (pp. VIII-IX). The work originated in northern India, possibly Bengal (XI).

The work describes rainfall as the basis of agriculture, classifies the clouds and mentions methods for estimating the rainfall. It describes agricultural implements and cowdung as manure. Methods of deciding the right time and seasons for cultivation are mentioned. A good deal is said about the collection, preservation and sowing of seeds. Prescriptions are detailed about weeding, levelling and watering. A lot is said about the various rites which must be observed from time to time in the course of the agricultural cycle.

Agriculture demands personal supervision (verse 80); keeping of gosala (vu. 87 ff); manure (vv. 109-111).

Instruments of agriculture—

Isāyugahal asthānumiyelistasya pāsikāh,
Addacallaśca śolaśca paccanī ca halāṣtakam.

Also included one *Kuddala* (v. 109), *yotra*, *rajju*, *phalaka*, *viddhaka* and *madika* (vv. 116-18).

42. *Gautama* Ed. L. Srinivasacharya with Maskari-bhasya, (Mysore 1917)—2.16 : Comy —*Vahiḥ sandhyatvam.* Comy.—*Grāmād bahireva saṁdhyopāsanam kartavya-mityekeṣām matam bahirabhyantare vā...... iti Gautama-matam. Ib.* 16.46 *Nityame ke nagare.*

Comy. *Eke nagare grāme saaivānadhyāyamicchanti. Na tu Gautamah grāmanivāsinām sadaivānadhyāya prasangāt. Tatra śūdrādibhūyiṣṭhe anadhyāyaḥ dvijātibahule adhyetavyamiti draṣṭavyam.*

43. *Vedah krṣivināśāya krsirvedavināśinī,*
Śaktimānubhayaṁ kuryādaśaktasu krṣiṁ tyajet.

44. *Gautama* 10.5-6. *Krsivanijye cāsvayamkṛte Kusīdam ca.*

45. Cf. see above.

46. Kautalya would restrict their activities—*Arthasastra.*

47. Cf. *Raghu*, 1.45—*Haiyaṅgavinam adaya ghasavrddhan upasthitan.*

48. Cf. *Arthasāṣtra* on *aryabhakta*, 2.15—one prastha of rice, a quarter of that as *supa*, 1/16th of that as salt, a quarter of *ghee* or oil.

49. Cf. Dr. Tara Chand, *History of the Freedom Movement*, Vol. I, p. 160.

50. A. N. Bose, op. cit. II, p. 9.

51. McCrindle, op. cit. p. 52-53.

52. Ibid. p. 53.

53. *Arthasastra*, 3.13.28; Ibid. 2.24.29.

54. R. S. Sharma, *Indian Feudalism* (2nd ed. 1980); Dr. Sharma regards 'serfdom' to be the economic essence of feudalism. He does not, however, prove the existence of 'serfdom' as a general institution for the period; cf. Coulburn, *Comparative Studies in Society and History*, Vol. X. pl. 356; D. C. Sircar (ed) *Land System and Feudalism in Ancient India*, pp. 57 ff.

55. *Journal of Indian History.*

56. See app.
57. *Manusmrti*, 7.115.
58. Watters, Vol I, pp. 176-77.
59. These have been called 'vassals,' but that term has implications which are not proved for *samanta*. See Dr. D. C. Sircar, *The Emperor and Subordinate Rulers* (Pub. Visvabharati).
60. This claim was often called *bhoga*—see, e.g. Harsha Stone Inscription of Cāhomāna Vigraharāja II (1973ff): *śrī Vatsasājah svabhogāvāpta-jayapresa-viṣaye*—For literary evidence, see B.N.S. Yadav in Sircar (ed.), *Land System* etc. pp. 72ff.
61. On forced labour or *visti* see G.K. Rai, Involuntary *Labour in Ancient India*.
62. Cf. L. Gopal, *Aspects of History of Agriculture in Ancient India*, pp. 42ff.
63. Cf. Mahalingam, *Readings in South Indian History* pp. 92ff; Burton Stein, *Peasant, State and Society in Mediaeval South India*, pp. 141ff. For northern India, an objective account of the conditions in the 12th century may be seen in Dr. B.N.S. Yadav's monograph *Society And Culture In Northern India*.
64. Marc Bloch enumerates the elements of the European feudal system as a subject peasantry, service tenament or fief, supremacy of a class of warriors, ties of personal obedience and protection, fragmentation of authority—*Feudal Society*, vol. II, p. 446.

6

The Urban Pattern

Although Harappan sites run into hundreds, less than half a dozen could qualify on present evidence to be called cities. Even of these, it has been suggested that except for Mohenjo-daro and Harappa, the other cities could hardly have had a population of 5,000. For Mohenjo-daro, an estimate of 40,000 has been made by Fairservis.[1] One is reminded of the *Jataka* story that the King of Videha had one big city but 16,000 villages. What accounted for the two big Harappan cities is not known. These could have been capital cities and also important commercial centres. There is plentiful evidence that the Indian merchants or caravan leaders carried their trade far beyond the frontiers of the realm.[2] Among the articles of this trade, precious metals and stones are evidenced most clearly. There is evidence of trade between Mesopotamia, Dilmun, Makan and Meluhha where the last-named country has been identified with the Harappan civilization.[3] "Among the imports from Meluhha are various kinds of timber, including a black wood identified as ebony", copper, carnelian and ivory.[4]

Behind the trade lay specialization of crafts. Working in stone, copper and bronze was as specialized as working in precious stones and metals. Pottery, brick-making and seal-cutting were highly specialized. The cities are a monument to the builder's art and the standardization of weights and measures and of writing suggests that traders, craftsmen and scribes must have belonged to groups with hereditary skill and education. The careful planning of the cities with their grid pattern and elaborate arrangement for water and sanitation imply a well-organized administrative authority. A formidable variety of artifacts were produced in the city where gold jewellery and silver vessels, bronze mirrors and razors, large and comfortable houses evidence considerable accumulation of wealth.[5]

Why and how this civilization declined and disappeared and what exactly it left behind as traditional skill, are speculative issues of which no satisfactory solutions are known. The Aryans have been blamed for destroying the Harappan cities and the Ṛgvedic *pur* has been construed to refer to them. But the relationship of the Vedic to the Harappan remains disputable.[6] Nevertheless, archaeological evidence at present clearly implies the disappearance of city life in the second millennium B.C. and its gradual revival towards the beginning of the first. This period of renewed urbanization has generally been placed in the later Vedic and Mahajanapada Age.

Later Vedic literature evinces a growing knowledge of crops and metals and mentions a large number of specialized crafts. It also mentions money as medium of exchange and names a few towns. Here then the thread of economic development is picked up once again as might have been the case more than a millennium earlier.

Even in the *Ṛgveda*, the crafts of the carpenter and the weaver were highly developed. The charioteer was a specialist carpenter and weaving of cotton as well as woollen wear was practised. The wool of Gandhara and the Indus region was famous.[7] Leather goods such as bow-strings, reins, bags and covers were made by the tanner or *carmamna.*[8] The smith or *karmāra* smelted metals, probably copper. We hear of an '*ayasmaya*' heating vessel. The smith is said to long for working with the bright metal (*hiraṇyavuni*) with the help of ancient plants and drugs; bird feathers possibly as bellows and glowing stones.[9] The epithet *ayodaṁṣṭra* for fire certainly suggests copper as the meaning of *ayas*. The axe or *svadhiti* used for felling trees could have been of bronze or copper.[10] *Vāśī* was probably the carpenter's awl. Gleaming spears (*ṛṣtis*) and arrows (*iṣu, didyut*) should have been tipped with copper. Thus working in wood, stone, and copper, cotton and leather were skilled crafts in the age of the *Ṛgveda*. The skills of chariot-making and weaving were so highly prized that they were used metaphorically for the making of prayers and hymns. The sacrifice was compared to a pattern of weaving. The carpenter and the smith furnished the image for the creativity of the gods.

Later Vedic literature mentions towns like Āsandivant, the capital of Pariksit, Paricakrā and Kampila. *Pur* meaning a city or citadal was familiar to the *Ṛgveda* as a metaphor applied to the clouds though it is not usually found in the context of normal human habitation. It was treated there as a demonic citadel destroyed by Indra. It has been concluded from this that the authors of the hymns themselves did not belong to the cities but knew of them and did not approve of them. It does not follow that the cities belonged to a different people, for the Vedic sages did not approve of cities even in later times. Nor do the *dāsas* mean non-aryans. They are merely demons of evil titanic forces.[11] That they should dwell in fortified cities and dry up natural creativity is appropriate enough in a context where moral and holy life was one of simplicity and spontaneity in the midst of nature. The seers did not share the modern outlook of the archaeologists who regard the city as the fount of civilization and progress.

The later Vedic age saw the growth of *Janapadas* and their capital towns like Hastinapura, Kausambi and Ujjayini. The beginnings of these cities go back to *c.* 1000 B.C. Attempts have been made to identify the archaeological period corresponding to the later Vedic age as that characterized by Painted Grey Ware. It has also been suggested that it was the knowledge of iron and its use in the ploughshare and axe that led to the colonization of the central Gangetic Valley and to increased productivity of agriculture, which, in turn, made the rise of cities possible. While the correspondence of the later Vedic age with that of Painted Grey Ware is chronologically reasonable, the other suggestions are speculative and unnecessary. The later Vedic and *Janapada* ages are continuous and saw the eastward expansion of settlements through the burning down rather than the cutting down of forests. The increasing specialization of crafts and professions and growing numbers must have been the basic factors behind the rise of trade and towns. The knowledge of metals, no doubt, increased. Iron and copper were clearly distinguished. Lead, bronze and tin are mentioned. A large number of occupations are mentioned on the occasion of the *Puruṣamedha*-Brāhmana, Rājanya, Vaiśya, Śūdra, Taskara, Ayogū, Māgadha, Sūta, Śailūṣa, Rebha, Kāri, Rathakāra, Takṣan, Kaulāla Karmāra, Maṇikāra, Vap, Iṣukāra, Dhanuṣkāra, Jyākāra, Rajjusarja, Mṛgayu, Svanin, Paunjiṣtha, Naiṣāda, Kitava, Vidalakāri, Kantakīkarī, Peśaskārī Bhiṣaj, Nakṣatradarśa, Praśnin, Abhipraśnanin, Praśnavivāka, Hastipa, Aśvapa, Gopāla, Avipāla, Ajapāla, Kīnāsa, Surākāra, Gṛhapa, Vittardha, Anukṣattā, Dārvāhāra, Peṣitṛ, Prakaritṛ, Upasektṛ, Upamanthitṛ, Vāsaḥpalpūli, Rajayitrī, Kṣattr, Anukṣattṛ, Aśvasāda, Bhāgadugha, Ayastāpa, Yoktṛ, Añjanīkāri, Kośakāri, Ajinasandha, Carmamna, Dhaivara, Dāśa, Vainda, Śanṣkala, Mārgava, Kaivarta, Ānda, Maināla, Parṇaka, Kirāta, Paulkasa, Hiraṇyakāra, Vāṇija, Carakācārya, Vīṇāvāda, Tūṇavadhma, Śaṅkhadhma, Vanapa, Dāvapa, Grāmaṇī, Gaṇaka, Pāṇighna, Talava, Cāṇḍāla, Vaṁśanartin; we notice here further sub-divisions of earlier known professions. Thus the making of bow and arrow now includes several specializations--arrow maker, bow maker and string maker. The smith may be Karmāra, or Ayogū or Ayastāpa (=smelter). Potters and bead-makers, goldsmiths, basket-makers of more than one kind, weavers, tanners, ropemakers, chariotmakers and carpenters are mentioned. Many kinds of hunters and fishermen as well as animal breeders and farmers are listed. Entertainers, jesters, dancers, acrobats and musicians comprise a number of distinct classes. Merchants with their balances, village herdsmen, astronomers, mathematicians and advocates or judges and wandering teachers, find distinct mention. Priests, rulers, tax-collectors and servitors of many kinds are mentioned as also farmers and ploughmen. The social scene implied here ranges over the woodland and pastures, fields and markets. It presupposes town life, and more a court life. The use of money is attested since *śatamāna* weighing a hundred *kṛṣṇalas* appears to have been used as such. *Pāda* referred to in *Br.* could have been a quarter of this. *Niṣka* could also have been used as a medium of exchange.[12] The use of gold and silver suggests the development of trade and of royal treasures.

The principal forms of property were land and gold, cattle and slaves. The difference between the life-styles of the rich and the poor was marked. The rich used jewellery, fine chariots, slaves and attendants and had food of high quality. Thus we hear of rice being eaten with milk or curd, sesamum or meat. On the other hand, during a famine an elephant-driver is found eating *kulmāṣa*. The rich included kings and noblemen and rich priests called *mahāśāla* and *mahāśrotriya*. These latter, however, seem to depend mainly on sacrificial fees and royal gifts. Mendicant sages who despised all wealth are also known and their teachings recorded.

From the sixth century B.C., we enter a period when city life, trade, money and banking and industrial guilds became an established and important part of Indian society. Taxila was the greatest city in the north-west. According to its excavator, the ancient city lay under the Bhir mound which stretched 1200 yards from north to south and 730 yards from east to west. The city was thrice built and destroyed before the Bactrians built a new city at Sirkap. Marshall thought the earlier city of the Bhir mound to have been haphazard in its layout and to have lacked wells, private as well as public, within the city.[13] This hardly squares with the far-flung renown of this metropolitan town of those days. The city at Sirkap was built in the second century B.C. and had city walls nearly three-and-half miles long built of solid coursed stone rubble. This city followed a chess-board pattern. The third city at Sirsukh belonged to Kushan times and was a rough parallelogram with a perimeter of about three miles.[14] Apart from Taxila, the only other city which has been excavated with some thoroughness though not yet uncovered horizontally is Kausambi. Here the beginnings of the city go back to the 11th century B.C. and the period of the NBP shows the magnificient 'palace of Udayana'. The city ramparts have been excavated and reveal the miniature history of the city.[15]

Turning to the literary evidence of the age of Buddha, we find the mention of a number of famous cities. When Buddha was about to enter *parinirvana* in the outskirts of the Malla city Kusinara, Ananda objected saying that it was a small, deserted, suburban town. There were a number of other 'great cities' (*mahānagarāṇi*) e.g. Campa, Rajagaha, Savatthi, Saketa, Kosambi and Varanasi which had numerous and affluent (*mahāśāla*) citizens.[16] Buddha reveals the ancient glory of Kusavati which had been a great capital town. It was a rectangle, 12 *Yojanas* long from east to west and 7 *yojanas* broad from north to south. It was "rich and prosperous, populous and crowded where it was easy to get alms". Day and night it always reverberated with ten kinds of sounds—of elephants, horses, chariots, drums, *mrdangas*, lutes, songs, conchs, *samma*(?), clapping and the cry 'eat, drink, enjoy a meal'. Valmiki describes Ayodhya as a narrower rectangle, twelve *yojanas* long and three broad.[17] The royal highway ran through the middle of the city which was surrounded by a wall pierced by gates. The city followed the grid pattern (*aṣṭāpadākāram*) in planning and had tall buildings of seven storeys. Markets were separately marked. Gardens, mango-groves and lines of *sala* trees beautified the city. A constant crowd of traders, craftsmen and nobles jostled in the streets. People came from far and near. The city was well-stocked with food and drink. Rice and sugar-cane were plentiful. It was well defended with towers and all kinds of engines of war and weapons. The citizens were prosperous and moved about well decked up with garlands, ornaments and perfumes.

Megasthenes described Pataliputra as a parallelogram 80 stadia in length and 15 in width, girdled with a wooden wall pierced with loopholes for the discharge of arrows.[18] It had a ditch for defence and sewage. The wall had 570 towers and 64 gates. The city had been founded in the days of Ajatasatru and was now, in the 4th century B.C., the greatest city of India. The Indo-Bactrian city of Sakala is similarly described in the *Milindapanha*.[19] It was surrounded by a deep moat, high ramparts and wall with towers and gates. The streets were well divided to meet in square crossings. The city included river and hilly portions, which Marshall has described for Sirkap as typically Hellenistic planning. Gardens, groves and tanks were in profusion. The shops displayed diverse goods. Tall buildings were like mountain tops. Elephants, chariots and horses crowded the streets. The markets were stocked with diverse kinds of cloth like *kasika* and *kotumbara*, flowers and perfumes, gems and jewellery *kārṣāpaṇas*, gold, silver and bronze, and all kinds of grains. Treasury and granary were full. Food and drink were plentiful.

Town-planning was a well developed science. *Dīghanikāya* and *Milindapañho* refer to town-planning (*nagaramāpana*). The *Arthaśāstra* and a number of treatises on *Śilpaśāstra* give eleborate directions about it,[20] which in practice naturally depended on the authority and continuity of the civic tradition. Repeated political upheavals and failure of authority could not but have had the result of uncontrolled changes in the older towns, till the very idea of a planned town was left only for an occasional ruler of vision. Fatehpur Sikri and Jaipur illustrate this. The usual mediaeval town, however, became a medley of narrow and tortuous streets with houses of all kinds encroaching on it, exhibiting squalor. Only palaces and residences of the rich remained subjects of planning.

The city was thus imaged in terms of the strength of its defence, its populousness, many-storeyed buildings, planned streets and quarters, prosperous markets, pleasure-gardens and tanks. Traders, adventurers, scholars and entertainers came to the city from far and near and it represented a high watermark of polish and culture. If the ascetic tradition condemned the city as 'a house on fire', men of letters and culture condemned the village as rustic and vulgar (*grāmya*), Vātsyāyana's *Kāmasūtra* gives a glimpse of the *nāgaraka* or townsman.[21] He is a man of wealth, leisure and sophistication, intent on leading a life of refined pleasure. He might dwell in a small or big town, and towns of four sizes are mentioned. His house should be ideally near a source of water. It should be with trees and a garden and it should have several functional rooms apparently for cooking, bathing and other house-work. There should be in addition two living rooms, exterior and interior. The interior living room was for the wife, the exterior one was the master's bedroom. The master's bedroom should have among other articles of furniture two beds, a chair with a cover and a head-rest, a stool, a wax-container, possibly for light, a spitoon, a lute hung from a peg in the wall, board and brushes for painting, some books, gaming boards, outside were to be birds in a cage and in the shade of the garden was to be a swing. The *nagaraka* observes cleanliness scrupulously, daily bathing and cleaning the teeth, shaving every fourth day and taking special care to be free from body odour. He ate twice, listened to the birds, watched cocks and rams fight and took a siesta during the day. He listened to music in the evening and assiduously pursued assignments of love. He participated in picnics, drinking parties, literary gatherings and theatrical shows. In the picnics hetaerae were freely admitted. Gambling and drinking were common. The *nāgaraka* lived in a mixed society of refinement but easy virtue. The village dweller is encouraged to follow the *nāgarka* so far as possible.

The rise of city life was due apart from political factors to the growth of professional specialization and consequent exchange of goods and services from far and near. The *Mūgapakkhā Jātaka* mentions eighteen guilds, a figure mentioned elsewhere too. Although these are not specifically listed, we can gather the names of many professions which were organized in guilds—workers in wood, stone, leather, metal or ivory, workers in bamboo, bronze or gems, weavers, potters, oilmillers, rush workers and basket-makers, dyers, painters and traders. Smiths and carpenters had many specializations. *Vaḍḍhaki* included architects, ship-builders, cartwrights, turners and ordinary carpenters. The guilds were well organized with a president called *Pamukha* or *Jetthaka*.[22] They even maintained arms for security especially for the protection of their caravans, and Kautalya has respect for the power of their forces. The guilds of the traders were probably the most important and the principal merchant or *setthi* had an important position at the court.

The hereditary character and guild organization of the crafts led to considerable localisation. We hear of "craft villages of wood-wrights, ironsmiths, and potters. These were either suburban to large cities, or rural, and constituting as such special markets for the whole countryside." To the ironsmiths' *gama* for example "people came from the *gamas* round about to have razors, axes, ploughshares, goads and needles made".[23] Within the towns too, certain trades were localised in certain streets. We hear, for example, of the *dantakāra-vīthi* in Varanasi. This principle of specialization applied to markets and we hear of the flower market, perfume market, markets for fruits, medicines, herbs, and jewellery. Some cities became famous for their products e.g. Kasi for its fine clothes.

When oceanic trade expanded during the Kusana and Gupta periods, we find a corresponding growth in specialization and guilds. The *Milindapanha* describes a great city as a cosmopolitan town where people came from all parts of the world—Scythia, Bactria, China, West Coast, Kasi-Kosala, Magadha, Saketa, Sorattha, Mathura, Alexandria, Kasmira and Gandhara. It lists numerous professions crowding the city—[24]

Khattiyā Brahmanā vessā suddā hatthārohā assārohā rathikā pattikā dhanuggāhā tharuggāhā celakā calakā pindadāvikā uggā rājaputtā pakkhavandino mahānāgā sūrā bammino yodhino dāsikaputtā bhattiputtā mallaganā ālārikā suddā kappkā nahāpakā cundā mālākārā suvannakārā sajjakārā sīsakārā tipukārā lohakārā vattakārā ayakārā manikārā pesakārā kumbhakārā venukārā lonakārā cammakārā rathakārā dantakārā rajjukārā kocchakārā suttakārā vilivakārā dhanukārā jiyākārā usukārā cittakārā rangakārā rajakā tantuvāyā tunnavāyā herañnikā dussikā gandhikā tinahārakā katthahārakā bhataka pannikā phalikā mūlika odanikā puvika macchika mansikā manjikā natakā naceakā langhakā indajālikā vetālikā mallā chavadāhakā puppha cchadakā venā nesādā ganikā lāsikā kumbhadāsiyo. This list invites a comparison with the list from the later vedic literature referred to earlier. This one is more elaborate in some respects showing a minuter subdivision in some of the crafts. It may also be compared with the list in the *Dīghanikāya*.[25]

"*Yathā nu kho imāni bhante puthusippāyatanāni—seyyathīdam hatthārohā assārohā rathikā dhanuggāhā celakā calakā pindadāyikā uggā rājaputtā pakkhavandino mahānāgā sūrā dhammayodhino dāsakaputtā ālārikā kappakā nahāpakā sūdā mālākārā rajakā pesakārā nalakārā kumbhakārā ganakā muddikā yāni panaññāni pi.*"

The list of Milinda is obviously more elaborate than the canonical list.

Inscriptions from the Śaka, Kusāna and Gupta times reveal

the importance and manysided activities of the guilds.[26] They acted as bankers and engaged in diverse kinds of social and civic works. They had considerable mobility and their members formed a community of which the members won renown in diverse fields. They patronized culture by their liberality and were proud of their products. Their role in municipal administration was no mean one. The copper-plates of the Gupta age from Bengal reveal that the representatives of the craft and trade guilds served in administrative councils.[27] In the post-Gupta period, however, they declined and were finally merged in *śūdra* sub-castes.[27a]

The craft of working in stone went back to prehistoric times. While stone tools and weapons were gradually replaced by metal ones in historical times, the craft of the stone-cutter remained important because of the new practice of building city walls, forts, temples, palaces etc. of stone. Nor could the art of the gem-cutter be separated from that of the stone-cutter. The perfection of the stone-cutter's art may be seen in the excavated and structural temples of ancient times, some of which have managed to survive. The carpenter's art was similarly ancient. Most of the buildings in the cities in the early historical period, especially in eastern India, seem to have been made of wood. The carpenters appear to have evolved a technique of standardization which enabled them to make all the parts of the house before-hand and number them.[28] Furniture, carts and chariots and ships were some other items which required the art of the carpenter primarily. The tools of the carpenter included *vāsī* (awl), *pharasu* (axe), *nikhādana* (chisel) and *muggara* (mallet), and, of course, the tape or *kāḷasutta*. The potter's was again an ancient craft and continued to be important even after the use of metals because earthenware remained in wide use and has remained so even now.

The weaver's craft again had a long and distinguished past. Cotton clothing with diverse designs was used in Harappan cities. Its use in the Vedic village is more than doubtful.[29] From the age of Buddha, we find the *Mahavagga* enumerating garments of linen (*khomāni*), cotton (*kāppāsikam*), silk (*koseyyam*), woollen (*kambalam*), hemp (*sāṇam*) and hempen cloths (*ghaṅgam*). Numerous varieties and quilts are mentioned. It is unnecessary to recount the fame which Indian textiles have enjoyed through the ages. The famous Mansre Inscription gives us a glimpse of the prestige and prosperity which a guild of silk-weavers enjoyed in the Gupta age.

Although copper was known and used earlier, it is iron that was plentifully available in India. "Probably in no country of the world is iron found more abundantly than in India and in none are the ores from which it is extracted of greater purity or more easily accessible." And from "a very early period India was famous for the high quality of its iron and steel".[30] Ktesias at the Akhaemenian court in the 6th century B.C. mentions two remarkable swords of Indian steel. The *Periplus* records the export of iron and steel from W. India to Abyssinia. In the 11th century Idrisi says, "The Hindus excel in the manufacture of iron....... It is impossible to find anything to surpass the edge that you get from Indian steel". According to Marshall, this literary evidence is fully corroborated by the analysis and micro-examination of selected specimens from Taxila and Besnagar. The superb Mehrauli Iron Pillar may also be mentioned in this context.

We hear of the *Kammāragāma* in the *Jātakas* and Megasthenes attests to the special protection of this industry by the state since it supplied the weapons to the army. The furnace of the smith is mentioned as burning inwardly, not outwardly. His bellows and hammerings find mention. Of the articles he fashioned, we hear of "razor, axe, spade, augur, hammer, instrument for cutting bamboos, iron weapon, grass cutter, sword, iron staff, peg and three-pronged iron fork (*Vāsi-pharasu-Kuddāla-nikhādana-muṭṭhika-velugumba-cchedana- satthi- tinalayana- asilonha- danda- Khānuka- ayas iṅghāṭaka*)".[31] If we turn to the actual finds of iron objects from Taxila, this is fully corroborated. According to Marshall[32], 221 iron objects were discovered from there and they included (A) household utensils, (B) arms and armour, (C) horse bridles and elephant goads, (D) carpenter's and blacksmith's tools, and (E) agriculture implements. In (A) we find cooking pots and cauldrons, tripod stands for these bowls, dishes and saucers, frying and baking pans, spoons and ladles, sieves, lamps, standard vase-shaped lamps with spherical body and handle, candelabra which Marshall attributes to a non-Indian prototype, incense burner, wheeled braziers of foreign origin, shovels, bells, locks, keys and lock plates, folding chair of foreign design, axle of spinning wheel. In (B) we find swords and daggers of diverse types, spears, javelins and butts where the heavier javelins have been assigned a foreign origin, arrow heads, some of foreign design, armour including plate armour for men and horses copied from Hellenistic designs, helmets and shield bosses of similarly foreign origin. Under (C) we find bits and cheek bars for horse bridles borrowed from the Greeks along with the word *Khalina*, elephant goads. Under (D) we find socketted axes, adzes, chisels, knives, saw, tongs, pliers and tweezers, scissors which appeared about the same time as in the Mediterranean area in the 1st century A.D., hammer, adze, pick, anvils, nails, nail-bosses and hooks, clamps and staples, hinges and chains. Under (E) we get spades, spuds and hoes, weeding forks (?) and sickles. Spades are considered by Marshall to have a Mediterranean affiliation. Among miscellaneous articles, we have needles, plummets, jumper and crowbar, shuttle and ingots.

Copper was rare although there were obvious sources in Rajasthan, Baluchistan and Kashmir. According to the Greeks, India imported copper, tin and lead from outside. Of copper manufactures, we get ornamental articles like brooches, pendants and clasps from Taxila. Articles of toilet show a large variety—unguent pots and bowls, flasks, mirrors, antimony rods, hair pins, jewel caskets. Copper utensils were common and we have cooking pots and cauldrons, handed jugs and ewers, spouted vessels with loop handles, drinking cups, goblets and beakers, bowls and cups, dishes and saucers, frying pans, ladles and spoons. We also get incense burners, inkpots, pens and styli, bells and keys. Surgical instruments of copper—spatula, forceps, decapilator, scale pans, clamps and chains—are found. Miscellaneous articles of copper are lamps, flutes, toy carts, staff terminal, vine leaves, winged eros, door ornaments, figurines.[33]

If we turn to an eastern city like Śrāvastī, the pattern of finds is similar. Of the 124 copper objects recovered from the site by K.K. Sinha in 1959, the majority are articles of toilet and ornaments including pendants, antimony rods, nail parers, barers and needles. The 156 iron objects recovered at the same site included knife blades, spear beads, nails, arrowheads, chisels, elephant goads, clamps and sockets.[34]

Turning to the precious metals, Marshall found the use of silver for jewellery rarer than that of gold.[35] Silver ware included ornaments, coins, goblets, bowls, cups, etc. Of gold jewellery, 213 pieces were recovered from Taxila[36] (op. cit. p. 616). Bone and ivory objects had a wide range. They were specially used for combs, handles of mirrors and fans, knife blades, spoons, bangles, hairpins, writing styli, gamesmen, toys, articles of toilet and ornament.

Industry using true glass appears to have developed at Taxila about the 5th century B.C[37] It produced beads, bangles, small vessels, tiles and miscellaneous articles. A variety of glass ware is met with—flasks and other vessels of blown glass, translucent and of sea-green or jade-green colour, lac glass bowls, ribbed ware imitating metal repousse ware, swirled or marbled ware in imitation of marble, branded agate etc. blue and white cameo-cut glass; coloured mosaic glass, colourless translucent glass, millefiori glass. We even have two plano-convex lenses of blue glass and it is not clear if they sought to imitate real lenses.

If the Panis of *Ṛgveda* signified traders, they were without doubt held in low esteem. In the later Vedic literature, the trader with his balance emerges quite clearly. No stigma attaches to him. In the age of Buddha, the position of the trader rises distinctly. The Brahmanical *sūtra* works, no doubt, impose numerous restrictions on his activity and do not reflect the status which he actually enjoyed in the civic life of the times.[38] This is probably due to the archaic rural background of the *sutras*. Gautama gives a long list of commodities which should not be turned into merchandise though barter is permitted in some cases and exceptions are allowed in times of emergency. Traders were recognized as a distinct class governed by their own traditions. In the *Jatakas*, the trader is called *seṭṭhi*, *satthavāha* and *vanija*. *Vañija* was the common term, *Seṭṭhi* had the sense of the capitalist and banker, *satthavāha* was the caravan leader. Mrs. Rhys Davids has shown that there was considerable mobility in the adoption of the traditional professions.[39] Brahmanas and ksatriyas too took to trade on diverse occasions. Apparently, what the *Dharmasūtras* called *āpad* or emergency was of not infrequent occurrence. Or rather, the emergency provisions were merely a legal fiction designed to reconcile a flexible reality with the theoretical stereotype.

Trade was felt to depend on initiative and enterprise and was full of risk. The *Cullakasetthi Jātaka* illustrates the rise of a merchant from penury to riches though astute and intrepid enterprise. The *Pancatantra* describes trade to be the secret of wealth with independence but it requires high intelligence and initiative.[40] It was in the caravans which ran along the highways between distant cities and ports that the prospects of much profit and risk lay. From Tamralipti and Campa in the east to Pataliputra, Varanasi, Kausambi and Mathura and thence to Taxila, Puskaravati and Kapisa in the distant north-west ran the celebrated Northern Highway (*Uttarpatha*). From Kausambi or Mathura to Vidisa and Ujjayini and thence to Pratisthana or Bhrgukaccha and Supparaka ran the Deccan Highway (*Daksinapatha*), Campa, Tamralipti and Dantapura were the great marts and ports in the east. Pratisthana, Tagara and Ujjain were the western marts and Patala, Bhrgukaccha, Surparaka and Muziris the ports on the west. Caravanas from Central Asia came to Kapisi, Puskaravati and Taxila. Mathura was the gateway to the north-west as well as the west. Oceanic navigation was opened in the Kusana-Satavahana period and trade reached its high watermark in the Gupta period when Indian ships sailed the Arabian Sea as well as the Bay of Bengal.

The *Milindapanho* speaks of the rich merchant having paid his port dues wishing to enter the great ocean and sail to Vanga, Takkola, Cina, Sovira, Surattha, Alasanda, Kolapattana, and Suvanna bhumi. It also mentions the cosmopolitan concourse at Sakala. Such international crowds gathered not only in the great towns of the north-west but also in the cities of the west and the Deccan. The Nagarjunikonda Inscription of Virapurusadatta of the regnal year 14 mentions monks going to Kasmira, Gandhara, Cina, Cilata, Tosali, Avaranta, Vanga, Varanasi, Yavana, Damila, Palura, Tambapannidipa, and of Ceylonese monks coming there.

The most important document about the trade with the west is the famous *Periplus oj the Erythraean Sea* written probably in A.D. 60. This work attributes the discovery of the monsoons and with them of the direct sea route across the Arabian Sea to Hippalus. "This whole voyage as above described, from Cana and Eudaemon Arabic, they used to make in small vessels, sailing close around the shores of the gulf; and Hippalus was the pilot who by observing the location of the ports and the conditions of the sea, first discovered how to lay his course straight across the ocean. For at the same time as the Etesian winds are blowing, on the shores of India the wind sets in from the ocean, and this south-west wind is called Hippalus, from the name of him who first discovered the passage across. From that time to the present day, ships start, some direct from Cana, and some from the cape of Spices; and those bound for Damirica throw the ship's head considerably off the wind; while those bound for Barygaza and Scythia keep along shore not more than three days and for the rest of the time hold the same course straight out to sea from the region" (p. 45). Warmington has proposed the following stages in the discovery of the use of the south-west monsoon by the Egyptian Greeks—Stage I: Coasting along Arabic from Eudaemon to Ras al Had and then along the coasts of Carmenia and Gedrosia to the Indus. Stage II: From Arabic Eudaemon or Cane to Szagros along the coast and then straight across the sea to Patala. According to Warmington, this breakthrough might have been the discovery of Hippalus. Stage III—Roughly about A.D. 41 and 50, sailing across the sea from Sagros to Sigerus or Barygaza on the Indian coast which was held to be 'shorter and safer'. Stage IV—About A.D. 50, from Ocelis or Eudaemon or Cane straight across the sea to Muziris on the Indian coast. This was done by throwing the ship's head off the wind with a constant pull on the rudder and a shift of the yard (thus sailing in the arc of a circle)" and thus they reached Malabar in forty days. This could also have been the discovery by Hippalus.[41]

We gather from the *Periplus* that from Ariaca, the north-west coast of India especially near the gulf of Cambay, were exported to the Abysinian ports "Indian iron and steel, and

Indian cotton cloth; the broad cloth called *monache* and that called *sagmatogene*, and girdles, and coats of skin and mallow-coloured cloth, and a few muslins, and coloured lac." (p. 24). The cotton industry was "one of the main factors in the wealth of ancient India and the transfer of that industry to England and the United States......is perhaps the greatest single factor in the economic history of our own time." (Schoff, p. 71). Mallow-coloured cloth has been explained as a coarse cotton cloth dyed purplish (ibid p. 73). From Ariaca and Barygaza in India, ships sailed to east African market-towns carrying "wheat, rice, clarified butter, sesame oil, cotton cloth, and girdles and honey from the reed called *sacchari*" (p. 27). *Sacchari* apparently refers to '*sarkara*'. To Ommana on the Persian Gulf ships came from Barygaza "loaded with copper and sandalwood and timbers of teakwood and logs of blackwood and ebony". (p. 36). The blackwood has been identified with *sisam* (Schoff, pp. 152-53.)

The market-town of Barbarieum lay near the mouth of the Indus. The Scythian metropolis of Minnagara lay inland behind it and was at the time of the *Periplus* subject to Parthian princes 'who were constantly driving each other out (p. 37). Into Barbarieum were imported "a great deal of thin clothing, figured linens, topaz, coral, storax, frankincanse, vessels of glass, silver and gold plate, and a little wine. On the other hand, there are exported costus, bdellium, iyclium, nard, turquoise, lapiz-lazuli, seric-skins, cotton cloth, silkyarn, and indigo." (pp. 37-38).

According to the *Periplus* "Beyond the gulf of Baraca is that of Barygaza and the coast of the country of Ariaca, which is the beginning of the kingdom of Nambonus and of all India" (p. 39). Behind the Saurastra coast lay the Abhera country which was very fertile and yielded "wheat and rice and sesame oil and clarified butter, cotton and the Indian cloths made therefrom, of the coarser sorts" (p. 39). From Ujjayini were brought to Barygaza "agate and carnelian, Indian muslins and mallow cloth, and much ordinary cloth."[42] (p. 42). The imports to Barygaza and Ujjayini consisted of "wire, Italian preferred, also Loadicean and Arabian; copper, tin and lead; coral and topaz; thin clothing and inferior sorts of all kinds; bright coloured girdles a cubit wide; storax, sweet clover, flint glass, *reolgar*, antimony, gold and silver coin, on which there is a profit when exchanged for the money of the country; and ointment, but not very costly and not much. And for the king, there are brought into those places very costly vessels of silver, singing boys, beautiful maidens for the harem, fine wines, thin clothing of the finest weaves, and the choicest ointments"[43] (p. 42). The exports are listed as "spikenard, costus, bdellium, ivory, agate and carnelian, lycium, cotton cloths of all kinds, silk cloth, woollen cloth, yarn, long pepper" (ibid).

Beyond Barygaza lay the Daksinapatha which had the important market-towns—Paethana or Pratisthana and Tagara. From Paethana to Barygaza was brought carnelian in great quantity; from Tagara, "much common cloth, all kinds of muslin and mallow cloth and other merchandise"[45] (p. 43).

Beyond Barygaza the market-towns were: Suppara, the city of Calliena (=Kalyana), Semylla, Mandagara, Palaepatma, Melizigara, Byzantium, Togarum and Aurundaboas; then the islands called Sesecrienae and of Aegiadii and of Caenitae opposite the place called Chersonesus (where there were pirates), and after that the white Island. "Then came Naura and Tyndis, the first markets of Damirica, and then Muziris and Nelcynda, which are now of leading importance" (p. 44). Tyndis and Muziris belonged to the Kingdom of Cerebothra, Nelcynda to Pandian Kingdom. Near the last was Bacare. "They send large ships to these market-towns on account of the great quantity and bulk of pepper and malabaturum. There are imported here, in the first place, a great quantity of coin, topaz, thin clothing, not much; figured linens, antimony, coral, crude glass, copper, tin, lead; wine, not much, but as much as at Barygaza; realgar and orpiment; and wheat enough for the sailors, for this is not dealt in by the merchants there. There is exported pepper, which is produced in quantity in only one region near these markets, a district called Cottonara. Besides this, there are exported great quantities of fine pearls, ivory, silk cloth, spikenard from the Ganges, malabathrum from the places in the interior, transparent stones of all kinds, diamonds and sapphires, and tortoise shells; that from chryse Island, and that taken among the islands along the coast of Daminca" (pp. 44-45).

Pepper brought the merchants unheard of profits and "was one of the most important articles of commerce between India and Rome, supplying perhaps three-quarters of the total bulk of the average westbound cargo" (Schoff, p. 214). Alaric had demanded pepper along with gold, silver, silk and scarlet cloth. 'And its popularity continued in later times. In *Piers Plowman*, the first thing the Glutton demands is pepper'. "Malabathrum and spikenard were the two most treasured ingredients of the ointments and perfumes of the Roman empire" (Schoff, p. 217).

Beyond Bacare lay the Dark Red Mountain and the district called Paralia which had a fine harbour called Balitta. Beyond this lay the Cape of Comari and a harbour further south was Colchi with its pearl-fisheries worked by condemned criminals. This belonged to the Pandian Kingdom. Beyond Colchi lay the district called the Coast country having an inland region called Argaru. Here pearls were gathered and muslins exported (p. 46). Argaru has been identified with ancient Uraiyur. Coast country is supposed to be *chola-mandalam*.

Further market-towns were Camara, Paduca and Sopatma. Palaesimandu or Taprobane produced pearls, transparent stones, muslins, and tortoise-shell (p. 47). Near about was the region of Masalia where a great quantity of muslins was made. Region of Dasarene yielded ivory. We hear of wild tribes like Cirrhadae (=Kirata?) and next of the market-town with the same name is Ganges where were brought "malabathrum and Gangetic spikenard and muslins of the finest sort, which are called Gangetic" (p. 47).

The balance of India's trade with Rome was favourable to India and a large quantity of Roman gold coins flowed into India. Pliny lamented that "in no year does India drain us of less than 550,000,000 *sesterces* ($ 22,000,000) giving back her own ware, which are sold among us at fully 100 times their first cost" (Schoff, p. 219). The reason for this was that "the general quality of Rome's exports was weight and bulk" (Warmington, p. 273). The Chinese annals confirm that the Parthian and Indian sea-trade with the Roman Empire reaped one-hundred fold profit (p. 274).

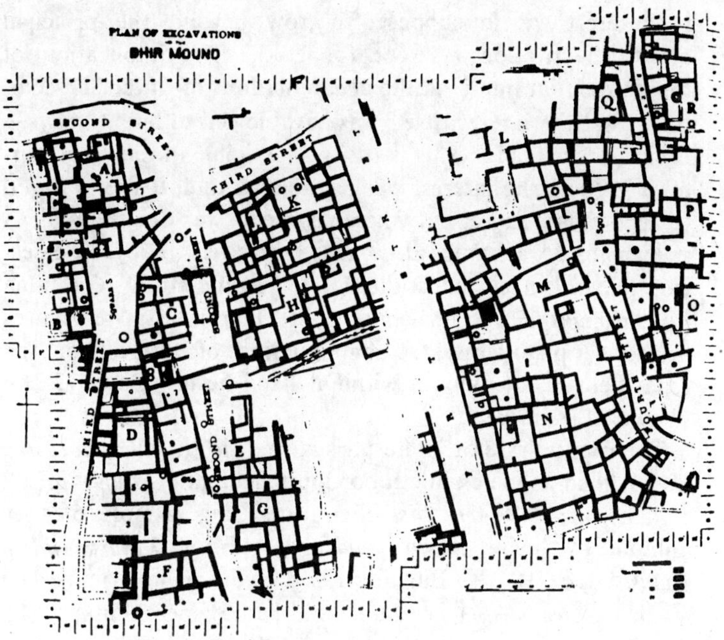

Taxila: Town-planning on the Bhir Mound, 1st century.

Money lending was recognized even in the *Dharmasūtras* as a distinct profession. Rural life as well as commerce in the cities required the borrowing of money. At the village level, the buying of articles like *ghee*, or wool or the use of bullocks for transport or the payment of rent in kind are visualized by Gautama as occasions of borrowing[46] (12.33). The accumulation of interest in such cases was not to exceed five times of the principal. Manu puts the limit at four times the loan.[47] Vasiṣṭha says "*dviguṇam hiraṇyam dhānyam dhānyenaiva rasā vyākhyātāh puspamūlaphalam ca tulādhṛtam: aṣṭaguṇam.*" Credit for buying grains, salt, sugar etc. and flowers, roots and fruits is here visualised. Only in the case of gold transactions, the increase of interest was limited to double the amount (*cirasthāne dvaigunyam prayogasya*).[48] Apparently, there was a great insistence on regular payment in these cases. Even normally the interest was to be paid monthly, not annually. This would protect the creditor from loss and the debtor from the accumulation of debt. Originally, the interest was not supposed to grow beyond the principal and this restriction was kept for gold. The implication of the differential limits on the accumulation of interest seems to be that the interest itself was payable in different ways—in kind or gold. This is easily intelligible in the rural context. Where the interest was payable in kind, it was allowed to accumulate more, but where payment was due in gold, a stricter limit was imposed because it was felt that the possession of gold itself constituted an accumulation (Gautama 12.29 : *bhuktādhirna vardhate*). The Dharmaśāstra recognizes besides simple interest, the compounding of interest or the repayment of the amount within a fixed term (Gau. 12.31 : *cakravāla vṛddhih*).

The normal rate of interest visualized in the *Dharmasastra* was defined as the eightieth portion per month (*Manu*, 8.140; *Yaj.* 3.16). The *Arthasāstra* endorsed this rate of 15% per annum by laying down *sapādapaṇā dharmyā māsavṛddhiḥ panaśatasya* (III.II). But for risky credit as in commercial lending (*vyāvahārikī*), the rate could be 60% per annum. To the foresters, the rate could be 120% p.a. while the rate among sea-traders is mentioned as 240% p.a. (ibid). Kautalya also lays down that where the loan was used to start a business, 50% of the profit was payable but this accumulated only upto twice the principal (ibid.).

Since physical labour was accepted as a mode of payment, insolvency could lead to slavery. The Buddhist texts relate many stories of the harassment of poor and insolvent debtors.

Borrowing often implied pledging a deposit and executing a bond or promissory note. The combination of accepting deposits and lending money to be invested in business constituted the function of bankers and the guild acted as such. They also received permanent endowments which were to be managed for the benefit of third parties, thus acting as trustees and executors. Several Satavahana inscriptions illustrate this. The actual rates of interest in some of the inscriptions tend to be lower than the customary 15% p. a., indicating the security and stability of business life. The high social position of the bankers is shown by their particpation in administrative councils.

NOTES AND REFERENCES

1. Cf. Fairservis, *Roots of Ancient India*, p. 443.
2. Wheeler, *The Indus Civilization*, (3rd ed.) pp. 74ff; cf. Possehl, (ed.) *Ancient Cities of Indus*, pp. 153 ff.
3. Allchins, *The Birth of Indian Civilization*, p. 270.
4. Ibid., p. 271; Cf. Lal and Gupta, *Frontiers of the Indus Civilization*, pp. 333ff.
5. Fairservis, op. cit., p. 292.
6. It is strange indeed that a great civilization with such a spread in space and time should have disappeared without leaving a trace in traditional memory. The almost unbelievable situation would become intelligible only if future researches reveal a closer relationship of the Harappan with the Vedic or the 'Dravidic' traditions. It may be noted that some scholars have discovered references to ruined cities in Vedic literature. *Naitandhava* and *Vyarna* are examples of such places.
7. R. 1. 126.6; 10.79.8.
8. Ibid. 8.5.38.
9. Ibid. 9.112.2
10. Cf. Fairservis, op. cit., pp. 347-48.
11. See below.
12. Cf. D.R. Bhandarkar, *Carmichael Lectures on Ancient Indian Numismatics*, pp. 64ff.
13. Marshall, *Taxila*, Vol. I, p. 95.
14. Ibid. 1, pp. 3-4.
15. G.R. Sharma, op. cit.
16. *Digha, Mahāparinibbānasuttanta.*
17. *Ramayana*, 1.5.5-23; 1.6. Lanka is described in Sundarakanda, 2. In *Raghu*, 16 one may see the state of Ayodhya in utter decline.
18. McCrindle, op. cit.
19. *Milindapañha*, see infra.
20. *Arthasastra*, 2.4.
21. *Kamasutra*, 1.4.
22. On guilds see the works of Fick, *Social Organization in Northern India* etc., Rhys Davids, *Buddhist India*, Mrs Rhys Davids in *C.H.I.* I, and Dr. R.C. Majumdar, *Corporate Life in Ancient India*.
23. *C.H.I.* I. p. 208.
24. *Milinda*, pp. 325 ff.
25. *Digha*, Vol. I. p. 44.
26. e.g. Mathura Stone Inscription of Huviṣka of the year 28, Nasik Cave Inscription of Nahapana of the years 41, 42, 45; Mandasor Inscription of the time of Kumaragupta, Indore copper-plate of Skandagupta.
27. Damodarpur copper-plates.

27a. Merchant guilds continued to be important in S. India, Nilakantha Sastri, *South India*, p. 164.

28. Bose, op. cit., II, p. 201.
29. Sethna, op. cit.
30. Marshall, op. cit., II, p. 534.
31. Bose, II, p. 193. *Jātaka*, V. 45.
32. Marshall II, pp. 540-44.
33. Marshall, II, pp. 564 ff.
34. *Excavations At Sravasti 1959*, pp. 66-68.
35. Marshall, op. cit., pp. 651 ff.
36. Marshall, op. cit., p. 616.
37. Marshall, op. cit., II, pp. 683 ff.
38. Buddhist and Jaina writings thus give a much higher status to the merchants.
39. e.g., *C.H.I.* I. pp. 20 ff.
40. *Pancatantra* (tr, Ryder), pp. 17 ff.
41. Warmington, pp. 45-46.
42. *Periplus*, p. 42.
43. Ibid. *l.c.*
44. *l.c.*
45. Ibid. p. 43.
46. *Gautama*, 12.33. *Kusīdaṁ paśūpajalomaksetraśadavāhyeṣu* : ***nātipañca-gunam.***
47. *Manu*, 8.151.
48. *Gautama*. 12.28.

7

The Standards of Living

India had the reputation of being a wealthy country in ancient times. According to Herodotus, the Indians who constituted the twentieth satrapy of the empire of Darius were "the most populous of nations in the known world" and "paid the largest sum : 360 talents of gold dust[1]." According to Megasthenes, Indians had abundant means of subsistence and exceeded in consequence the ordinary size. They were skilled in the arts and famine rarely visited them. There was little theft and they left their houses and property generally unguarded. Being simple in their manners and frugal, they lived happily enough. They did not drink wine and their food was principally a rice pottage. According to Arrian, they dressed in three pieces of cotton. Fa-hien similarly described the people of the middle kingdom as "prosperous and happy". If Greeks had noticed the absence of slavery and much crime, Fa-hien noticed the absence of vexatious interference by the state as well as the mildness of punishments. He also noticed that the people did not drink and were given to vegetarian diet.

The abundance and natural fertility of land in relation to the population was the standing cause of prosperity, as the Greeks noticed. The absence of any considerable extent of slavery, skilled handicrafts and light taxation helped to maintain the standard of well-being in the countryside. Nevertheless the slaves, servants and labourers constituted the poorest class which owned little or no property. Slaves existed from Vedic times as a form of property, acquired originally through captivity in war and secondarily through gifts and purchase. Manu mentions seven kinds of slaves

(8.415) captured in war, serving for subsistence, born in the house, bought, gifted, hereditary and punished to slavery. Slavery through indebtedness was the principal form of the last variety. Manu would like to think principally of the śūdras as *dāsas* (8.413). Kautalya's interdiction on the enslavement of the *ārya* goes much further (3.13.4) because *arya* for him means just a free man including the śudra. Only foreigners or *mlecchas* were free to sell or pledge their children to slavery. No free minor of any caste could be sold into slavery. A free person could, however, in dire distress, pledge himself to work for another as a slave but his or her work was regulated to ensure the personal dignity of the slave. If a free person were to sell himself into slavery, he would still retain his personal inheritance and the title to "What is earned by himself without detriment to his master." And he can always become free on paying the price. One who is punished into slavery can redeem himself by work and a captive in war too could be redeemed by work or half the price. For Kautalya thus the slave retains personal as well as property rights. This must be the reason why Megasthenes declared "All the Indians are free and not one of them is a slave. The Lakademonions and Indians are so far in agreement. The Lakademonions, however, hold the helots as slaves, and these helots do servile labour; but the Indians do not even use aliens or slaves, much less a country man of their own." The *dāsa* in India was "not the same as Greek *doueos* and was certainly no Helot" (Kangle, III, p. 187).

Between Kautalya and Manu, the latter has definitely a sterner view of the slave who could hold no property "like a wife or son" (8.416). But this seems to be due to Manu's identification of the slave with the śūdra, "bought or unbought" and his general theory of keeping down the śūdra. Since he seeks to reduce the slave to virtual if not formal slavery, he could not be expected to mention the rights of the slaves. His dictum, "*Śūdraṁ kārayet dāsyam*" may be understood as a modification of Kautalya's "*na tvevāryasya dāsabhāvaḥ.*" By implication Manu maintains the right of a *dvija* to freedom. In fact, there is proper punishment for one seeking to enslave a person of the upper castes (8-411-12). Gautama prohibits the sale of a slave of the male sex.

Yājñavalkya says that if one is enslaved by force or sold by robbers, he is entitled to freedom naturally (2.14.182). Any slave who saves the life of the master is entitled to freedom. Freedom could similary be won by giving up subsistence or through redemption by payment. Nor could slavery be valid when contrary to the hierarchy of castes. Nārada gives a most elaborate description of the slaves, mentioning fifteen types of slaves instead of the seven mentioned by Manu. Moreover, in his view in the case of four varieties of slaves—born in the house, obtained by purchase or hereditary right, or one who has sold himself—there could be no redemption except through the master's sweet-will. Nārada also justifies the employment of slaves of slaves in dirty work. In all these respects, Nārada shows a worse condition for the slaves than the *Arthaśāstra*. Perhaps this worsening was due to Bactrian, Saka and Kusana rule.

In the *Jātakas*, the slaves appear mainly as domestic servants. Their treatment differed according to the "disposition and capacity of both master and slave." Of "actual ill-treatment there is scarce any mention" (*C.H I.I.* p. 205). There are no runaway slaves. Slaves could be manumitted or free themselves by payment.

It may be concluded that slaves in India were neither numerous nor plentiful and that they were mainly employed in domestic work rather than in fields or mines. The customary price of a slave was 100 Kārṣāpanas, which made them fairly expensive.

Labourers were employed in fields or mines, in looking after cattle or in shops or streets. According to the *Arthaśāstra*, they were to be paid as contracted. In the absence of any contract, the rates were to be 10% of the grain harvested or of the produce or the goods handled. (3.13.27-29). For labourers in fields, ranches and orchards, the *Arthaśāstra* (2.24) prescribes wages of one and a quarter silver *paṇa*s per month plus provisions according to the person. This was for unskilled labourers. For king's servants, apparently skilled workers, Kautalya prescribes the minimum wage of 60 *paṇas* which have been interpreted as silver *paṇas* per annum or copper *paṇas* per month. It would amount to 2 or 2.6 copper *paṇas* per day. This could be partly converted into kind by the payment of one *āḍhaka* of grain per day. Manu prescribes that the wages were to be from one to six (copper) *paṇas* per day plus clothes every six months and one *droṇa* of grains every month (7.126). The commentator says that the clothes and grains too would vary from one to six and that the average payment would be three *paṇas* per day, three outfits of clothes every six months and three *droṇas* of grains every month. In the *Nāradasmṛti*, the labourer is distinguished from the slave and could not be made to do dirty or degrading work. Three types of wage-earners are mentioned: the highest are soldiers, the middling farm labourers, the lowest porters.

The *Jātakas* tend to confirm these rates. In *Gangamāla Jātaka*, a water-carrier and his woman are both paid half a silver *māsaka* or copper *paṇa* each for the day. The man ran singing under the scorching sun and the two planned to buy a garland, perfume and strong drink with their saving. The *Mahāummagga Jātaka* relates that a potter's hireling after a full day's work with clay and the wheel 'sat all day besmeared on a bundle of straw' eating '*appasūupaṁ yava bhattaṁ*', barley gruel with just a little broth. The *Visahya Jātaka* mentions the daily earning of a grass-cutter as one silver māsaka.[2]

From other evidence too, it appears that the daily wage of an unskilled labourer was two copper *paṇas* a day. From the Sanchi Stupa Inscription of Amrakardava, Dr. Pran Nath has shown that the daily food of a monk cost one-half or one-quarter of a copper *paṇa*. He has also argued that the standard food prescribed by Kautalya for an *ārya* or for a man of a low caste (*avara*) would have cost about one fourth of a copper pana.[3] The standard food is:

> *Taṇḍulānāṁ prasthaḥ caturbhāgah sūpaḥ*
> *sūpaṣoḍaśo lavaṇasyāṁśaḥ caturbhāgaḥ*
> *sarpiṣastailasya vā ekamāryabhaktaṁ-*
> *Ṣaḍbhāgaḥ sūpaḥ ardhasneha-*
> *mavarāṇām. Pādonaṁ strīṇām. Ardhaṁ bālānām.*
> (2.15.43-46).

Rice, broth, some *ghee* or oil and salt, this constituted the standard food. For the poorer classes, the amount of broth

Sanchi, Stupa 1: Yaksha on the west pillar of the northern gateway, Ist century B.C.

and ghee was less.[4] A *prastha* was roughly equal to a 'pound. When the lowest paid worker in royal pay getting 60 *paṇas* was partly paid in kind, he was given an *āḍhaka* or 4 *prasthas* of rice, apparently assuming that his family consisted of husband, wife and four children. If this wage in kind is set off against 45 silver *paṇas* for the year, as suggested by Kangle, we could have an *ādhaka* for two copper *paṇas*, i.e. 1 *prastha* for 1/2 copper *paṇas*. In case of daily labourers, the wage of the man was lower but his wife also worked to supplement the earnings as the *Jātakas* show. Although the income of the labourer was low, it was not too low for securing the amount of food normally supposed to be required since food was cheap.

For food, thus, we see a variety of patterns. At the upper level, we have cakes of wheat and barley, fine rice with milk or curd or meat or pulses, milk and milk products, meat and fish, fruits and vegetables, sugar, salt etc. along with drinks of various kinds.[5] At the lowest level, we see the elephant-driver in a famine-hit country subsisting on Kulmāṣa,[6] or the poor potter's assistant getting down with a little barley gruel and broth. In between, we find rice or *saktu* with salt and ghee or oil, broth or sour, and vegetables. While the poor man's food was cheap, the royal dish was fantastically expensive.

Similarly, in the matter of clothes, three pieces of cotton cloth covering the lower and upper parts of the body and the head constituted the normal clothing.[7] The rich wore clothes of fine stuff like muslin or silk which could have embroidered designs and they also put on ornaments of precious metals and stones. Elephants, horse and carriage, big houses and expensive household equipments, furniture, perfumes, slaves and servants, were the other costly items distinguishing the rich from the poor. Kings, noblemen and rich merchants indulged in conspicuous expenditure also and lived ostentatiously.[8]

Thus, although the gap between the very rich and very poor was quite marked, there was no dearth of land for cultivation or building and no over-population. Village grants flourished and there was only a marginal class of slaves and landless labourers. Taxation was mild. There was no scarcity of coarse food or cloth. Economic life ran on customary lines and wealth was not overvalued. Peasants and labourers, craftsmen and traders worked hard but were aware of the philosophy of resignation.

Notes and References

1. Herodotus, op. cit., p. 215.
2. Dr. Pran Nath (*A Study in the Economic Condition of Ancient India,*

p. 148) has argued, by comparing the evidence from a variety of sources, that the daily wages of an unskilled labourer varied between half and one *pana* a day and that taking into account the rise in the general price level, this rate was comparable to the rate in the 11th century and again that worked out for the 16th century. He calculates a seven-fold price rise from the 5th to the 11th and a two-thirds price rise from the 11th to the 16th centuries. Moreland has calculated the rise from the 16th to the 20th centuries.

3. Pran Nath, op. cit., p. 150.
4. The evidence of Kautalya is supported by the Mathura Stone Inscription of Huviska : two permanent endowments of 5500 silver *panas* each for feeding 100 Brahmanas every full moon day and distributing every day 3 adhakas of *saktu*, 1 *prastha* of salt, 1 *prastha* of *śukta* or sour, 3 jars of green vegetables and 5 vessels of a drink. If the rate of interest be assumed to be 15%, we have roughly 1 copper *paṇa* for one person's food and as the price of 1 *āḍhaka* of *saktu*.
5. *Samanta pāsādikā* mentions the best alms as one *ādhaka* of old *sāli* rice which was bright and polished, boiled and eaten with 1/4 of *mudga* broth, with dainties (vyañjanas) like meat, fish, vegetables, fruits, *karūra* and ghee, oil, butter milk, *rasa*, *kanjika* etc. (II pp. 712-13). *Vinaya* describes goọd or fine food as *ghee*, butter oil, honey, sugar, fish, meat, milk, curd etc.
6. *Iśādi*, p. 379. *Samantapāsādikā* mentions stale *kulmāsa* as illustrating the poorest kind of food. I pp. 200-01.
7. Buddhist monks were *Antarvāsaka*, *Uttarāsaṅga* and *Sanghāti*.
8. Cf. "The houses of the laity are sumptuous inside and economical outside. The inner rooms and the central hall vary in their dimensions and there is no rule for form or construction for the tiers of the terraces or the rows of the high rooms. The houses were built of bricks, bamboo or wood (Watters, I, p. 147)". For seats, all use corded benches. The royal family, the grandees, officials and gentry adorn their benches in different ways, but all have the same style. The press and ornaments of the kings and grandees are very extraordinary. Garlands and tiaras with precious stones are their head-adornments and their bodies are adorned with rings, bracelets and necklaces. Wealthy mercantile people have only bracelets. Most of the people go barefoot and shoes are rare." (p. 151).

8

The Development of Socio-ethical Ideas

The notion of *dharma* embodies the tradition of the pursuit of moral values and constitutes one of the most distinct and essential aspects of Indian culture. The concept of *dharma* is not merely theoretical but intensely practical. Embodied in rules and institutions and illustrated by popular character-types from epic stories, Puranic myths and legends and folk-tales, the notion of *dharma* reaches every man, the illiterate peasant and housewife as much as the learned philosopher and minister. *Dharma* like *sadhana* is one of those golden threads which bind the elite and the common folk together and which are available at the level of every day life but reach up to the heavens.

Hegel had pointed out that the subjectivity of pure morality and the objectivity of pure law are both abstractions and find their concrete reality in institutional ethos or *sittlichkeit.*[1] This concept of *sittlichkeit* or 'social ethics' is very near that of *dharma* which includes morality and law, convention and courtesy. Revelation, tradition and convention have all gone into the making of *dharma* which thus constitutes the essential social bond. "It is called *dharma* because it is the principle of cohesion (*dharma*). *Dharma* holds the people together."[2]

Early Vedic society had a highly developed moral consciousness which is reflected in the hymns of *Ṛgvedasaṁhita.* This moral consciousness was integrally bound up with religious consciousness. Man must act as the gods act and the gods act by a fixed and eternal law called *ṛta.*[3] Thus the

Sarnath: Preaching Buddha, Gupta Period

idea of Natural Law, at once moral and cosmic, was reached early. *Ṛta* and *Satya*, law and truth, were thus held to be the foremost virtues. The belief in *Ṛta* produced a belief in a just ritual order for all human life and actions. Social life was thus sought to be regulated ritually and sacramentally. The major *śrauta* sacrifices covered the seasonal cycle of economic life as well as the need for firm authority and victory in the political sphere.[4] The *pākayajñas* reminded man of his obligations to other men and creatures.[5] The system of domestic *saṁskāras* or sacraments punctuated the personal life of the individual.[6] This ritualization of social ethics remained a permanent part of the tradition of *dharma*. Through its symbolism and authoritative suggestion, the ritual sought to educate the raw and instinctive attitudes of man. Thus when men reaped the fruits of the earth, they must remember the bounty of the gods.[7] The king must remember that all authority proceeds from the gods.[8] The groom must know that the bride is given to him by Soma, Gandharva and Agni and that marriage is a permanent relationship with moral obligation.[9] Children and wealth are the gifts of gods.[10] Nor is death the end of life which in a different form extends beyond it. Funerary rites, therefore, constitute a necessary though final part of life.[11]

Not only does the notion of *Ṛta* lead to a ritualized scheme of social ethics, it makes piety the first of all virtues. Piety implies faith or *śraddhā*, 'placing the heart' or placing in the heart.[12] It implies further attuning the mind (*dhi*) to the will of the gods and the readiness to serve them. Truth or *Satya* is often mentioned as coordinate with *Ṛta*. They were the first-born of the creative effort of the gods.[13] "By Truth is the earth upheld, the heaven propped up.[14]" Truth meant the conformity of thoughts to the Natural Law and the conformity of speech and action to the mind. Truth implied not only the objectivity and openness of the mind but sincerity and consistency. Truth is opposed to lying or deceit or crookedness, which are resorted to harm others. Non-violence as pacifism or passivism as such is not a virtue emphasized in the *Ṛgvedasamhita* but avoiding unjust or unfair harm to others is.

The *Ṛgvedic* attitude to morality is heroic. It prized virtue in the original sense of manliness which corresponds to the notion of *vīra* or *nṛ* or *vṛṣa*.[15] Life is conceived as a struggle between the forces of light and darkness. This is more than a mythical conception. The myth is, in fact, nothing except the expression of the idea of moral struggle.[16] Life is a constant and hard choice between right and wrong. Goodness consists in the right and strenuous exercise of the will.

Hence good life is essentially a life of action[17] and the good man must aspire to be a hero. This mythical representation of the moral life in terms of the struggle between the gods and the demons became a familiar and permanent element in the Indian tradition.[18] It may be mentioned here that modern historians consider this ethical understanding of the myth to be a late product and tend to regard the myth as the reflection of primitive fancy and at the same time inconsistently enough of a historical struggle between human tribes especially Aryan and non-Aryan, or as simply the expression of a superstitious fear or poetic wonder created by the spectacle of the alternation of darkness and light, draught and rain.[19] This view is apparently based on the assumption that surviving primitive tribes are culturally nearer the early Vedic age than the later Vedic and post-Vedic traditions.

Generosity is another great virtue in the *Ṛgveda.* Goodness is giving; the evil man is he who does not give. Since gods give to man, man must give back to them and to those who have need.[20] A whole hymn is devoted to the virtue of charity. "The unwise obtains wealth in vain. Truly that becomes his death. He nourishes neither *aryaman* nor friend (i.e. neither gods nor men). Eating alone, one only accumulates sin (*Kevalāgho bhavati kevalādi*)."[21]

Family and the state were the principal institutions of social cohesion and the two were linked together by the village community. Family, *kula,* was the chief of the kinship groups which included *gotra* and *jana.*[22] The family was patrilineal and extended. Loyalty to the ancestors was strongly emphasized and the worship of the *pitṛs* was an essential ritual. Agni symbolized the Father, the lord of the house. He is expected to be wise and kindly, leading his folk by the proper ways.[23] At the same time, he is the fierce defender of the family. The father had absolute authority over the son as the story of *Śunaḥśepa* illustrates.[24] He was also the teacher of the children. Daughters were also educated although their position was lower than that of sons. Childhood was ideally required to be spent in acquiring Vedic learning and this period of education was one of stern discipline. The *brahmacārin* or Vedic student was highly respected.[25] *Brahmacarya* began with the sacrament of

Upanayaṇa which was deemed a second birth for the individual. Great value was placed on the student's observance of celibacy, obedience, poverty and industry. Memorization, accuracy, eloquence and the power of original composition were encouraged. The ends of education were the cultivation of *medhā* or understanding and retention, *dhī* or intuition and *tejas* or the force and lustre of a cultivated mind. For society, the purpose of education was the preservation of the learning of the sages and seers. By helping in the continuation of this tradition, one was absolved of the first of the Three Debts which everybody incurred by virtue of being a social creature. This first obligation was termed the 'obligation to the sages' (*Ṛsi-ṛṇa*).[26]

The other two obligations were—'obligation to the ancestors' (*pitṛ-ṛṇa*) and the 'obligation to the gods' (*deva-ṛṇa*). The former required the procreation of children to maintain the continuity of the family, and the latter required the setting up of the sacrificial fire so that worship of the gods could be maintained unbroken. Both of these could be done by the householder only. For this purpose, marriage was required. Marriage was sacramental and indissoluble. Girls were married when they were grown up. A maiden is said to win a husband through *brahmacarya.*[27] Women are found even as seers. The glorious dawn was held up as an example of the bustling and brightly bedecked young maiden, waking up early in the morning, milking the cattle and loosening them for the pasture, cleaning and looking after the household.[28] There was no segregation of men and women but they were expected to abide by a chaste life till marriage. The married woman was given an honoured position in the household. She was expected to be the mistress of the household and to produce many children.[29] She participated in the Vedic religious rites with the husband. She was the alter ego, the other half of the husband.[30] The rivers with their bright and changing glances, purifying and fertilizing power, cool and delightful, are compared with the loving mothers.[31]

Indra and Varuna were the prototypes of the rulers. Indra is the impetuous warrior who is assisted by his companions, the Maruts. He is the leader in war, a mighty hero who protects the realm from enemies. Varuna is the emperor of a vast realm.[32] He abides by fixed laws by which he governs. He moves among the people, discerning the righteous and the wicked (*satyānrte avapaśyan janānām*).[33] The human ruler was a free man among free men, leading and governing with the help of popular bodies, enforcing the law which was above him in source and majesty.[34] While the king's authority and the trust which lay on him were of momentous import, he was expected to discharge them with the help and counsel of the priests. Heroic and popular, the king was to be wise and in wisdom he was to acknowledge the superiority of the brahmanas.[35]

Early Vedic social and moral ideas have continued down the ages. The idea of Natural Law, truth as the supreme virtue, the importance of charity, the ideas of studentship, loyalty to the family, the ideal of the ruler who would be strong, wise and popular, all these are permanent elements of the tradition. During the later Vedic period, moral ideas become more internalized and spiritualized. The conception of the gods and sacrifice changed. The gods were seen to be the projections of a single and universal spiritual reality directly accessible in the hearts of men.[36] With this, the symbolic nature of sacrifice and worship became subordinate to philosophical understanding and tradition.[37] Morality thus came to be an inward matter of the heart.

In the early Vedic period, it was held that gods willed by law and the good man must will accordingly. Morality was essentially a matter of right willing and its paradigm was illustrated in myth and ritual. While the behavioural rules and ancient rituals were maintained, their understanding underwent a great change. Morality was no longer simply external conformity but a subjective state of feeling, knowledge and choice. The distinction between right and wrong was held to be a rational distinction, a matter of objective knowledge.[38] What enabled a person to exercise this faculty of discrimination properly was the purity of his heart. Moral reason was not simply intellectual, it involved an intuitive element. The element of willing as choice was still held to be important. This again emphasized that although moral life depended on knowledge, it was quite different from a simply speculative or intellectual life. Moral values were regarded as ends which are the objects of choice in accordance with intuitive reason.[39]

The kinds of moral values may be distinguished. The first comprises ideal dispositions or qualities of the soul, which may be called virtues. The second comprises duties and obligations in the context of social life. Virtues are values which one must realize in one's own being in order that one may realize one's own real nature. Moral life is here a stage in the development of spiritual life. The obligation under which man acts here is universal and absolute because it arises from his spiritual nature. It is the obligation which the higher self of man places on his lower self, the obligation which man must universally feel as a spiritual being. On the other hand, man's membership of society imposes specific obligations on him corresponding to his situation. These obligations are largely concerned with the functions and relations of classes and subserve essentially social values like common security, prosperity and justice. Moral values are thus seen to arise from spiritual as well as social needs. On the individual, however, they impinge as obligations of personal character and social conduct sanctioned by revelation and tradition.

The moral end—*artha*—is an ideal or rational end (*śreyas*), not an empiric satisfaction (*preyas*); *anyacchreyonyad utaiva preyaḥ*).[40] *Preyas* includes the objects of egoistic desires, sensuous, and social. The *Kaṭhopaniṣad* illustrates this most vividly by the story of Naciketas. He is offered long life for himself and his children, wealth of all kinds, dominion, slaves, damsels and all the things which men want and find it hard to get. Naciketas is not tempted. He declares pleasures to be ephemeral and the life of instinctive seeking to be imprisoned in the valley of death. "Man cannot be satisfied by wealth or gain (*Na vitiena tarpanīyo manuṣyaḥ*".[41] Hoping to preserve and add to his satisfaction the fool chooses *preyas* (*preyo mando yogaksemād vṛṇīte*). The wise man, the man endowed with Reason, chooses *śreyas* after due discrimination (*tau samparītya vivinakti dhīraḥ*). *Śreyas*, thus, has both the characteristics of an ideal end—it is rationally determined and not ephemeral; satisfactions, on the other hand, are instinctive and momentary. The ideal end continues and grows. Empiric satisfactions keep slipping, however much we may seek to preserve and increase them (*Śreya ādadānasya sādhu bhavati hīyate rthād yau preyo vṛṇīte*). Further, choosing the ideal end is an expression of inner freedom and extends it whereas seeking satisfactions is bondage ('*hṛdayasyeha granthayaḥ*', '*anīśayā śocati*').[42]

If this distinction of *śreyas* and *preyas* were logically pushed to the extreme, the good would become identical with the realization of a pure spiritual condition free from all desires. This is the state of freedom or *Mukti*. Since this lies beyond desires, it lies beyond action and hence beyond all kind of prescription and regulation. The state of spiritual freedom thus becomes transmoral. *Śreyas* as *summum bonum* transcends the realm of moral distinctions but the path to it lies through that realm. "No one who has not desisted from evil actions, no one who is not at peace and inwardly collected, no one who has a restless mind, can attain to the Self by intellect alone."[13] The search for the good begins with the distinction between the Good and the Pleasant, proceeds through the cultivation of virtues, and leads on to the realm of the Pure Spirit beyond the dualities of moral consciousness.

Prajapati is said to have summed up the moral requirements of men, gods and demons in three *Das* viz. *dāna*, *dama* and *dayā*.[44] Gods or the divine side of human nature is prone to be led away by enjoyment and needs training in the restraint of the senses. The demonic part of man is prone to violence and needs to cultivate compassion. Man seeking egoistic ends within a network of social relationships needs above all to give and sacrifice. Charity or *dāna* represents this altruistic need of man. Self-control, charity and compassion are, then, the three great virtues which man must cultivate.

At another place it is stated that there are three "stems of Dharma".[45] A reference to the *āśrama* has been seen here. *Yajña*, *adhyayana* and *dāna* constitute the first stage, *tapas* the second and staying with the teacher the third.[46] At other places, again, *tapas*, *brahmacarya* and *satya* have been emphasized. The *āśramas* represented the stages not only of man's biological life but their integration into social and moral patterns which would constitute a gradual approach to the condition of spiritual self-sufficiency. While the first two *āśramas* doubtless go back to the ancient Vedic age, the third *āśrama* too appears to have been formulated by the later Vedic age when the emergence of symbolic sacrifices and meditation gave it emphasis. It is generally supposed that the fourth *āśrama* was also an accepted part of the Vedic scheme of life in the age but this seems not to have been the case.[47]

The theory of the *āśramas* postulates that to move from instinctive and appetitive life to desirelessness, intermediary stages of controlled desires and actions are necessary. The duties for the *āśramas* accepted desires and the actions directed to satisfy them as valid within certain limitations. *Āśrama-dharmas* or the duties prescribed for the *āśramas* are largely regulatory. They accept the validity of the basic human and social seekings—*putraiṣaṇā*, *vittaiṣaṇā*, and *lokaiṣaṇā*.[48] Family, wealth, and social recognition are basic ends which men seek. The householder may seek all these ends combining them with the worship of the gods, charity and compassion. As a preparation for the life of the householder, a period of stern discipline was required. As old age approached, one could retire to the forests to meditate, abandoning the life of earning and procreation.

While no clear and systematic description of the four *āśramas* can be traced in later Vedic literature, the theory of the four *Varnas* finds it *locus classicus* in the *Puruṣa-sūkta*.[49] Here *Puruṣa* is the source of the cosmos as well as of society. There is a correspondence between the functional parts of *Purusa* and the *varnas* in society. The order of the *varnas* thus comes to be an organic unity and the relationship of the different *varnas* comes to be one of functional correlation. At the same time, the functions relate to ends or values and since these form a hierarchy, the *varnas* too form a hierarchy. Spiritual authority, temporal power, production of wealth, and labour are the four chief social functions where the first two were held pre-eminent while the last two were held as necessities rather than values.

Thus conceived, society was held to be engendered by a primordial sacrifice which was regulated by the First Laws or *Dharmas*. "The *Varnas* were created for the sake of work.

That work called *Dharma* regulates every one as duty and is the means of obtaining human ends or values."[50] *Dharma* came to replace the early Vedic concept of *Rta.* If *Brahman* is the original substance of creation in its ultimate unity, *Dharma* is the law that governs the created world in its dynamic inter-relationship. It is the law that underlies Nature as well as Society.

Although society consists of four orders, it is held together and flourishes by the principle of *dharma.* "In the beginning this (the Ksattriya and other castes) was indeed Brahman, one only. Being one, He did not flourish. He projected an excellent form, the Ksattriya—Therefore, there is none higher than the Ksattriya—Yet He did not flourish. He projected the Vaisya—He did not still flourish. He projected the Sudra caste—Yet he did not flourish."[51] "So He created *Dharma,* the form of the good. *Dharma* is the ruler of the ruler. Therefore, there is nothing higher than *Dharma.* So even the weak hopes (to match) the stronger one through *Dharma* as one might through the king. *Dharma* is the same as Truth. Hence when one speaks the truth, he is said to speak what is right or just and speaking justly one is said to speak the truth. Both these—Truth and Justice—are the same."[52] Sankara comments "Truth is understanding a thing in accordance with the scriptures. The same thing when it is practised, is called justice, and when it is understood to be in accordance with the scripture, is truth....Therefore, that justice in its double aspect of theory and practice controls all, those that know the scriptures as well as those that do not. Therefore, it is the "Controller of the Ksattriya."[53]

Sreyas or the moral good is here identified with *Dharma* which is explained as the principle of social justice grounded in Truth. The word *dharma* corresponded to the Greek conception of justice or *dike*[54] and there is an obvious similarity between the Platonic explanation of justice and the conception or *dharma* as the just social order correlating human classes based on aptitude and functions.[55] Even the hierarchy of the classes is the same except that the Indian conception distinguishes the philosopher from the king and would keep them distinct. There is much speculation in the *Brahmanas* about the relationship of the brahmanas and the

Ksattriyas. They are said to be related as Intelligence (Mitra) and Will (Varuna). Both were superior to the rest. As for their mutual relationship, the king was declared to exercise supreme social power in a physical or administrative sense but the real source of that power was held to be in spiritual authority. Since the Brahmana represented that authority, he was to be given due respect by the Ksattriya.[56]

The post-Vedic period saw a number of diverse developments. On the one hand, Vedic orthodoxy sought to formulate and systematize the conception of *dharma* in the *Dharma-śāstra*. On the other, materialists and political scientists questioned the orthodox views and sought to explain the social order in terms of contract, utility and force. Sramanas and reformers sought to develop an ascetic or liberal interpretation of *dharma*.

Jaimini's *Mimāṁsā-sūtras* undertook to investigate the nature of *dharma*. They define *dharma* as "*Codanā-lakṣano rtho dharmah*",[57] i.e. *dharma* is the good which is made known by the *Vedas*. The commentator Śabara explained that *dharma* is what leads to good—'*Yaḥ śreyaskaraḥ sa eva hi dharma-śabdeno-cyate*',[58] and Kumarila says "The good is the satisfaction of the person. The substances, qualities and actions which the *Vedas* reveal as the means to its realization constitute *dharma* in this aspect."[59] An object becomes a *dharma* not by virtue of its empirical reality but by virtue of its transcendental efficacy in producing happiness, an efficacy which can be known only through the *Vedas*. Where the satisfaction is simply an empirical effect, the causal object is just natural, not moral. The *Prābhākaras* identify *dharma*, not with things and actions but with a transcendental entity called *apūrva* which is participated by prescribed actions. They explain *artha*, not as satisfaction, but as non-dissatisfaction, which may be hedonically neutral. It is the earlier Bhatta view which is, however, more usually accepted by the Mimamsakas.

Śreyas on this view is not radically opposed to *Preyas*, which is clearly opposed to the Upanisadic view. Apparently, the ritualistic tradition represented by Jaimini did not accept a purely idealistic ethics. It defined *dharma* as a revealed means of attaining the good. This tradition was significant for analysing the nature of moral prescriptions and the principles of their interpretation. The implied ethical theory is formalistic. The moral good is not characterized in subjective terms or in terms of its content. In fact, it cannot be recognized by experience or reason. *Dharma* can be recognized only in terms of an imperative of which the authority is not derived from any natural source of knowledge, i.e. the imperative must belong to Revelation or the *Veda*. Unlike the Kantian imperative, the imperative for the Mimamsakas is not devoid of explicit or implicit reference to a desired end. Good as satisfaction may be moral or non-moral just as evil may be. When the good is attainable only through following a revealed prescription, it becomes a moral good or *dharma*. Thus the apparent hedonism of the view with respect to the end, is more than annulled by the rejection of empiricism with respect to the means. Similarly the analysis of moral obligation in terms of the forms of imperative statements is joined to the postulate that only Vedic imperatives can transcend empirical knowledge. Thus Mimamsaka formalism is joined to dogmatic supernaturalism and was much criticised in the rival philosophical schools.

Thus *dharma* came to be defined as a system of rules deriving their authority from the Vedic tradition and regulating personal conduct as well as social relations and business. The definition in terms of obligatoriness or instrumentality referable to the scriptures, was wide enough to include moral as well as legal matters and the codes of *dharma* which were compiled in the *sutras* and the *smrtis* came to have this mixed aspect. Gautama's *Dharmasutras* have been reckoned as the most ancient. They state "*Veda* is the source of *dharma*. So also are the memory and conduct of those who are versed in the *Veda*. It is true that celebrated persons have occasionally transgressed morality but that does not constitute an example to lesser persons".[60] In matters of doubt, it is recommended that a *parisad* of at least ten learned and selfless persons was to be convened to give its judgement. If that were impossible, even one learned and righteous Vedic scholar might be called to give a decision.[61] Baudhayana says "*Dharma* has been taught in each *Veda*. It shall be explained accordingly. Secondly, *dharma* has been handed down by memory. Thirdly, there is the tradition of the *śiṣṭas*. *Śiṣṭas* are those who are free from envy, egoism, greed, pride, stupidity and anger, and whose accumulation of grains will suffice for a few days only. In their absence a *Parisad* of at least ten should be consulted."[62] "Since *dharma* is manifold, subtle and difficult, it should not be pronounced upon by just one person."[63] Vasistha categorically states "*śiṣṭaḥ punarakāmātmā*", i.e. the authentic person is one who is passion-free. He also seeks to define the boundaries of Aryavarta, apparently because that was the region which provided the standard for conduct.[64] This juxtaposes the duality of *dharma*, as inner morality and as outward conduct.

The *sutras* thus enlarge the sources of *dharma* to three—scriptures, traditions and example. It is obvious that in this age of the compilation of dharma, past traditions and contemporary practices were both taken into account. That is why occasionally even divergent practices are noticed and sometimes disapproval expressed. The nomenclature of the *āsramas* and the opinions expressed with respect to them also suggest that the scheme of four *āśramas* was still in the making. Thus Baudhyāna mentions '*Brahmacārī gṛhastho vānaprasthaḥ parivrājaka iti*'[65] while Āpastamba says '*Gārhasthyām ācāryakulam maunam vānaprasthyamiti*'.[66] Again both Gautama and Baudhāyana mention with respect the view that there is really only one *āśrama*, that of *gārhasthya*.[67] Haradatta argues that this doctrine of one *āśrama* only is true enough of the *śruti* which stresses the continuity of the family, but not of the *smṛti*—"*Śraute nāstīti yuktam na punaḥ smartepi nāstīti*".[68] Similarly, the description of the *jātis* in the *sūtras* presents divergences and shows an evolving situation.

Apart from rules of conduct relating to the *āśramas* and the *varnas*, the *sutras* go on to describe the regulation of business and livelihood for the various castes and advise the king about taxation and the administration of law and juttice. Quite fierce laws are proposed to prevent the miscegenation of castes. Otherwise too, the laws are unequal between the castes, especially between the Brahmanas and the Sudras. It seems that the underprivileged status of the sudras had an essentially ritualistic origin. The basic exclusion of the sudra was from Vedic study and ritual, which seems to have come to prevail towards the end of the Vedic Age.[68a]

The *sūtras* clearly belong to a period (*c.* 600 B.C.—200 B.C.) when the economic and political conditions were undergoing change and the structure of society was becoming more complex. On the other hand, family life and Vedic schools still ran in their accustomed ways except that mendicancy had become more widespread. Society had also expanded towards the Deccan and some regional peculiarities were beginning to be noticed. The *sūtras* seek to preserve and codify traditional rules relating to the personal and social conduct of the individual and at the same time introduce modifications which would take note of the important changes which were occurring.

While the *śrauta sūtras* systematized the details of the Vedic sacrifices, the *gṛhya sūtras* recapitulate the "rites and superstitions connected with home life". "Every important phase of a man's existence is accompanied with its appropriate rite; and what to do and what not to do, injunctives, prohibitives, taboos, are taught as general rules of conduct. The greater events, birth, marriage, death, are described in their religious setting; each with minute detail."[70] The picture is essentially of the rural folk and the ethos must represent immemorial Vedic customs except that the references to crude images of some deities could be a later development. It is more likely, however, that these, like the folk deities themselves, belonged to the folk life from an ancient period. In some respects, thus, the *Grhyasutras* supplement the elite priestly tradition which the *Brahmanas* record, just as the epics derive basically from the bardic tradition of the ruling class. The variations of these texts are not merely of time and region but of aspect and tradition. Nor must the *gṛhya* ritual and superstitions be deemed simply as the expression of a primitive mentality. As mentioned earlier, ritual was a mode of religious as well as moral consciousness and enables one to have a glimpse into the traditional domestic ethos of a rural folk belonging to the upper castes. We notice, for example, the value placed on the birth and upbringing of children, the constancy of marriage, the reverence felt for the ancestors; the stress on hospitality and the recognition of the claims of all beings on man. The principal features of the domestic ethos of the Indian tradition may be firmly traced back to this period.

Manusmrti completed the task which the *sutras* had begun and it did it so well that in practice it replaced them. Unlike the *sutras*, the *Manusmrti* is not only detailed and systematic but places the rules of *dharma* within a theoretical structure. Here we have not only a socio-ethical code but a philosophy.

Manu begins with the account of creation which depends on the *Nāsadīya* and *Puruṣa-sūktas*. The account is Vedantic but takes the help of Sankhya too. Creation is bound by the dualities of pleasure and pain. Underlying these is the distinction of right and wrong actions. There is a succession of four human ages *Krta*, *Treta*, *Dvapara* and *Kali*. These take up a total of twelve thousand years, a modest figure which the commentators and later understanding inflate fantastically by interpreting the years to be 'divine years'.[71] *Krtayuga* was a golden age when the *Dharma* was in full swing. In each succeeding age, a quarter of *Dharma* was lost. *Tapas* was the principal *dharma* in *Kṛta* age, *jñāna* in the *Tretā*, *yajña* in *Dvāpara* and *dāṇa* in *Kali*. The duties of the four *varnas* are thus described. The Brahmana has to study, sacrifice and give alms in common with the other two twice-born castes. His characteristic duties are to teach, officiate at sacrifice and receive alms. The distinctive functions of the Ksattriya are to protect the people and avoid addiction to pleasures. The Vaisya is privileged to engage in agriculture, keeping cattle, trade and money lending. The Sudra has the sole function of serving the upper castes "without envy". To the Brahmana belongs the supreme position in society. "By virtue of *dharma*, he is sovereign" (*Dharmataḥ brāhmaṇaḥ prabhuḥ*).[72] In describing the glory of the Brahmana, Manu becomes rapturous. The Brahmana is the visible embodiment of eternal righteousness. All property in society really belongs to him and consequently what he gets is not a gift. What others get must be deemed an act of grace on the part of the Brahmana. What this extravagance really means is that as the custodians of education, religion and the laws, the Brahmanas are entrusted with the higher social functions and deserve appropriate respect and authority. The Brahmana must be endowed with learning and virtuous conduct or *ācāra* which is the highest *dharma*.

Dharma is defined as what is practised by good and learned persons who are free from attachment and hatred and what is approved by one's heart.[73] Manu here implies that *dharma* has to be discovered not only through tradition but also through conscience. This would conform with Jaimini's definition if we understand his use of *artha* to correspond to the Upanisadic usage. As Mrs. Rhyṣ Davids has shown, the word *artha* anciently meant the ideal object of desire, not *any* object of desire. The desirable, however, lies within the sphere of desire and Manu asserts categorically that while sensuality is not good, nor is total asceticism, since Vedic values and the Vedic path of action depend on the acceptance of some desires.[74] Desire and ritual, moral rules and laws, all arise from *saṅkalpa* which may be explained as the act of volition including the idea of the object or end to be realized through action. This assertion of Manu "*Saṅkalpamūlaḥ kāmaḥ*" is in line with the *Gita* or early Buddhism but whereas these latter condemned *karma* and *sankalpa*, Manu upholds them as the basis of moral and religious institutions.

The sources of *dharma* are—the *Vedas*, the tradition and practice of those who know them, the conduct of good people and the satisfaction of the *Atman*.[75] Here too, Manu clearly reiterates the role of conscience in determining what is right and what is wrong. Revelation, tradition, example and conscience, all co-operate in the discovery of *dharma*. "*Vedaḥ smṛtiḥ sadācāraḥ svasya ca priyamātmanaḥ*".[76] But, one should not, like the atheistic revilers of the *Vedas*, disregard the sacred tradition on the basis of merely rational philosophy (*hetuśāstra*). Here again is an implied reference to the Buddhist view which sought to ground morality on subjective feeling alone and defended the view rationally, criticising the *Vedas*.[77]

When practice is taken to be a standard, one should look to the practice current in *Brahmāvarta*.[78] *Brahmarṣideśa, Madhyadeśa, and Āryāvarta* too are holy lands and relevant in the determination of *dharma*. Manu, however, uses the word *dharma* beyond the *Varnasrama dharma* to include also the rules and customs current in different regions, castes and families also. "*Deśa-dharmān jātidharmān kuladharmānśca śāśvatān Pāṣaṇḍa-gaṇa-dharmānśca śāstre sminnuktavānmanuḥ.*[79] *Varnasrama dharma* itself includes *Varnadharma*, *āśrama-dharma*, *varṇāśrama-dharma*, *guṇadharma* and *naimittika dharma*.[80]

The purpose of the *saṁskāras* and other ritual is to purify the body from hereditary and embryonic taints. The various rules of discipline and ritual prescribed for the *brahmacarin* and *grhastha* serve to render their bodies fit to attain to holy knowledge (*'brahmīyaṁ Kriyate tanūh'*).[81] *Jata-karman*, *Namakarana*, *Niskramana*, *Annaprasana* and *Cudakarman* represent the *saṁskaras* to be performed by the first or the third year of the child. Then must follow *Upanayana* or initiation into studentship. For the Brahmana, it should be performed in the eighth year, for the Ksattriya in the eleventh and for the Vaisya in the twelfth year. The *Upanayana* could be preferably performed earlier, but in no case after double the normal age. The present version of the *Manu-smrti* denies *Upanayana* to women. "Marriage is their *Upanayana*, serving the husband is staying with the teacher, doing the household work is their performance of sacrifices."[82] Manu, however, has been quoted also to refer to the ancient practice of the *Upanayana* of women.[83] The denial of *Upanayana* to them and marrying them early was a fateful change. It was a change in the conception of the very role of women in society and of what constituted their ideal of life. The woman loses education as well as independence. She is only a daughter, wife and mother living under the authority of parents, husband and children. She is no longer an independent person who could aspire after knowledge or sacred learning. Nor is she allowed economic independence since by and large she does not own property. The fulfilment of her life lies in serving men in different relationships. In finding her fulfilment through service alone in a condition of dependence, the woman is indeed like the *sudra*. In Manu's view at least, five-eigths of society must be perpetually condemned to a virtually servile status.[84] It is, of course, possible to argue that the dependence of women in Manu is within the conduct of domestic relationship and affection, a situation best calculated to fulfil feminine nature. It is even possible to argue that feminine independence tends to mar the beauty and virtue of feminine character and that it is only a snare to turn women into wage-earning labourers and burden them with an avoidable burden. This, however, exaggerates the difference between men and women and tends to be unfair to the latter.

Education means for Manu not merely the acquisition of learning but the building of a sound moral and spiritual character. The student must abide in strict discipline and observe poverty, obedience, charity and regular habits of study and worship. He must respect the teacher. Much stress is laid on *sāvitrī-japa* and *japa-yajña* is declared much superior to other sacrifices. *Prāṇāyāma* is praised as the highest *tapas*. Acquisition of knowledge thus becomes primarily the acquisition of spiritual knowledge. One of the pre-conditions of a sound moral and spiritual character is the cultivation of self-control and habitual restraint over the senses. Wealth, family, age, actions and learning constitute a five-stepped ladder of values in which each succeeding step is higher than the preceding one.[85] Thus wealth is of least consequence while learning comes highest. *Acarya* and *Upadhyaya* are distinguished, the former teaching the whole of the *Vedas*, the latter only a part. The teacher gives a man a veritable second birth and is the true spiritual father. "Not by years or age or wealth or family did the seers give the Law. He who knows is for us great" ('*Yo' nūcānaḥ sa no mahān*).[86] While the Brahmana must cultivate learning, he must avoid the desire for recognition which is like poison.[87]

Manu mentions three points of view about values or *puruṣārthas*. "*Dharmārthāvucyate śreyah Kāmārthau dharma eva ca/Artha eveha vā śreyah trivarga ititusthitih*".[88] He himself regards *trivarga* as constituting the good of man. Duty, interest and pleasures, all three are thus admitted as valuable human ends.

Love, respect and service to parents and the teacher constitute the highest duty. "*Triṣvete-ṣvitikṛtyaṁ hi puruṣasya samāpyate/Eṣa dharmaḥ paraḥ sākṣād upadharmonya ucyate.*"[89] These three sum up human duty and constitute the primary meaning of *dharma*.

Learning, skill and righteousness should be acquired from

everywhere, even the *candala.* In times of emergency, we may study even under a non-Brahmanical teacher.[90]

The teacher should be paid at the end of the course. Land, gold, cattle, horse, umbrella, shoes, seat, grains, vegetable or clothes may be offered to the teacher.[91]. But the teacher was no salesman, nor a mere technician. He carried forward the torch of tradition and what was given him was a sign of gratitude.

The rules about marriage stipulate that the girl should not be a kin "*Asapiṇḍā ca yā mātu-rasagotrā ca yā pituḥ*".[92] She should preferably be of the same *varṇa—savarṇa.* Else the wife may come from a lower *varna.* Manu permits a sudra wife for the upper caste men but goes on to contradict himself by prohibiting her for Brahmanas and Ksattriyas, especially for the former.[93] Eight types of marriages are then formulated—"*Brāhmo daivas tathaivārṣaḥ Prājāpatyas-tathā-surah|Gāndharvo rākṣaśaścaiva paiśācaścāṣṭamodhamaḥ.*"[94] The first six are permitted to the Brahmanas, the last four to the Ksattriyas, those very four without the *Rākṣasa*, i.e. *Āsura*, *Gāndharva* and *Paiśāca* to the Vaisyas and the Sudras. Another view is then mentioned that the first four alone are valid for the Brahmanas, Raksasa alone for the Ksattriyas, *Asura* alone for the Vaisya and Sudra. Then again *Paisaca* and *Asura* are condemned while *Gandharva* and *Rākṣasa*, are permitted to the Ksattriya.

Brāhma was the normal Vedic form of marriage where the bride was presented with clothes and ornaments to a groom of learning and character and after he had been invited by the bride's father himself and suitably honoured. In *daiva* the groom was the priest. In the *Ārṣa* the bride was given for a nominal consideration of a pair or two of cattle. The *daiva* and the *ārsa* were obviously exceptional or vestigial. In the *prājāpatya* "the offer of marriage comes from the wooer". This form is omitted by Apastamba and Vasistha. In all these forms, marriage consists of the bride being presented to the groom by the bride's father without any consideration. *Vivāha* is *Kanyādāna.* It has been suggested that originally all these four forms were really only one and represented the form current among the Brahmanas.

Āsura or *mānuṣa* form was the acceptance of a bride by

giving suitable gifts to the bride and her relations. This is said to represent the common or plebian form of marriage by purchase but the *Dharma-śāstras* condemned the sale of a daughter very strongly.[95] *Gāndharva* was love marriage and *svayamvara* may be included in it. *Rākṣasa* or *kṣātra* form was marriage by capture and in the heroic epics, not uncommon among the Ksattriyas. *Paiśāca* was merely a euphemism for seduction and was counted as marriage only for legitimizing a fact.

The ideal of monogamy is generally assumed. Love between man and wife is held up as an important value. The wife should be loved and honoured and kept happy, for she is the root of domestic felicity. "*Yatra nāryastu pūjyante ramante tatra devatāḥ*".[96]

The householder must perform the five *mahāyajñas*, viz. *brahmayajña*, *pitṛayajña*, *daiva*, *bhūta*, *and* "*Adhyāpanam brahmayajñaḥ pitṛyajñastu tarpaṇam / Homo daivo balir bhauto nṛyajño tithipūjanam*".[97] One should not eat alone but also offer food to the gods, guests, dependents and ancestors. Man has a moral relationship not only to gods and sages and the departed ancestors but owes hospitality to all men and must assist life in all its forms. "*Svādhyāyenārcayetarṣīn homair devān yathāvidhi / Pitṝn śrāddhaiśca nṝn annairbhūtāni balikarmaṇā.*"[98] It is interesting to note that among the gods to be propitiated are included Śrī, Bhadrakālī and Vāstoṣpati. Charity too must be sedulously given to the *brahmacarin* who comes abegging. Elaborate conventions are prescribed for hospitality. Maidens, young brides, pregnant women and the sick must receive priority in the matter of feeding. To cook only for oneself is sinful.[99]

In connection with *śrāddha*, Manu lists the Brahmanas who deserve to be avoided as *apāṅkteya*.[100] We have here a cross-section of the brahmanas who had adopted professions held in low esteem by the tradtionist high-brow. Those who ministered at the sacrifices of *Pūgas* and *Gaṇas* were held in disfavour. Physicians were similarly held in low esteem. Perhaps the physicians like the *Pūgas* and *Gaṇas* included or associated with the unorthodox. Traders were similarly considered low, especially those who sold meat or the *rasas*.[101] Sellers of *soma* or those who cross the high seas presumably for trade are objects of disfavour.[102] Temple priests were also considered unfit for Vedicists' company, which shows the tradition of temple worship was quite distinct from that of Vedic ritual. Or, perhaps, this condemnation arose from the fact that the temple priests used the money gifted to the temple. The expression "*Devakośopabhoji*" indicates this. The exclusion of money-lenders is more easily understood. Those who live by cattle-rearing, service, acting and dancing, sale and manufacture of oil and the makers of bows and arrows are other classes held in low esteem just as are astrologers or the teachers of the science of war. Cultivators too are included in this category. To be involved in a livelihood which cannot avoid violence, impurity or a plain mercenary outlook was in effect condemned. A proper livelihood is one which does not involve violence to creatures or involves only a little violence. The accumulation of wealth should be limited to what is required for life and what can be earned by proper work and without physical labour. "One may live by *ṛta* and *amṛta, mṛta* and *pramṛta*,., *satya* and *anṛta* but never by *śvavṛtti*."[103] *Ṛta* is the collection of grains singly or in sprays from where they grow, i.e. *uñcha* and *śila*. *Amṛta* is what one gets without asking. *Mṛta* is what one gets as alms. *Pramṛta* is tilling the soil. *Satya* and *Anṛta* are trade while *Śvavṛtti* is service. The accumulation of wealth should be for the day, for three days, for the year or at the most for three years. The Brahmana should live in extreme simplicity, even poverty. He should not seek to please the world or adopt crooked and impure ways of living. He should learn contentment and avoid attachment to pleasures. He should abandon all business which clashes with study. His fulfilment lies in living by teaching, however hard that might prove to be.

Dependence on others constitutes unhappiness while independence is the essence of happiness "*sarvam paravaśaṁ duḥkḥam sarvamātmavaśam sukham etad vidyāt samāsena laksaṇam sukha-duhkhayoh.*"[104] The satisfaction of one's conscience (*Paritoṣontarātmanaḥ*) must be the basis of one's actions. Respect must be shown to parents and teachers, Brahmanas and cows and ascetics. Atheism and criticism of the Vedas should be avoided, Hatred, pride, anger and sharpness of temper should be avoided. One should not hit anyone except a child or a student and those only to discipline them. No one who is unrighteous and violent and earns wealth by wrong means can be happy. One should not move from the path of righteousness even if one suffers, for ultimately it is the truth that wins. "*Adharmeṇaidhate tāvat tato bhadrāṇi paśyati. Tataḥ sapatñāñjayati samūlastu vinaśyati.*"[105] Hence *artha* and *kāma* should be abandoned where they clash with Right. Even "those practices of *dharma* should be avoided which produce painful consequences and are disapproved socially. ("*Dharmaṁ cāpyasukho-darkaṁ loka-vikruṣṭam eva ca*).[106] This sounds dangerously like utilitarianism. As already mentioned, a school of Mimamsa tended to be utilitarian but sought to understand the relationship between means and ends supernaturally. Manu seems to recognize here that the traditional body of *dharma* contained elements which did not find rational or social approval in his times. Such elements were allowed to become obsolete. The best test of what was to be adopted out of the practices and rules included in *dharma* was furnished by sticking to the family tradition.[107]

The family was a big establishment including relations and servants. Harmony must be maintained within it by avoiding all quarrels and litigations. One must patiently bear the anger and criticism of family members, dependents and even servants.[108] A most important aspect of family ethos was charity. In course of time more and more emphasis was placed on it as the very archetype of good works. It was, however, held that alms should be given or received only with the greatest circumspection.[109]

Of purely moral rules of conduct, Manu says that the *yamas* should be observed without any exception or failure. The *niyamas* are relatively secondary. *Yamas* are basic 'don'ts' while *niyamas* include positive duties.[110] Virtue has to be cultivated gradually and continuously. It alone helps in afterlife provided one does not engage in injury to any beings. The soul is a lonely being and only its moral quality accompanies it beyond death. To reach the *summum bonum* we must devote thought to one's good in solitude.

Ahimsa was generally recognized as the principal *yama.*

Manu fully endorses the virtue of *ahimsa*, repeatedly stressing that one should not harm other beings in any way and should cultivate gentleness, mildness and pity. *Ahimas* was by this time recognized to imply vegetarianism. Here Manu compromises by saying that the preparation and eating of meat for sacrificial purposes should be accepted but beyond that strictly avoided.[111] Even professions involving the slightest injury to living creatures were declared unclean. The acceptance of vegetarianism outside ancient Vedic ritual by Manu represented a major step in the development of vegetarianism in India.

In laying down the rules for the third and the fourth *asramas*, Manu makes it clear that the renunciation of the world is justified only for one who has fulfilled the three basic obligations.[112] Study, worship and family duties must be satisfactorily concluded before one has the right to renounce the world. It is also clear that the *grhasthasrama* is the basic *asrama*. Nor should the *Vedas* be ever renounced. In fact, Manu speaks of *Vedasannyasikas* who remain engaged in *Karmyoga*.[113] The meaning of the term Veda has been diversely interpreted,[114] but, in any case, it is undoubted that such an ascetic continues Vedic study and stays at his son's place.

The universal essence of *dharma* is described by Manu to consist of ten virtues: "*Dhṛtiḥ kṣamā damosteyam śaucamindriyanigrahah | Dhīr vidyā satyam akrodho daśakaṁ dharmalakṣanam||*[115]" These ten virtues, it may be noted, include not only truth but the means to it, viz. intuitive reason and knowledge. These virtues along with three obligations constitute the whole of social ethics in its essence. The virtues are universal, the obligations relative to basic social situations. In the course of fulfilling the obligations, other socio-ethical rules have to be observed. Beyond this lies the attainment of spiritual emancipation.

The structure of *varna-asrama dharma* presupposes a stable social order and that implies the state. Unless there is a firm and just political authority, there would be no order; anarchy will prevail. There would be no security, no justice, no property and no hierarchy. The ruler thus performs functions analogous to the gods and his authority or *danda* is a divine blessing.[116] The king is a great divinity in human shape and deserves respect and obedience. But he must act wisely and justly.[117] *Rajadharma* is the duty of the king, the ethos of the state.

The king must be educated and disciplined. He must master *trayī*, *daṇḍanīti*, *ānvīkṣikī*, *ātmavidyā* and *vārtā*. Of these, *daṇḍanīti* or political science is called *'śāśvatī'* or perennial.[118] Other sciences can flourish only when the state functions properly and in this sense, the science of the state is the First Science which must be preserved to the last. Manu is haunted by the spectre of anarchy, a fear which can be disregarded only by those whom chance might have placed in some era of peace and security. Manu, however, is quite clear that a lawless king precipitates the very anarchy which it is his duty to prevent.[119] Hence Manu's highlighting the need for authority does not mean an advocacy of despotism. The very notion of *rajadharma* implies the existence of rights which limited the authority of the ruler because it is his duty to protect those rights. The king is required to act within a framework of laws and justice and that is why he is required to be educated and enlightened in the first place. Secondly, he must acquire self-control and avoid the addictions arising from passions and anger. Hunting, gambling, sleeping during the day, fault-finding, women, drinking, music and dance, travelling about for pleasure these are the ten evils of passion.[120] Calumny, violence, enmity, envy, jealousy, taking away property, scolding, punishment and harshness—these eight are the evils arising from anger.[121] All of these evils arise from greed which must be controlled. Wine, gambling, women and hunting are the worst of the former group, while violence, scolding, and inflicting economic loss, these are the worst of the second group. The worst of these are wine and physical violence. The king, in short, must have learning as well as character.

He must then seek due counsel and appoint seven or eight ministers (*sacivas*) who ought to be hereditary and able.[122] He should also appoint a *purohita* and various *amātyas* and *adhyakṣas*. A *dūta* too should be appointed, a fort built and above all Brahmanas should be kept pleased by liberality, which is like filling a treasury of spiritual merit.[123] The king should regard the welfare of the people as his good.[124] Taxation should be light and the officers just. He should fight bravely but righteously.[125] War should be avoided as far as possible. Manu forbids the use of deceptive weapons and of poisonous and burning arrows as also of a special type of arrow called *Karnin.*[126] He also forbids the use of force against an enemy who has already suffered much loss or who is retreating. These chivalric rules sound strange when we remember the method which the Bactrians followed in Manu's times.[127] These rules also establish most clearly the moral elevation of Manu.

The king is required to dispense justice in the *sabhā.* The king should be assisted by a specially appointed learned Brahmana and three other learned men. Decisions should be based on equity (*dharmaṁ śāśvatam āśritya*) and on the actual laws and customs of the castes, regions, guilds and families—"*Jāti-jānapadān dharmān Śrenī-dharmaṁsca dharmavit/ samiksya Kula-dharmāṁśca svadharmam pratipādayet//*[128] In cases of violent and sexual crimes, the punishments were harsh and included mutilations and death. Fines were common for diverse types of crimes relating to the right of property and contract.

All moral and spiritual means are subsumed in Vedic *karmayoga* 'which is two fold *pravṛtta* and *nivṛtta* and leads respectively to temporal as well as eternal good."

Vaidike karmayoge to sarvānyetānyaśeṣatah/
Antarbhavanti kramaśaḥ tasmin tasmin Kriyāvidhau
Sukhābhyudayikam caiva Naihśreyasikam eva ca/
Pravṛttam ca nivṛttaṁ ca dvividham Karma Vaidikam
Iha cāmutra vā kāmyam pravṛttam karma kīrtyate/.
Niṣkāmam jñānapūrvam to nivṛttam upadiśyate//
Pravṛttam Karma samsevya Devānāmeti sāmyatām/
Nivṛttam sevamānastu bhūtānyatyeti pañca vai//[129]

Thus *dharma* in the sense of practising virtues and fulfilling obligations leads to happiness in life and heaven after death while *dharma* as desirelessness and self-knowledge leads to emancipation. The former or *pravṛtti-dharma* consists in the control or limitation of desires, the latter or *nivṛttidharma* in the eradication of desires totally through the transcendence of the personality based on physical and social identification. The former paves the way for the latter. Man begins with an animal consciousness which seeks gratification by a natural instinct. The rules of *dharma* give him a moral and social personality in the first instance and lead him towards true self-knowledge ultimately. The whole tenor of *dharma* is towards transcendence through regulation and negation but it is transcendence in graduated steps. Hence Manu says "*Na māṁsabhakṣaṇe doṣo na madye na ca maithune/ Pravṛttireṣā bhūtānāṁ nivṛttistu mahāphalā//*[130] Instinctive life is not evil but transcending it is a great good. "Seeing the Self in all beings and all beings in the Self, seeing equality, the self-sacrificer attains to self-government."[131] Practising the *Vedas* and practising self-knowledge in peace, this is the whole path of *dharma* leading from the bondage of animal life to spiritual freedom through the intermediate stage of social ethics.

To discover the *dharma*, one must use reason to understand revelation but reason should be in consonance with faith. "*Ārṣam dharmopadeśaṁ ca Vedaśāstrāvirodhinā/ Yastarkeṇānusandhatte sa dharmaṁ veda netaraḥ*".[132] Formal decision in *dharma* may be obtained from a panel (*pariṣad*) of at least ten consisting of three scholars each connected with one of the *Vedas*, a logician, a *Mimamsaka*, a *Nairukta*, a *dharma-pathaka*, and three persons, one from each *asrama*. A smaller panel could consist of the first three. *Dharma* is what even a single learned man may decide, *not what may be opined by multitudes of fools.*[133] Mere numbers do not constitute a *parisad* or assembly with authority. Subsequent *smrtis* follow Manu basically. Yajnavalkya is more concise and polished. He distinguishes *ācāra*, *vyavahāra* and *prāyaścitta* as the three main divisions of *dharma*. The distinction arises from the attempt to define legal matters and procedures clearly. It is thus clearly seen that the transgression of a law entailing punishment is distinct from a transgression involving an expiation. The advance is conceptual and theoretical.

The source of *dharma* is defined to be desire arising from right mental determination (*Samyak-samkal-pajah Kāmaḥ dharma-mūlam idam smṛtam*)[134] and its sources are the same as recognized by Manu. Of all the *dharmas*, the highest is self-knowledge through *Yoga*. *Dharma* includes virtues and obligations and the traditions of families, castes, guilds, corporation (*ganas*) and regions.[135] If the king conquers a new territory, he should protect its established usages and law—"*Yasmin deśe ya ācāraḥ vyayahāraḥ kuleṣviti Tathaiva paripālyo sau yadā vaśam upāgataḥ.*" It is clear that although Yajnavalkya defines legal procedures, he continues to regard law as essentially a pre-existing tradition, canonical or social, not as the command of the sovereign. Narada, however, shows the influence of the *Arthasastra* and admits royal command as one of the sources of law (*vyavahara*)[136] Brhaspati makes a clear distinction between civil and criminal law—"*Tadāha Bṛhaspatiḥ Dvipādo vyavahāraśca dhana-himsā-samudbhavaḥ*". Katyayana elaborates Narada's adopted dictum in the four 'parts' of *vyavahara* and shows how royal command is the most authoritative.

The *smrtis* after Manu are chiefly remarkable for the systematization of *dharma* in the context of litigation and expiation, rather than in the delineation by *dharma* as social ethics. *Dharma* as social order had already crystallized and formulated its traditions. It is the development of the state and the growing indirectness of administration and the formalization of law and legal procedures which are reflected in the *smrtis* now. If the *Dharmasastra* views social ethics from a Brahmanical point of view, emphasizing religious life, Vedic authority and the position and privileges of the Brahmanas, the *Arthasastra* viewed the same spectacle from the point of view of the ruling class which meant the Ksattriyas. It is true that both the *dharma* and the *artha* have on the whole a public rather than a class point of view and both are interested in social justice above all. Nevertheless, the view of each is to a certain extent coloured by the circumstances of its origin and authorship. *Dharma* has little original interest in the details of statecraft where it is content to borrow the standard categories evolved in the *artha*. The administrative structure assumed in the *Dharma* too is relatively simple. The greatest difference, however, lies in the more realistic, even cynical approach of the *artha* especially to such issues as of war, diplomacy and espionage. While the ethical outlook of the *dharma* is idealistic, the outlook of the *artha* tends to be utilitarian.

It has been argued that the original name of the science of polity was *Ksattra-Vidya* and that its antiquity goes back to the age of the *Chandogya Upanisad.*[137] By the sixth and fifth centurtries B.C., the ethos of the heroic rulers and warriors called *Kṣāttra-dharma* was rivalled by the growth of a science of Policy or of the Polity of using Power (*nītiśāstra* or *daṇḍanīti*). In course of time, this science of policy came to include the science of the management of economic resources (*vārtā*) and was termed *Arthaśāstra.* Between the 6th and 4th centuries B.C., there was a great development of the science of polity and it ramified into many schools. Some of its schools appear to have been influenced by materialistic doctrines (*Lokayata*). The *Arthasastra* of Kautilya represented the high water-mark of the science of polity, after which it appears to have stagnated and declined, till even its ancient literature was lost. Even the *arthaśāstra* was virtually lost.[138]

Vedic reflection over political authority had sought its moral basis. This could only be earthly conformity to the heavenly paradigm of the authority of Indra and Varuna and this 'limitation' was expressed ritually. This relationship of the royalty to divinity being mediated by ritual naturally implied a close relationship between royalty and priesthood.[139] The two were regarded as complementary orders because ultimately authority implies the union of will and knowledge. In the later Vedic age, it came to be clearly realized that the ultimate source of authority lies in law which is revealed to and interpreted by the brahmana but enforced by the ksattriya.

With the change in the position of the ruling class in the sixth and fifth centuries B.C., the older sacerdotal thinking tended to be removed from reality. The emergence of political adventurers was accompanied by that of professional administrators and soldiers. For these, the state was essentially a structure of power rather than that of moral obligations and behind political power lay military force, wealth astuteness of policy and a changeable public opinion. The state was an objectification of *artha* rather than that of *dharma*; what its management needed was *dandaniti* rather than *rajadharma*. *Dharma* implies a stable order, permanent principles and disregard of merely ephemeral or empirical consequences. *Niti*, on the other hand, relates means to ends and *dandaniti* relates power as means to the attainment of ends conceived as *artha* or as *trivarga*.

For a philosophical justification of political power, we have to turn to the *Mbh*. After the war, Yudhisthira was apalled by the spectacle of violence which the search for political power had produced and thought that renunciation would be better than the acceptance of a position which depended on such violence.[140] The king must use force, which needs obvious justification. The question here is not that the authority of the king takes away the liberty of the subject but that the authority of the king requires force to maintain itself. The question of liberty is a larger one and belongs to the context of man's search for law as such.[141] Moral as well as social life requires subjection to rules which would restrain the liberty of the individual in some sense but confer value in consonance with the nature and source of the rules. The question here, however, is that political authority uses force which may deprive all those who defy it of not only their liberty but their life as well. It is this implied ruthiessness and violence which bothers Yudhisthira who is the incarnation of *dharma*. The answer which ultimately satisfies him is that life and property, liberty and virtue all require a secure social order. This security can be given only by political authority and human nature being what it is, force must be used to check anarchy.

Bhisma says to Yudhisthira, "I know your mind which values compassion greatly. However, pure compassion cannot succeed in attaining great objectives. Moreover, knowing you to be mild, disciplined, very noble and very virtuous, people will disregard you as a powerless person full of virtue and pity. You should therefore, look to the traditional duties of the kings." Even Yudhisthira ultimately wants to know how successful captains of war lead the armies even at the expense of righteousness. In answer to this Bhisma speaks of expedience and of the need of knowing the crookedness and evil of others and meeting it adequately. The whole tenor of the argument is that to remove the evil of anarchic insecurity, the evil of political force has to be used necessarily. Looking at its purpose and necessity, political force or *danda* is not evil at all. In fact "sincc well employed and equitable *danda* protects the people, it is the same as *dharma*." "*Danda* is divine (*daivam hi paramodaṇḍaḥ*)".[142]

It is interesting to note that a more cynical view of the situation also finds mention. It is stated that the ruler should look only to visible or empirical considerations of virtue and gain and should not bother about considerations of transcendent virtue. He should concentrate on power and could even employ a force of brigands, provided they could be disciplined.[143]

We know from the *Arthasastra* that there were quite cynical schools of political thought which regarded religion and morality as only a cloak to be used by the ruler to his own advantage.[141] In this tradition, power is the prime value and considerations of a transcendent kind, moral or religious tended to be disregarded.

The *Arthasastra* tends to hold a middle position, seeking to reconcile gain with virtue, although Kautilya clearly announces the priority of *artha* on the ground that *artha* is the source of *dharma* and *kama*.[145] The priority which Kautilya has in mind rests on the fact that the politico-economic order is the pre-condition of virtue and happiness. The instrumental character of *artha* is recognized within the scheme of values. Nevertheless, within the scheme of political science, *Artha* is the principal value, and political science itself is as fundamental a science as the state is foundational to social ethics. Curiously, while *Manu* described *dandaniti* as *śāśvatī*, the *Arthasastra* reserves that category for *ānvīkṣikī*.[146] Kautilya mentions the view of Usanas that all sciences rest in *danda-niti*, but does not agree with this. For him *trayi* is the source of *dharma*, and it is the protection of *dharma* which furnishes the basic justification of the state.

Although Kautilya does not accept that *danda-niti* is basic to the other sciences, he does maintain that *danda* is the pre-condition of all the sciences, as well as of the realization of Virtue, Interest, and Pleasure. *Danda* itself, however must be grounded in discipline and this implies a proper education for the ruler.

While virtue can be promoted only indirectly through the prevention of lawlessness, the welfare and happiness of the people must be promoted by a sound policy. The state of the *Arthasastra* is above all a welfare state which engages in wide-ranging social and economic policies. According to the *Dharmasastra*, *dharma* is the sole means to welfare and happiness. But the efficacy of *dharma* as also its consequences are not amenable to empirical knowledge. The *artha*° holds that the policy of *niti* should promote *hita-sukha* in the empirical realm so that the people remain pleased with the ruler.[147] This is a whole range of new concepts, public policy (*niti*) and social good (*prajā-hita*) are now brought within the scope of a utilitarian outlook. A rational analysis seeks to relate means to ends on the basis of empirical investigation and is not content merely with immemorial tradition. The end of policy is not merely preservation but increase.

The *Artha*° accepts the traditional *varnasrama dharma* but evinces a more enlightened outlook. The Sudras are regularly expected to engage in agriculture, trade and crafts.[148] Their industry is recognized and their lawful protection is recommended. Slavery is discouraged and the existing slaves are subjected to humane laws.[149] The Brahmanas are brought within the scope of capital punishment where treason is concerned, but otherwise their special advisory position in administration is sought to be protected and furthered.[150] The business of merchants is sought to be stringently regulated. The mendicants are not looked at with much favour.[151] Nor has the *Artha*° any thought for considerations of 'purity' and 'non-violence' which weigh so much with the *dharma*. The ruling class comprises not only the kings and their relations but also a large and complex class of administrative officials at various levels. Their ethos is a new factor. The higher ranks were susceptible to treason, the lower to corruption. The *Artha*° spends much ingenuity in seeking to control these endemic evils.[152]

Loyalty and satisfaction among the officials and the people is now a prime consideration and it is sought to be constantly ascertained and tested and promoted by a suitable policy of rewards. For the dissatisfied, the Four Means are to be used.

The development of an economic policy based on detailed empirical knowledge was one of the most important contributions of the *Artha*°. The economic welfare of the people and the resources of the state are sought to be systematically promoted. Agriculture, irrigation, mining, trade, industries, forest wealth, taxation, regulation of prices, wages and interests, management of state factories giving employment to the poor and needy, control of market, etc., all come within the purview of the *Artha*°. The task of administration in the *Artha*° is not the collection of customary taxes or dispensation of rough and ready justice but the sensitive and multiform adjustment of a complex and diversified social and economic order. In the process, an elaborate administrative structure of rules and policies was evolved. Royal orders and edicts as well as usage and precedents came to be important elements in the decision of legal matters. *Artha*° thus says in a well-known verse "*Dharmaśca vyavahāraśca caritraṁ rājaśāsanam| Vivādārthaścatupādah paścimaḥ pūrvabādhakah||*" Equity, testimony, usage and royal orders constituted the four parts of a legal dispute where the latter over-ruled the former (or vice versa). Where custom is opposed to canonical or secular law, law should take precedence. If law should appear unjust, equity should be upheld." *Śāstram vipratipadyeta dharma nyāyena Kenacit| Nyāyastatra pramāṇam syāt tatra pāṭho hi naśyati||*[153]

While the *dharma-śāstra* analyses society into *varnas* and *asramas* as the basic stations from which duties and moral relations flow, the *Arthaśāstra* analyses the state into *prakṛtis* or constituents. These are essentially elements endowed with functional efficacy in the context of policy formation. The seven *prakrtis* are the Sovereign, the Ministry of Officials, Country, Forts, Treasury, Force and Ally.[154] Of these, the first three may also be rendered as the sovereign, the administrative personnel and the land and the people. The other four stand for the defensive, financial and military resources and foreign relations. It is a comprehensive view of the political order in its several dimensions, administrative, economic, military and international.

In an ideal state, the sovereign should be of noble lineage, endowed with intelligence, strength and firmness, virtuous, energetic, dependable and disciplined. He should have high qualities of the intellect and will. Such a sovereign could be produced only by adequate education and training. The administrative officials should be loyal, efficient and resourceful. The people should be pure and loyal, industrious as agriculturists with a majority of population belonging to the lower castes.[155] The treasury should be full and the army should consist largely of experienced Ksatriya soldiers. In this scheme, society is functionally divided into rulers, administrators, soldiers and the tillers. They are mutually connected by organic relations and the purpose of political policy is to develop them and keep them loyal *vivṛddhāścā-nuraktāśa)*. The *Arthasastra* is further aware of the fact that the state is part of an inter-state system, and that security does not simply mean preventing the violation of law, but also ensuring the safety of the realm in the inter-state context.

The forms of social ethics in the *Arthasastra* are distinct from, though connected with those represented in the *Dharmaśāstras*. The performance of duty as determined by one's station in terms of *varna* and *asrama* is not the same thing as the performance of actions successfully though even the performance of duty in a purely moral sense requires the help of prudence and conditions of security and adequacy of resources. The world of *artha* is more extensive than that of *Dharma*, and in part functions as the precondition for its realization. *Dharma* is prior to *artha* in an ideal sense, but *artha* is necessary to its implementation. Further, the actual social order being far more complex than that visualized in the *Dharmasastras*, the interpretation of *dharma* in practice necessarily requires the study of means and ends at a secondary level. Without the help of *niti* or prudence and experience, it would be impossible to act by *dharma* in practice. In the *Dharmasastra*, the *ksatriya*, for example, has the right to rule and fight by birth. Actually a ruler or soldier must immediately face the possibility of removal from position or life itself and finds himself in the midst of a chain of authority, dangers and tasks. His task is not simply to rule or fight in the abstract according to pure conscience but to take numerous particular decisions and determine in each situation what constitutes the best. To be a good king or soldier, therefore, he must possess not only basic virtues and the sense of obligations to ultimate ends but also the ability to see which particular means from among the available ones will best serve the purposes of his station without jeopardizing his life or position. The discrimination of moral right and wrong to become real must be joined to the discrimination of the efficient from the inefficient. This at least is the situation where public duties and public good are concerned. In private life, mere feeling or conscience may be adequate provided one chooses to disregard practical consequences, including success and ultimately life; in public life, however, the good which needs to be accomplished extends beyond the consciousness of the agent, and cannot be equated simply with the subjective movements of his conscience. This is, of course, not to say that this harmonious dichotomy of *dharma* and *niti* constitutes a complete solution. The lives of martyrs, for example, provide an easy counter-example. But, then, martyrs function as independent individuals, not as determinate cogs in the wheel of a public order.

It is a pity, however, that after Kautilya, the tradition of the *Artha* ceased to develop. Kamandaka follows the school of Kautilya, though his treatment especially of education, the *Prakṛtis* and *Maṇḍala* shows a certain freshness.[156] While Kamandaka gives evidence of the continued study of the *Artha*, it is clear that there is already a divorce between theory and practice, *lakṣya* and *lakṣaṇa*. The older definitions and theories continue but no note is taken of the changing structure of polity and the problems arising from it. Much later authors like Somadeva and Hemacandra[157] show not only the same petrified state of theory but a virtual reduction of the science to the unprincipled principle of expediency for all practical purposes and the older science was lost in course of time. The new political realities departed far from ancient conceptions in some respect. The *Śukranītisāra* evinces the prevalence of the 'feudal-federal' structure.[158] What the *Arthaśāstra* had called *Dharma-vijaya* had become widely prevalent in Gupta and post-Gupta times and converted empires into virtually loose federations of principalities of which the rulers preferred loyalty to the emperor.[159] This was a new structural feature which was radically at variance with the jealous conception of sovereignty which the *Artha* upheld. Similarly the mode of payment which it implied and also the consequent change in military organization were a far cry from the *Artha* tradition. The knowledge of political and military conditions of distant areas declined sharply. Royal and aristocratic arrogance increased with ignorance and only flattery and servility flourished in the new courts. The *Artha* had stood for the idea that governance is a matter of knowledge and skill, of political wisdom, diplomatic astuteness, and administrative expertise. This older tradition was now submerged in the tide of clannish aristocracies, often emerging from backwoods, and petty though pretentious monarchies.

The *Artha* had premised the proper education and moral training of the prince as the basis of enlightened monarchy. "*Nayasya vinayo mūlam*".[160] The prince was to have learning, self-control and devotion to popular good. The nobility was to be kept under firm control and officials paid in cash and their work supervised and checked. The emphasis on hereditary rights and their connection with land tended to upset this whole structure. The glorification of royal pomp and power tended to dwarf the role of the ministers, priests and scientists. The moral character of political authority tended to be over-shadowed by the characteristic evils of hereditary, personal rule.

According to the *Dharmasastra*, *dharma* as virtue consists in every one doing one's duty according to one's own station. Correspondingly, social justice consists in keeping the orders (*varnas*) distinct and unmixed. The prevention of social miscegenation or confusion (*samkara*) was thus regarded as the principal value to be realised in the maintenance of public life. In essentials, this idea of non-confusion is comparable with the Platonic idea of justice[161] and the Confucian idea of the Rectification of Names.[162] Unfortunately, the identification of functional classes with rigidly hereditary groups produced a system of 'castes' which could neither be fully real nor represent the ideal. This was a plain perversion of the notion of *dharma* and was criticized by liberal and enlightened thinkers. The *Mahabharata* and Buddhist and Jaina works reflect this critical and enlightened outlook which protested against the perversion of the notion of 'social order'.[163]

In the *Mbh. dharma* is not obvious or conventional. It is subtle and profound.[164] What it requires is a mode of understanding, an inner attitude, rather than a new set of prescriptions, or formulae or institutions. From an objective point of view, thus, the attitude is conservative. It does not seek to supersede the divisions of the *varnas* and *asramas* by any new ones. It lays much store by the mendicant's life but even that had been codified already. It notices the contradiction between the ascetic and secular ideas of life and seeks to reconcile it in terms of the directive of action without any passion, a doctrine which the *Gita* has made so well-known.[165] For the person who would seek to act by duty alone without reference to personal desires and ambitions, the content of the duty must be determined by some other source. The doctrine of *varnasrama dharma* was the obvious source to appeal to. The doctrine of *niskama karman* finds its complement in that of *svadharma* which in turn finds its content from *varnasrama dharma*. The ethical speculation of the *Mahabharata* emphasizes not the social or economic behaviour in its causal aspect but the subjective attitude and the transformation which it effects on character. The Righteous Hunter (*Dharma-vyādha*) thus explains that what he actually does for livelihood is morally immaterial because he only conforms to his duty.[166] In the *Śākuntala* an indignant fisherman defends the dignity of his vocation and compares it to that of the sacrificial priests.[167] Thus the attempt is not to discover or re-distribute vocations but to perceive in all of them a uniformity from the moral point of view. At the moral level, the socially given *varnas* cease to constitute a hierarchy. A true hierarchy based on spiritual values is not denied but the very example of the Righteous Hunter illustrated the contrast between social assumption and moral reality. *Dharma-vyādha* belonged to Mithila, the realm of Janaka who was himself a sage in the truest sense though functioning as a ruler. Similarly, we find a woman who has gained spiritual perfection without Vedic study or rituals and is actually superior to a proud Brahmana who has studied the Vedas and practised austerities.[168] Here thus we have a woman and a Sudra engaged in their much despised routine duties attaining to a moral perfection beyond that of the Brahmana. *Svadharma* thus constitutes the real *dharma*. What is ethically important is that one does one's work whole-heartedly as duty, not the nature or content of the work. And a true Brahmana is one who has attained moral self-control and spiritual detachment. "*Yaḥ krodha-mohau tyajati taṁ devā brāhmanaṁviduḥ*".[169] Brahmanahood is here defined in terms of moral and spiritual qualities, not heredity. The perennial *dharma* is verily hard to know and it is grounded in Truth "*Durjñeyah śāśvato dharmaḥ satu satye pratisṭhitaḥ*".[170]

When Yudhisthira, the incarnation of Righteousness, is asked by the Snake, to define a Brahmana, he answers, "He is considered a Brahmana in whom one can see truth, liberality, forgiveness, character, non-violence, self-control and pity—"*Satyaṁ dānaṁ kṣamā silam ānṛśaṁsyaṁ damo ghṛnā/Dṛṣyante yatra nāgendra sa brāhmaṇa iti smṛtaḥ*.[171] At this, the Snake logically points out that these qualities may be found in a Sudra. Yudhisthira then goes on to declare, "In that case the Sudra is not a Sudra, nor the Brahmana a Brahmana, where this conduct can be discerned, he is a Brahmana, where it is not found that one is to be indicated a Sudra." In that case, the Snake argues, *jati* would be quite meaningless. Yudhisthira replies by saying that *jati* is impossible to discern since all men constitute a single species. Hence, according to Yudhisthira, Manu rightly stated that all are Sudras by birth till they are spiritually regenerated.[172] It is conduct, therefore, that really distinguishes the *varnas*. Otherwise, their confusion is unavoidable.

Here we can clearly see the realization that the original distinction of the *varnas* rested on moral qualities which makes them purely ideal. The socially available *varnas* are seen to be mixed hopelessly. This appeal from birth to conduct is clearly protestant and highlights the distance between ethical idealism and social reality in the early post-Vedic age.

Early Buddhist literature presents similar protestant views. In the *Ambattha-sutta*, the Buddha declares "Among those who follow the lineage of both, the Kshatriya has superiority. However, the person who has learning and character is superior to gods."[173] This is a double rebuttal of Brahmanical orthodoxy. It places character above birth and in the matter of birth, places the Kshatriyas above the Brahmanas. In the *Sona Danda sutta*, it is mentioned that the conventionally accepted Brahmanhood depends on five qualities viz., *varna*, *jati*, *mantra*, *sila* and *panditya*. Of these five, the Buddha argues that the last two are the really essential qualities.[174] In the *Assalayana sutta*, we find a full-fledged rational critique of the caste system. It represents the Brahmana Assalyana asserting that according to the Brahmanas, Brahmana is the highest *varna*, that the Brahmanas alone get liberated, that they have been born from Brahman himself. Against this, Buddha is represented as upholding emancipation for all the *varnas* (*Cāturvarnim Suddhim*). Buddha argues that Brahmana women conceive and produce children in the same manner as all the rest. It is further pointed out that among the *Yavanas* and *Kambojas*, as also among other countries beyond the border, the system of *varnas* does not exist. Their societies have only two classes—freemen and slaves. By implication, the *varna* system ceases to be natural. In the moral realm, laws applied equally to all the *varnas* and their destiny after death is determined by the quality of their deeds, not by the accident of their birth in life. Buddha further argues that if a person of the upper castes were to produce fire from sandal wood and a person from the lowest castes were to produce fire from the wood of an *eranda* tree, the fire would still be the same. Similarly, the moral and spiritual attainments of men belonging to the different *varnas* do not have any connection with the accidents of birth. It is also obvious that all men constitute the same species and are capable of interbreeding unlike different natural species. Finally, it may also be recognized that gifts given to a person of learning and character produce much merit but not when given simply on the basis of birth. Buddha thus concludes that since *tapas* is more significant than *mantra* and *jati*, it follows that the principle of universal liberation is valid.

In the *Vasettha sutta*, the Buddha is asked whether one becomes a Brahmana by birth or by deeds. The Buddha points out the difference between species and caste. Among the species, there is a clear difference in physical features which enables one to distinguish them. Among human beings, on the other hand, distinction rests on vocations. A man may live by tillage or industry, trade or service or he may be a soldier or a priest; but all this does not qualify one to become a Brahmana. One does not become a Brahmana or a non-Brahmana by birth. It is by deeds that one becomes or ceases to be a Brahmana. It is through austerity, chastity, self-restraint and control of senses that one becomes a Brahmana. The importance of the *Vasettha sutta* may be gauged from the fact that it is found repeated in the *Majjhima* and the *Suttanipata*.[177]

In the *Brahmanadhammika sutta*, the Buddha declares before the assembled Brahmanical elite of Kosala that the Brahmanas of his time no longer followed the customs of the ancient Brahmanas (*porānam brāhmaṇānam brāhmaṇa-dhammam*). The ancient Brahmanas were seers who practised austerities. They did not accumulate wealth but devoted themselves to sacred studies. Even as house holders, they followed a life of discipline. They did not sacrifice animals. In the *Sundarika-bharadvaja sutta* Buddha says, "do not ask about birth, ask about conduct" "*ma jātim pucchi caranam ca puccha*".[179]

The Buddhists held that human nature is naturally good and that the source of evil is the force of untamed desire. They, therefore, assumed a golden age when men lived in peace and righteousness. Decline took place as men became selfish and acquisitive. With property began crime and that necessitated the establishment of political authority. Kingship was created by the people for the protection of life and property and the king appointed by the general approval of the people. In course of time, kingship too declined.[180]

The Buddhist notion of political authority was thus utilitarian and popular. Republicanism was accepted as an alternative to an elective and popular monarchy. Great stress was laid on the ancient tradition and laws and the need for amity. War was condemned as violence.

The Buddhists thus upheld the twin social ideals of the "True Brahmana" and the 'virtuous ruler'. The former stood for the morally perfected and the spiritually enlightened person such as the Buddha was. This idea rejected birth or conventional social position or traditional learning as grounds for claiming esteem. What makes a person valuable is the degree of his enlightenment, not social position.

The notion of the ideal ruler was defined as one of righteous universal ruler. Such a ruler governs by moral, not physical authority. The ideal was developed in contrast with that of the Brahmanical ideal of universal ruler conquering by force of arms.[181] It was, however, realized that the actualization of the ideal of rulership by virtue alone was beset with great difficulties. It is reported that the Buddha himself could have exemplified such a ruler but rejected the idea as a temptation.[182] From the other side, Asoka sought to achieve the victory of *dharma*, which merely promoted a particular religion in practice and did not prove permanent. Rulership is a temptation for the saint while sainthood is equally a temptation for the ruler. And yet the world has been waiting for such a combination of the saint and the ruler.[183]

The most sustained Buddhist critique of caste is to be found in the *Vajrasūcī* attributed to Aśvaghoṣa.[184] It begins by asking whether the Brahmana is to be identified with the soul or *jāti* or the body or knowledge or conduct or *karma* or the *Veda*. It is obvious that the first alternative must be rejected because the soul may transmigrate among gods, men and animals. *Jati*, again, cannot confer Brahmanhood because otherwise even the sage Vyasa would cease to be a Brahmaṇa, nor can we ascertain of the purity of anyone's parental lineage.[185] The body cannot be regarded as Brahmana for obvious reasons, otherwise burning the dead Brahmana would lead to *Brahmahatya*. Knowledge, conduct and action may be found in a person belonging to any caste. Similarly, professions are found in a mixed condition. It is thus concluded "Brahamanhood is not by scriptures, or sacraments or birth or family or Vedic learning or profession. Brahmanhood is avoidence of sins."[186] In fact, all men belong to the same race. There is only one human order or world which gets functionally divided into four. An ancient Brahmanical authority is quoted to the same effect.[187] The Jainas too had an ancient tradition which traced the distinctions of the *varnas* from an original distinction between the rulers and the ruled. In fact, the Jaina tradition is similar to the Buddhist with respect to the question of social distinctions. They also held that "one becomes a *sramana* by equanimity, or Brahmana by chastity.... and by one's actions one becomes a Brahmana or a Ksatriya or a Vaisya or a Sudra...... here who is exempt from all *karma* we call a *Brahmana*."[188]

This controversy about the nature of caste between the Brahmanical and non-Brahmanical thinkers continued into classical times. The *mimaṁsaka* champion Kumarila argued that Brahmanhood is not a mere collection of moral qualities but a physical class character which is not to be identified with any physical form. *Jati* is thus neither an acquired character nor a species or race but a distinctive heredity. It has a physical and genetic base but it is not a characteristic bodily form."[189] It assumes that pure heredity exists and has a distinctive physical and genetic basis. Buddhist and Jaina thinkers criticised such views severely. Thus, *Prajnakaragupta* argues that Brahmanhood is neither a *jati* nor a *gotra* nor a distinctive capacity.[190] The difference from *jatis* like animal species is obvious. The purity of lineage or *gotra* cannot be established nor do the *Brahmanas* evince any special capacity. Brahmanhood is thus simply a social convention.[191]

In the same strain, the Jaina philosopher Prabhacandra argues that a Brahmana cannot be distinguished from a non-Brahmana as a cow from a buffalo, nor is there any way of showing purity of lineage. Brahmanhood is just a social description depending on social functions. There is only one human *jati* which becomes many *varnas* through functional difference (*vrttibheda*).[192]

It is commonly assumed that the social ethics of the *Dharmasastra* represents the socially accepted ideals of ancient Indian society and that reality tended to approximate to the prescriptions of the *Smrtis*. It is then naturally assumed that the divergent views found in Buddhist and Jaina literature represent merely ineffective criticism on the part of some dissidents. For such a view, there is in reality no warrant. A careful examination of Buddhist literature clearly proves that the Brahmanical notion of *dharma*, specially *varnasramadharma* represented merely Brahmanical opinions, usages and recommendations. What the *Dharmasastras* spell out as *dharma* should not be identified with commonly accepted opinions of the whole of society. The Kshatriyas clearly disputed these and the Buddhists and the Jainas who had wide following sought to understand the nature of *dharma* and the divisions and positions of the social classes differently. Nor should the prescriptions of the *Dharmasastras* be confused with law enforced as such by the state. The *Dharma*° themselves have a large body of recommendations which they do not place in the context of law-enforcement but only of sin and expiation. In viewing the *dharma* as formulated by the *sastras*, we should neither *ipso facto* identify it with representative social ideals nor regard it as the description of real social institutions or prevalent laws. *Dharma* indicated norms of many different kinds and these were formulated and interpreted differently by different sections of society. It would be wrong to continue the error of over-emphasising the stereotype of *dharma* presented in the *smṛti* literature.

The heart of *dharma* consisted of universal moral ideas such as truth and non-violence, self-control and charity. Asoka sought to define this universal core as '*saṃyama*' and '*bhāva-śuddhi*'.[193] The *Dharmaśāstras* called it *sādhārana dharma*[194] and the Buddhists and Jainas called it with greater accuracy simply *dharma*.[195] The emphasis which was thus placed on non-violence and ascetic self-restraint represented the accepted ethos of the society and defined its characteristic orientation.

The whole of *dharma* was often summed up as *ahimsa*, or *paropakāra* or *ātmaupamya* or *samatā*, i.e., as non-injury based on non-discrimination between self and another.[196] The virtue of non-violence grounded in the unity of being led to altruism and tolerance. The emphasis on charity and compassion strengthened the practice of altruism.[197] The first hospitals for men and animals were thus started by Asoka[198] and the state as well as the rich were regularly expected to look after the widows, orphans, the handicapped and the destitutes.[199]

Arising from the same source, tolerance embraced social as well as religious differences. As Asoka phrased it 'Concordance is indeed good,[200]' and Indian society has ever presented a unique spectacle of the harmony and co-existence of diverse social, ethnic and religious groups. Each group was thus allowed to preserve its traditional way of life which was also called *dharma*. The multiplicity and separateness of *jatis* was the other side of the coin. While *dharma* as virtue proceeded from the spontaneous knowledge of the heart and led to disciplined and altruistic social behaviour, it also stood for duty laid upon a man by his social position and relationships. The *Dharmasastra* laid great stress on this aspect and in this sense sought to preserve a concrete tradition of social life, of its structure and institutions. Unfortunately, in the later Vedic and more so in the post-Vedic period, they tended to prevent the original ideal of *Varna* by turning it into *jati*. The functional superiority of the Brahmanas was sought to be converted into that of a hereditary priesthood. A similar attempt was made on behalf of the ruling aristocracy. But these represented class distortions of the ancient view.

As a matter of fact, the notion of *varna* was originally a solvent of the diversity of primitive distinctions of clans and tribes. The re-emergence of *jatis* was a retrograde phenomenon. To seek to accommodate them among the *varnas* as intermediate entities arising from miscegenation was already a contradiction because it denied in effect that only the *varnas* had social validity. The result was that whereas the rise of the *varna*-system in the Vedic age had created a universal society out of primaeval particularism, the recognition and expansion of the *jati*-system reintroduced social fragmentation. But the actual triumph of Brahmanical ideas was a long and gradual process which met with much resistance from non-Brahmanical and heterodox ideas.

If *varna-dharma* was an ancient—and revealed—tradition of obligations arising from the fundamental classification of social functions, the diversity of *jatis* and their modes of life were simply a matter of social usage and convention. Similarly, in the case of *asrama-dharma*, the basic articulation of obligations corresponding to the natural stages of life, rested on the perception of the three debts' but institutional details again were a matter of usage. *Varnasrama dharma* thus, is a combination of moral as well as conventional rules. It was not in any case a system of 'laws' to be enforced by the state.

In post-classical times, however, we hear of claims of maintaining the *varnasrama dharma* intact, whatever that might mean. As the evidence of Śaṅkara shows, such claims had little effect in reality.

While little semblance to the ideal was preserved with respect to the *varnas* and only *jatis* proliferated with their strange customs and usages, of the *asramas* these of *brahmacarya* and *vanaprastha* had a declining reality in post-Vedic times. The householders preserved the *paka-yajnas* and the *sandhyopasana* better than the cycle of Vedic rituals and the effective values of domestic life came to be affection and dutifulness, hospitality and charity. The mendicants grew in numbers and diversity and despite the existence of ignorant and deceitful beggars among them, they stand for the ideal of renunciation as also of service through imparting spiritual knowledge and solace.

The Indian tradition of social ethics or *dharma*, thus, identifies morality with the cultivation of higher emotions and the performance of socially imposed obligations. In one sense it identifies virtue with Knowledge, in another, with the disciplinned application of the will. It places much emphasis on ascetic conduct and highlights the struggle between duty and temptation. It encourages much preoccupation with the self so that one could be selfless. At the same time it disparages casuistry and moral doubt and promotes a sense of duty and devotion to rule which tends to be literal and encourages a legalistic attitude.

Affection and hospitality, tolerance and acceptance, charity and philanthropy, non-violence and compassion have been widely accepted values in the Indian tradition. Virtual autonomy of groups in regulating their accustomed mode of social life and harmony between them have been a marked feature of that tradition. The modern notions of the struggle of the individual against the group or of groups against groups, whether classes, races, religions or nations, were largely strangers in the context of the ancient ethos. The freedom which the individual sought was ideal freedom, not the freedom to maximize his competitive gains by any means. Instead of the notion of right, that of duty was pre-eminent. It was accepted that justice means non-discrimination but this did not lead to any notion of social or economic equality. Inequalities in these respects were accepted as inevitable on account of the diversity of human capacities, effects and virtue.

Notes and References

1. e.g., Hegel., *Encyklopadie der philosophischen Wissenschaften in Grundrisse* (Hamburg, 1969), pp. 402 ff.
2. "*Dhāranād dharma ityāhuh Dharmo dhārhyateprajāḥ.*" It is a precise reversal of the current behaviourist and positivist outlook of the social sciences. What determines social form is the apprehension of 'ideal law'. The *Purusa-sukta,* thus, traces the social order to the divine *Purusa,* Cf. Maitland (tr.) *Gierke's Political Theories of the Middle Ages,* p. 8.
3. Cf. Coomaraswamy, '*Vedic Examplerism*' in Vol. II, pp. 177 ff.
4. Cf. Keith, *Rel. & Phil. of the Veda and the Upanishads,* Vol. II, pp. 321 ff.
5. Cf. Kane, *Hist. of the Dh. S*' Vol. II, pt. II, p. 746, and fn., 1782. Also Ibid p. 735, "It is on account of these sentiments, that no Poor Law and no work-houses were required in India."
6. This sacramental system from *garbhādhāna* to *antyesti* remained acceptable even to the heterodox as remarked by Udayana in his *Ātmatattvaviveka "Nāstyeva taddarśanaṁ yatra, sāṁvṛtam etad ityuktvāpi grabhādhanādyantyeṣtiparyantāṁ Vaidikīṁ Kriyāṁ nanúṭiṣṭhati janaḥ.*"
7. The *Agrayana isti* ensures this.
8. The best account of Vedic political theory may be seen in Coomarswamy, *Spiritual Authority and temporal Power in the Indian Theory of Government.*
9. *R.* X. 85, 41.
10. Ibid. X. 85. 41-44, and *ad.* in the *R.*
11. Ibid. X. 14 ff.
12. Cf. Benveniste, *Indo-European Language and Society,* pp. 138 ff. where Darmasteter's equation of *srat* and heart is questioned.
13. *R.* X. 190.
14. Ibid. X. 85.1.
15. Indra is the archetypal figure for heroism. It has been suggested that *vrse* originally had the sense of 'sire', not 'male'—E. Benveniste, *Indo-European Language and Society,* 1973, pp. 19 ff.
16. Cf. Sukhthankar, *The Meaning of the Mahabharata.*
17. So Indra's advice is '*Caraiveti*', Keep 'moving'—(*Aitareya Brahmana, Pancika,* 7.)
18. So in the Puranas, e.g., in the *Markandeya* Purana in the famous *Saptasati*. *Gita* plainly speaks of god-like and demoniac natures.

19. See. e.g., *Vedic Index*, passim. cf. Keith, op. cit., Vol. I, pp. 231 ff.
20. Thus *arati* is the enemy. Men and gods are part of a cycle of mutual giving. The *Isopanisad* and the *Gita* state explicitly that the consumption of goods must be preceded by sacrificial parting.
21. *R.* X. 117.6.
22. This is according to the usual modern interpretation which regards *jana* as clan. In ancient commentaries *jana* simply means 'people'. For discussion, see *infra*. Delbruck's *Indogermanische Verwandtschaft-verhaltnisse* pub. in 1890 argued that the Indo-European family, was a large patriarchical joint family. cf. Benveniste, op. cit., pp. 165 ff.
23. *R.* I. 189.1.
24. *Aitareya Brahmana*, 7.13-18.
25. Cf. *Atherva*, XI. 5.
26. "*Jāyamano ha vai brāhmanas tribhir ṛnavānjāyate.*" (*T.S.* 6.3.19.5)
27. *Atharva* XI, 5.18.
28. Svami Dayananda has specially brought this out in his comy. on the hymns to Dawn.
29. *R.* X. 85. 45-46.
30. *Satapatha* (5.2.1,10) '*ardho vā esa ātmano yajjāyā.*
31. *R.* III. 33.
32. e.g. *R.* I. 17 etc.
33. Cf. *R.* 7.60.2 : *ṛju marteṣu vṛjinā ca paśyan.*
34. See Jayaswal, *Hindu Polity*.
35. See Coomarswamy, op. cit.
36. Cf. *Br. Upa.* 3.9.
37. Cf. *Studies in the Origins of Buddhism*, pp. 279 ff.
38. *Katha*, 1.2.2.
39. In *Katha* 1.3. This faculty is called *Vijnana* or *Buddhi*. Cf. Jaidev Singh, '*The Concept of Buddhi in the Bhagvadgita*', paper presented at the Indian Philosophical Congress.
40. *Katha*, 1.2. 1-2.
41. *Katha*, 1.2.27.
42. *Katha*, 2.6.15; *Mundaka* 3.1.2. cf. *Svetasvatara*, 1.8—'*anīśaścātmā badhyate bhoktṛbhāvād.*"
43. *Katha*, 1.2.23.
44. *Brhadaranyaka*, 5.2.
45. *Chāndogya*. 2.23.
46. Cf. my *Sramana Tradition*, p. 5.
47. Vide my *Studies in the Origins of Buddhism*, pp. 322 ff.
48. *Brhadaranyaka*, 4.4.22.
49. *R.* X. 90.
50. Sankara, *Isadi-dasopanisadah*, p. 684 (ad *Br*. 4.15)
51. *Brhadaranyaka*, 4.11-13.
52. Ibid. 4.14.
53. *Sankara*, op. cit., p. 683.

54. This is how the Indo-Greeks equated *Dike* and *Dharma* in their coins. Asokan *dharma* has been translated by *eusebeia* at Kandhar.
55. Professor Urwick has expounded thls similarly in detail.
56. See Coomarswamy, op. cit., also my *Aspects of Jaina Political Thought*.
57. *Mimamsa-sutras*, 1.1.2.
58. *Sabarabhasya* (Anandasrama ed.) Vol. I. P. 17.
59. *Slokavartika* (Varanasi 1978), p. 37.
60. Gautama, *Dharmasutras*, 1.1.1-4.
61. Ibid.
62. Baudhayana, *Dharmasutras* 1.1.1 ff.
63. Ibid. 1.1.13.
64. *Vasistha, Dharmasutras*, Also *Baudhayana*, op. cit. 1.2.12 ff.
65. *Baudhayana*, op. cit. 2.6.14.
66. *Apastamba, Dharmasutras*, 2.9.21.1.
67. *Gautama*, op. cit., 1.3.3. : Ib. 1.3.35. *Baudhayana*, op. cit. 2.6.29-30.
68. Haradatta.

68a. The *Apaśūdrādhikarana* of the two *Mīmāmsās* shows that the exclusion of the *śūdra* could not have been original.

69. Bühler, SBE, Vol. II, pt. 1, Introduction; *Camb. Hist. of India*, Vol. I, p. 227.
70. *Camb. Hist. of India*, I. p. 228.
71. *Manu*, 1.6.9. Medhatithi says—'*Varsasankhya ceyam divyamanena*'.. But actually *Manu* 1.71 defines one *daivayuga* as consisting of 12,000 human years of *Caturyugi*.
72. *Manu*, 1.93.
73. *Manu*, 2.1.
74. *Manu*, 2.2.
75. Ibid. 2.6.
76. Ibid. 2.12.
77. Ibid. 2.11.
78. Ibid. 2.17-18.
79. Ibid. 1.118.
80. Cf. *Bhavisyapurana*, quoted by Kulluka ad *Manu*, 2.25.
81. *Manu*, 2.28.
82. Ibid. 2.67
83. Quoted *Smrticandrikā* : *Manu, pariśista*, p. 14.
84. If we take sudras to be a quarter of the whole and upper caste women to be half of the remaining three-quarters, we have : 1/4+3/8 = 5/8.
85. Ibid. 2.136.
86. Ibid. 2.154.
87. Ibid. 2.162.
88. Ibid. 2.224.
89. Ibid. 2.236.
90. Ibid. 2.38, 241.
91. Ibid. 2.246.
92. Ibid. 3.5.

93. Ibid. 3.13-14.
94. Ibid. 3.21.
95. Cf. ibid. 3. 51-53.
96. Ibid. 3.56, cf. *ibid*. 3.60.
97. Ibid. 3.70.
98. Ibid. 3.81
99. Ibid. 3.115, 118.
100. Ibid. 3.149 ff.
101. Cf. *ibid*. 4.210-24; 4.253.
102. Ibid. 3.158.
103. Ibid. 4.4.
104. Ibid. 4.160.
105. *Manu*, 4.174.
106. Ibid. 4.176.
107. Ibid. 4.178.
108. Ibid. 4.174-85.
109. Ibid. 4.186-200; 4.226 ff.
110. Ibid. 4.204.
111. Ibid. 4.258.
112. Ibid. 5.41; 44-46.
113. Ibid. 6.1.
114. Ibid. 6.86, 95.
115. Ibid. 6.92.
116. Ibid. 7.3 ff.
117. e.g. Ibid. 7.32.
118. Ibid. 7.43.
119. Ibid. 7.27.
120. Ibid. 7.47.
121. Ibid. 7.48.
122. Ibid. 7.54.
123. Ibid. 7.82.
124. Ibid. 1.19.
125. Ibid. 7-88-89.
126. Ibid. 7.90. The Indo-Greeks used doubled-tanged arrows—cf. G. R. Sharma, *The Reh Inscription of Menander*.
127. G. R. Sharma, op. cit.
128. *Mannu*, 8.41.
129. Ibid. 12. 87.90.
130. Ibid. 5.56.
131. Ibid. 12.91.
132. Ibid. 12.106.
133. Ibid. 12.113.
134. *Yajnavalkya*, 1.1.7.
135. Ibid. p. 97, 102.
136. Kane, op.cit. Vol. I, P. 208.
137. A.D. Pant, Introduction, Beni Prasad's *Theory of Government in Ancient India*.

138. Vide Coomaraswamy, *Spiritual Authority and Temporal Power in the Indian Theory of Government.*
139. Vide Coomaraswamy, *Spiritual Authority and Temporal Power in the Indian Theory of Government.*
140. *Mbh, Śāntiparvan.*
141. Liberty as 'doing what one wants', *Kāmakāra,* was not deemed a value. Value arose from the principle which the will followed. The *Gita* thus contrasts *śāstravidhi* and *kama-kāra.* So Mbh., *śāntiparvan,* 91.3 contrasts *dharma* and *Kāmakārma.*
142. *Santiparvan*—Chapters 56 ff; 101; 121.
143. Ibid. chap. 132.
144. *Artha* 1.2.5.
145. Ibid. 1.7.7.
146. Ibid. 1.2.12.
147. Cf. *Artha* 1.4.4; ibid. 1.5.17; *Ib.* 1.19.34.
148. Ibid. 1.3.8.
149. Ibid. 3.13.
150. Cf. Ibid. 1.9.
151. Ibid. 2.1.32.
152. e.g., Ibid. 2.8.
153. Ibid. 3.1.39.
154. Ibid. 3.1.45.
155. Ibid. 6.1.8.
156. Kamandaka, I, 21.60, VIII. 1 ff.
157. *Nitivākyāmṛta, Laghvarhanniti.* —See my *Aspects of Jaina Political Thought.*
158. Cf. Beni Prasad, *State in Ancient India,* pp. 486 ff. Cf. Lallanji Gopal monograph questioning the authenticity of the *Śukraniti.*
159. Cf. U. N. Ghoshal, op. cit. pp. 365-56.
160. Kamandaka, I. 21.
161. Cf. Coomarswamy, op. cit.
162. Cf. Fung Yu-Lan, *History of Chinese Philosophy,* Vol. I.
163. Cf. G.C. Pande, *Sramaṇa Tradition,* pp. 52 ff.
164. Cf. *Santiparvan.* Chap. XIX—*Vanaparvan,* dialogue of Yudhisthira and Nahuṣh (*Ājagara parvan*).
165. *Bhagavadgita,* Chap. II.
166. *Mbh.* I. pp. 666 ff.
167. *Abhijnana-Sakuntala.*
168. *Mbh.* Vol. I. p. 664.
169. Ibid. I. p. 665.
170. Ibid. *l.c.*
171. *Mbh.* I. p. 628.
172. *Mbh.* Vol. I. p. 628. The view attributed to Manu here does not occur in the present *Manusmriti* but may be traced in other *dharma-śastrā* authors, see Kane, op. cit., Vol. II. pt. I. pp. 188-89, and 439-44.
173. *Digha* I, p. 86.

174. Ibid. pp. 104-5.
175. *Majjhima* II, pp. 403 ff.
176. *Majjhima* II. pp. 462 ff.
177. *Majjhima*, l.c. ; *Khuddaka* Vol. I, pp. 362 ff.
178. *Khuddaka* I, pp. 311 ff.
179. *Khuddaka* I, pp. 334 ff.
180. *Digha* Vol. III, pp. 66 ff. Cf. *Digha* II, pp. 60-61.
181. Cf. Ghoshal, U.N. op. cit., p. 268.
182. Cf. *Samyutta*, I, pp. 115-16.
183. Cf. Plato, *Republic* Bx. IX, final remarks, Jowett, *Dialogues* Vol. I, p. 851.
184. *Vajrasuci*, *Visvabharati*, 1960.
185. Cf. my *Sramana Tradition*, p. 56.
186. Ibid. p. 57.
187. Ibid l.c.
188. Jacobi, *Jaina sutras*, Vol. II, pp. 130-40.
189. *Sramana Tradition*, p. 62.
190. *Vārtikālaṅkara*, pp. 10-12.
191. Ibid.
192. *Sramana Tradition*, p. 63.
193. *Fourteen Rock Edicts.*
194. Cf. Kane, *History of the Dharmasastra*, Vol. II, pt. I. pp. 3 ff.
195. Cf. *Studies in the Origins of Buddhism*, pp. 466 ff.
196. e.g., cf. *Yogabhasya* and Y. S. 2.30.; Aryadeva, *Catuhsataka*, *Mbh.* "*paropakāraḥ puṇyāya parapīḍanam*".
197. Cf. *Chandogya* Prajāpati's Sermon on the three *Da's*; *Dana* was counted a *pāramitā* by *Mahāyāna*, and the *Dharmaśāstra* placed an increasing emphasis on *dāna* in the early mediaeval period.
198. *Rock Edict.* II.
199. Cf. Kane, op. cit.
200. *Samavāya* is the word which Asoka uses.

9

Socio-Historical Order : Vedic

"Indian social history has a very different rhythm, a very different tempo from that of Western history. In the West social changes have been faster and at times revolutionary... In its aspiration after rationality, Western thought has erected the incoherences of ethos and attitudes into irreconcilable contradictions demanding absolute choice. The Indian mind, on the other hand, has sought to govern social relations not by an abstract reason but by intuition and compromise. It has met new challenges by modifying rather than rejecting older solutions......In the social and cultural tradition of India......the older and the newer forms have continued side by side and this continuity stretches back to prehistoric times. Conservatism with the readiness to reinterpret the past have prevented revolutions, and the caste-system has damped the growth of class antagonisms and conflicts.[1]"

How the development of social differentiation in India assumed the peculiar pattern of castes and subcastes and provided the historical background for the emergence and crystalization of the concept of *dharma*, is difficult to trace in the absence of ampler social records, though the broad outlines of the history may be recovered from the religious, legal and general literature of the successive epochs.[2] It is generally believed that early Vedic literature reveals a system of three social 'orders' or 'estates,' viz. *Brahman*, ***Kṣattra*** and ***Viśaḥ***. In *R*. 8.35, thus, the **Aśvins** are entreated to quicken the *Brahman* and prayers (*brahma jinvatam uta jinvatam dhiyo*), quicken the ***Kṣattra*** and the heroes (***Kṣattram*** *jinvatam uta jinvatam nṝn*), and to quicken milch cattle and the *Viśaḥ*, (*dhenūr jinvatam uta jinvatam viśo*). In *R*. 1.157, again the Aśvins are entreated to sprinkle the *Kṣattra* with glowing mead (*ghṛtena no madhunā Kṣattram ukṣatam*) and to quicken the *Brahman* in contests (*asmākam brahma pṛtanāsu jinvatam*). In a hymn to Bṛhaspati (*R*. 4.50) it is stated that the *Viśaḥ* themselves give obedience to the king who follows the *Brahman* (*tasmai viśaḥ svayam evā namante yasmin brahma rājani pūrva eti*).

This division of 'orders' was represented among the gods too. Agni, Mitra, Bṛhaspati and Soma represented the *Brahman* while Indra and Varuna represented the *Kṣattra*[3] Aśvins, Maruts and Viśvedevāh represented the *Viśah*. Indra and Agni,[4] Mitra and Varuna[5] are represented as complementary pairs. Asvins are seen to be connected with ploughing, sowing, agriculture and food.[6] The Maruts and Viśvedevāḥ are described as forming troops or masses. Rudra, the father of the Maruts, is the lord of cattle.

This notion of the three 'estates' was ritually formulated and was symbolically connected with a notion of the division of the divine and hence of human powers and functions. The S'B thus asserts that these three orders being comprehended in Indra-Agni constitute the whole, i.e. these three divisions reflecting a divine prototype exhaust the human collectivity or society—"*Yāvad brahma ksattraṁ viḍ indrāgnī vā idaṁ sarvam*" (4.3.2.14). Mitra and Varuna, *Brahman* and *Ksattra* are called Kratu and Daksa. "Counsel and Power". "Mitra is the Counsel and Varuna the Regnum (*Ksattra*). Mitra the Knower (*abhigantr*) and Varuna the Executive (*Kartr*).[7]" The *Viśah*, on the other hand, were the subjects of this bipartite sovereignty, the people as a mass when distinguished from those among them who had authority. They were connected with the function of providing nourishment and hence with agricultural production and cattle. Their mode of existence was also conceived as essentially one of being in mass or troops (*gaṇaśaḥ*). Hence they were represented by the Maruts or the Viśvedevāh. Literally the *Viśah* meant 'settlements' and indicated sometimes the whole community ruled by the sovereign, sometimes the common people or the third estate.[8]

The origin of this three-estate system has been attributed to an ancient Indo-European or Indo-Iranian tradition, or more plausibly to the conditions naturally resulting from the facts of war and conquest which lead to the emergence of warlike rulers and a conquering aristocracy imposing itself on the conquered people.[9] A good illustration of this process can be seen in the growth of Frankish and Norman nobilities in later times. The Vedic system of estates, however, does not quite conform to this. Vedic thought does not confound sovereignty and property, and unlike the wide-spread tradition of the ancient Near Eastern civilizations, Vedic thought sharply contrasted the priestly with the royal power. In the earlier period, this contrast was not so much of exclusive classes as of functions. Persons from the same class could be kings or priests as, for example, in the case of Devāpi and Śantanu,[10] but the offices of the king and the priest were held distinct. This sharp contrast between holiness, sovereignty and property is a distinctive idea unparalleled anywhere else in pre-modern times and helped to mould Indian social development in a characteristic pattern.

Holiness proceeds ultimately from Logos, the most essential and primordial expression of divine reality. There is a Law in the highest heaven which is revealed by the Word, and which has to be followed on earth as it is followed in heaven.[11] The seer and the priest have a natural leadership (*purohita*) inasmuch as they reveal the Law and help its ritual enactment on earth. The archetypal order is reflected in ritual and society and every householder must kindle and keep up the Fire as its symbol.[12]

Order in the created world has to be mainitained and protected against the forces of darkness and chaos. Social order too must be maintained and protected and the duty devolves on the *Ksattra*, or Sovereignty. The human ruler is not the source of law but subject to it.[13] The law is known from Revelation and the ruler has only the obligation of protecting it.[14] Political power is, thus, executive and judicial, not legislative in nature. Priestly and Royal authority, the Sacerdotium (*brahman*) and the Regnum (*Ksattram*) are distinct but complementary.[15]

The acquisition of wealth or the production of food was not regarded as a specialized function. Nor was any special class based on it. Just as fighting was not a specialized function even in the epics where kings and priests, nobles and commoners are found to fight equally; similarly 'productive' activity was not socially specialized.[16] In the epics, the *brahmacarins* are found to tend the cattle of the teacher and the early Buddhist writings show Brahmanas as agriculturists or ranchers.[17] The stigma against these professions appears first in the *Sutras* which, however, compromise with reality by accepting: these professions for the Brahmanas in 'exceptional times'. The *Viśah*, thus did not mean 'producers' but simply the community or people as a whole, guided and protected by the *Brahman* and *Ksattra*, priesthood and royalty, neither of which was hereditary. In this sense, the early Vedic social system was a two-office rather than a three-estate system. Since the people who were not priests or rulers constituted an undistinguished common mass, it might be called a system of 'orders'[18] of social functioning.

The acquisition of wealth or food was, in fact, regarded as a gift of the gods expressed in the bounty of nature.[19] Unlike governance or prayer or even craftsmanship, food production was not supposed to require any special technology. If anything, it required ritual magic. The food which the gods eat is ambrosia *amṛta*, *madhu*, *soma*.[20] It belongs to the highest heaven and has been brought to the earth by the Bird or fire in the form of the fertilizing flood of rain.[21] The Asvins shower *madhu* and bear food in their chariots.[22] Rain falling through the clouds is the cosmic counter part of the drops of *soma* falling through the woollen strainer.[23] The fertilizing fluid energy or sap enters the plants and makes them food, fit again to be offered to the gods.[24] The cycle of solar heat, rain and vegetations is the cosmic sacrifice which is imitated in the human ritual which is an expression of human gratitude and a celebration of divine bounty.[25]

Specialisation was undoubtedly known for the crafts such as of the carpenter, the chariot-maker and the smith. Tvastr and the Rbhus were the divine counter parts of the craftsmen.[26] Nevertheless, despite the distinct existence of such professional groups, they were, in terms of social recognition, merged in the *Viśah* and were not treated at par with the first two orders. *Ksattra* or dominion was held by the king. Whether the kinsmen of the king constituted a ruling nobility or aristocracy in the early Vedic period, is more than doubtful. On the other hand, in the later Vedic period, the existence of an aristocracy is undoubted.

In the *Ṛgveda*, the word *rājanya* occurs only in the famous *Puruṣa-sūkta.* In the later Vedic literature, *rājanya* and Ksattriya stand for the ruling nobility but in the *Ṛgveda*, Ksattriya is synonymous with the king or *rājan.* Thus Varuna, Mittra and Aryaman are called *rājānaḥ* as, for example, in *R.*1.41.3 or *R.*7.40.4. In *R.* 4.42.1 we have *mama dvitā rāṣṭram Ksattriyasya*'. In *R.* 7.64.2. *rājānā* and *Ksattriyā* are plainly indentified. *Ṛ.* 8.25.8 says "*dhṛtavratā Ksattriyā Ksattramāsatuḥ*".. *R.* 8.67.1 speaks of the Adityas as Ksattriyas, *R.* 7.10.4.13 speaks of the '*Ksattriyam mithuvā dhārayantam*'. *R.* 10.68.8 speaks of the ksattriyas who are *dhṛtavratā, R.* 10.109.3 speaks of the '*rāṣṭram gupitam Ksattriyasya*'. These are all the occurrences of the word Ksattriya in the *Ṛgveda* and it is clear that the word simply means the king and is exchangeable with *rājan.*

The word *rājan* or king occurs frequently in the *Ṛgveda* and often stands for the divine rulers Mitra, Varuna, Aryaman and Indra.[27] Soma too is sometimes called rājan.[28] The king holds sway over the people who are called *Craṣani, Kṣiti, Kṛṣti, Jana* or *Viśah*[29] He is the protector of the people and the law.[30] He is the leader in war, heroic and pious. He doubtless had warlike companions just as the Maruts were for Indra.[31] Maruts constitute a troop of youthful warriors who are all alike and equal.[32] Perhaps they reflect the king's companions and were an incipient 'functional' nobility. One may recall the *comites* of the Frankish invaders of Gaul.

The basic question is the extent to which the hereditary principle obtained among the kings during this period.[33] There is clear evidence of the election of the king by the assembly of the people called *samiti*[34] which along with the *s. bhā* constituted the two popular organs of government of the period.[35] While the *sabhā* was apparently the King's council of companions, the *samiti* was the gathering of the whole people, deriving from the archaic tribal assembly.[36] There are examples of kings being expelled and also of states which were republican.[37] At the same time, there is evidence of some kings whose fathers were also kings.[38] It may be safely presumed that in the course of time, the original principle of election became one of selection and ultimately transformed itself into that of approval. As the hereditary principle grew stronger, the elective principle must have become a mere conventional formality by the later Vedic age, a tendency which may be paralleled elsewhere.[39] The territorial expansion and settlement of the clans also must have lent an air of unreality and impracticability to ancient tribal customs and gradually strengthened the rule of heredity and primogeniture which slowly came to the fore. At the same time, the kings and their kinsmen became an ever larger class with political, administrative and military functions. Distinctions of family and clan among them came to be more than matched by their common position and function in the social hierarchy and they came to constitute a distinct class cutting across their separate kingdoms and principalities, a ruling aristocracy proud of its birth and position. This was the *ksattriya* class in the later Vedic age, seeking to convert itself into a 'caste'.

The usual word for priest in the *Ṛgveda* is *Brahman* but the word 'Brāhmaṇa' too is found used for priest at a number of places, most of which belong to the first and tenth *mandalas* but some come from admittedly older portions of the *saṁhita*. Thus *R*. 6.75.10, which is used in the performance of *tarpana* and *śrāddha*, says *'brāhmaṇāsaḥ pitaraḥ somyāsaḥ*." *R*. 7.10. 3.1, which is equally famous compares the Brahmanas to the frogs—*'saṁvatsaram Śaśayānā brāhmaṇā vratacārinaḥ*'. It is clear that the priests not only used the hymns in the sacrifices but as 'seers' or *ṛṣis* composed them. They were an obviously specialized class since they required long training in myth and ritual,[40] theosophy, metrics and poetry. Ṛgvedic hymns are no untutored warblings but the compositions of an educated and self-conscious tradition with an eye on the formal aspects of poetry. The line quoted above already speaks of the year-long training of the Brahmanas under a vow. To acquire the art of hymn-making which was regarded as exacting as that of the carpenter and the chariot-maker, must certainly have required a long period of training. This period of training called *brahmacarya* constituted the earliest educational institution, although the word *brâhmacarin* as such seems to occur only once in the *Ṛg.* i.e. in 10.109.5. The earlier reference to *Vratacārin Brāhmaṇa*, however, had apparently the same sense. In later Vedic literature, the word is common.

In the earliest period, Vedic education probably usually began in the family and helped the growth of the hereditary principle within the priestly class. At the same time, it cannot be doubted that the Brahmanas were not in that period a wholly hereditary class. A well-known hymn of the ninth *mandala* says "I am a priest, my mother is a stone-grinder, my father a physician" (*kārur aham tato bhiṣag upalaprakṣinī nanā*).[41] The growing elaboration of the ritual, however must have accounted for the need for specialised training, tending to convert the priests into a kind of professional guild.[42]

In later times, Brahmanas are found divided into *gotras* but the word does not have that sense in the *Ṛgveda.* At the same time, the Ṛgvedic seers are clearly seen to emphasise their separate lineal descent and an ancient tradition spoke of the Seven Seers. Perhaps it was natural for later priests to seek to connect themselves with the families of ancient seers.[43]

European scholars have debated the position of the caste system in the *Ṛgveda* at great length. Zimmer and Muir[44] argued that the early Vedic age was wholly caste-free, the caste system having developed only in the later Vedic age when the Aryan migration had reached the east. This was contested by others who sought to discern a continuity of development between the earlier and the later period.[45] As argued above, the development of the priesthood and aristocracy appears to be continuous, being the natural consequence of a growing hereditary position. It does not, however, amount to saying that Brahmanas and Ksattriyas already existed as castes in the early Vedic period. To say that "all the elements of the caste system were already in existence[46]," is highly misleading, because historical structures are not simple aggregates of "elements". Some kind of social differentiation is inevitable but one should not interpret such data anachronistically.

On the other hand, the attempt to trace the Śūdras to the *dāsas* of the earlier period is based on an unsubstantiated hypothesis about an invading and colour-conscious Aryan race in strife with the pre-Aryan natives of the country. Nowhere in ancient Indian literature does the world *arya* have a racial sense. Modern scholars, on the other hand, assume that a branch of the Indo-Europeans called themselves 'Ārya' as a racial designation. Prof. Spiegel held that Ārya meaning 'honourable' and derived from *ārya* meaning lord in the *Vedas* is to be identified with the Avestan *Airya* which was a name the ancient Persians applied to themselves and from which the more modern Iranian has arisen.[47] The undivided Indo-Iranians or Āryans inhabited "the vast plains of the Oxus and the Jaxartes, the land Eranvej of the two rivers Vahvi-Datiya and Ranha[48]". As evidence of the ethnic meaning of *ārya* or Airya, it has been mentioned that Darius called himself not only Persian but 'Aryan, of Aryan descent.'[49] However, the meaning 'noble' would fit the context fully. Again, Herodotus has been quoted "The Medians were once universally known as Arians, but they, too, changed their name."[50] But Herodotus does not say this of the Persians or Bactrians or Indians'. In any case, Vedic language and society are so far removed from the hypothetical extra-Indian wanderings of the Indo-Iranians, that they have no memory whatever of that period.

The etymology and meaning of the Vedic word Ārya have been debated but it seems reasonable to accept that Arya as 'master of the house' derives from *arya* meaning 'hospitable' which itself goes back to *Ari* meaning 'stranger'. Hence the god Aryaman represented the 'host' and was the god of hospitality.[51] This is in line with the view of the *Nighantu* (2.22). "*Rāṣṭrī aryaḥ niyutvān inaḥ iti catvāri īśvaranāmāni.*" "Thus in explaining *R.* 1.117.21 "*abhi dasyum bakurenā dhamanto-ru jyotis' cakrathu rāryāya*"—Yāska says "*Ārya īśvara-putrah.*"[52] It is tempting to read in this interpretation a reference to the 'nobility' but most probably *ārya* as houselord corresponded to the Vedic and classical *grhapati* to which the Pali and Prakrta *gahapati* and *gāhāvai* correspond. The later *Kutumbin* had the same sense. The meaning of the word *ārya* seems to have had two components from the beginning. On the one hand, it had the sense of 'being worthy' indicated by the suffix, and on the other, of being 'master' or 'free'. Since the sense of 'being worthy' was specially in the context of hospitability, and the sacrifice to the gods was conceived on the analogy of hospitality to an honoured guest, Ārya developed the meaning of 'pious', a meaning which it often has in the *Ṛgveda.* Thus in *R.* 4.26.2 "*aham bhūmim adadām āryāyā ham vṛṣṭim dāśuṣe martyāya*", *āryāya* is plainly paraphrased by '*dāśuṣe martyāya*'. The gods shower their gift of means of sustenance—land and rain-fall—on the men who are liberal in sacrifices, which reminds one of the *Bhagavadgita.* On *R.* 2.11.18 *apāvṛnojjyotirāryāya ni savyataḥ sādi dasyur indrah*"—Sayana comments "*āryāya karmaṇām anusṭnātre janāya*". Sayana and other commentators generally interpret Vedic *ārya* as 'pious' or 'noble.'[53]

In later literature too the word *arya* has a similar spread of meaning. Thus it is used for 'noble' as e.g. in "*Yad āryam asyām abhilāsi me manah,*"[54] or 'freeman' as in "*natvevāryasya dāsabhāvah*",[55] or 'enlightened' as in the Buddhist *Āryadharma* and the contrast of *ārya* and *prathagjana.*[56]

To assume that the Vedic seers were race-conscious and colour-conscious and that *ārya* and *dāsa* in the Vedic hymns stand for the fair Aryan and the dark non-aryan races respectively must need more evidence than the mere fact that the modern representatives of the cognate European races happen to suffer acutely from race and colour prejudices.[57] Prof. K. Chattopadhyaya analysed the 148 separate and 33 compound occurrences of the words Dasa and Dasyu in the *Ṛgveda Samhita* and came to the conclusion that the traditional interpretation of the word as 'demon' appears to suit most of the occurrences.[58] The ancient commentators take the conflict of *dasa* and *deva* to be the same as the later Vedic or Puranic *devasura-samgrama.* They do not think of this conflict as one between human races. That the *dāsas* are described as *ayajvan, avrata, akarman* etc. is easily intelligible because opposition to sacrifice or worship is the essential nature of ungodly forces. Just as gods are the luminous powers underlying worship, the demons are the dark powers opposed to it. Their description as black-hued followed from this and the epithet noseless applied to them is in consonance with their traditional image of hideousness or even noselessness. The contrast of *Ārya* and *dāsa* is the contrast of the pious, godly person with the unholy and the ungodly. The notion that the Aryans in India described those who did not worship their gods as unpious and ungodly seeks to import the kind of outlook which was common enough in the Semitic races into India when even in the Vedic age the gods are nowhere conceived as tribal or ethnic, standing in contrast with the gods of other races or tribes. Vedic gods are universal and superhuman and they have no interest in ethnic conflicts. Their conflict is only with the powers of darkness and sterility.

When it is said that the *dāsa varna* was placed below, the reference is not to the lower social position of the conquered race but to the gods banishing the demons to the underground below the earth (2.12.4).[59] When the sage Agastya is said to nourish both the *varnas*, the reference is to both the modes of spiritual life, not to Āryans and non-Āryans (1.179.6).[60] Indra is asked to know the *āryas* from the *dasyus* so that he may destroy the lawless (*avrata*) for the sake of those who are ready to worship (*barhismate*, 1.51.8).[61] Gods create or unveil light for the pious, driving away the *dasyus* (1.117.21; 2.11.18; 7.5.6). Ārya sometimes could simply have had the sense of 'man', 'pious' or 'free' as distinguished from both gods and demons e.g. in 6.18.3 or 4.26.2, "You alone controlled the demons (forces of chaos) and saved the folk for the pious (ruler)". Here the conflict of Light and Darkness becomes the model for the conflict of chaos and order in the human realm. "I gave the earth to the *ārya*, I gave rain to the liberal man." Sometimes *ārya* meaning, 'lord' or 'holy' even becomes the epithet of the gods e.g. in

5.34.6 where Indra is the *ārya* who subdues the *dāsa* at will. The reference is either to the 'master' controlling the 'slave' or to holiness triumphing over demons. Sayaṇa prefers the former.[62] In 10.43.4 we hear of the winning of happiness[63] and holy light for man ('*vidat svar manave jyotir āryam*') Sometimes *dāsa* and *ārya* are put together as supernatural and human enemies—'*hato vrtrāny āryā hato dāsāni*' (6.60.6)[64], '*dāsā vrtrāny āryā jigetha*' (10.69.6),[65] '*yayā dāsāny āryāni vrtrā*' (6.22.10),[66] *dāsā ca vrtrā hatam āryāṇica* (7.83.1).[67]

It is true that *dāsa* occasionally also has the sense of slave or servitor as in later times,[68] but it has been suggested that it might have been an altogether different word.[69] The usual words *dāsa* and *dasyu* come from a root meaning to cause injury as Sayaṇa states and the hymns themselves use the root *das* or *dās* in this sense e.g. 10.102.3—'*antar yaccha jighāṁsato vajram indrā bhidāsatah*'. Here *jighāṁsatah* and *abhidāsatah* seem to have the same sense.[70] This meaning continued in the word *dasyu* or 'plunderer' in later times. On the other hand, the word *dāsa* meaning servitor completely replaced the earlier word *dāsa* meaning 'enemy, demon', for which the word *asura* came to be used. The word '*ārya*' on the other hand tended to generalize its meaning from 'pious' to 'noble'. At the same time, *ārya* as 'free man' contrasted with *dāsa* as servitor or slave, came also to mean a person of the upper three castes.

With this reinterpretation of the distinction between *ārya* and *dāsa*, it also follows that the distinction of *varnas* did not reflect a colour consciousness. There was undoubtedly a word *varṇa* meaning 'colour'[71], but whether the word *varṇa* meaning 'estate' or 'class'[72] is the same word, must leave some room for doubt. Even if the two words be assumed to be the same for the sake of simplicity, the connection between the two must be supposed to lie in the fact that the gods were bright and the demons dark.[73] Man too was created for light and followed it. Hence the distinction of the human order from that of the powers of the dark was also a distinction based on 'colour' or rather 'brightness of aspect'[74], in some sense.

The later Vedic age saw the emergence of numerous

specialized professions and, by their side the noticing of numerous tribal groups engaged in primitive but characteristic professions. *Rathakāra*, *Iṣukāra* and *Karmāra* are examples of the former kind, *Niṣāda* and *Dhīvara* are examples of the latter. The *Vājasaneyi saṁhitā*, for example, gives a comprehensive list of both kinds of groups, which are not distinguished. At the same time beginning with the *Purusasukta* and generally accepted, we have the theoretical formulation of the four *varnas* as constituting the divine and perennial order of society.[75] No other theory in human history has been so widely accepted as a fact, although the Marxian theory of two warring classes bids fair to win wide acceptance as a matter of fact. The word *varna* now definitely acquires the meaning of 'one of the four social classes.'[76] Brahmanas and Ksattriyas were already real, functional classes and were accepted as such in the new theory with some generalization which could well reflect actual conditions. *Brahman* and *Ksattra* are now clearly identified with the Brahmanas and Rajanyas, as for example in *Taitt.* B. 3.9.14. The Brahmanas were not merely poets and singers or seers; they were a specialised class of priests and teachers. The Ksattriyas, again, were not only rulers but a ruling nobility composed of the king's kinsmen. They were also warriors and administrators. The very growth of learning in priestly schools ensured that they should become teachers not merely for their own children but for others as well. Changes in political fortunes, the growth of settled territorial life and the development of the art and weapons of fighting would help the development of a hereditary class of rulers and administrators, warriors and soldiers.

It has been argued above that early Vedic society was not aware of itself as constituted by fair Aryans warring against dark non-aryans. Even if there was such a stage of conflict between 'Aryan' speaking invaders and 'non-aryan' speaking inhabitants of the country, that stage must be held to have been forgotten by the time the Vedic hymns were collected in their present form. Vedic society conceived of itself not in terms of ethnic conflict but of ritual harmony. For Vedic social self-consciousness, the human order imitated the divine order. What men did was ideally grounded in what the gods did "in the beginning." It is this ritual mode of thought which underlies the *Purusa-sukta* and dominates the social consciousness of the later Vedic age. Society was thus conceived as a hierarchy in the true sense of the word, i.e. in the sense of a society governed in accordance with sacred principles, not in the sense of a society governed by priests. From the beginning Indian social theory and practice sharply distinguishes between Two Powers which are kept seperate. This prevents the emergence of priest-kings or king-priests, of priestly hierarchy and royal aristocracy. The reality of the Vedic system depended on the learning and character of the Brahmanas and the piety of the king and the maintenance of mutual respect and harmony between them.

Later Vedic literature asserts the primacy of the Brahmanas in the social order and formulates that the prosperity of the realm depends on the harmony of the Brahmanas and the Ksattriyas. This merely continues an ancient idea but the *Brahmana* texts illustrate it in a variety of ways from ritual symbolism and at the same time seek to *define* relations between the classes in terms of the notion of four *varnas*, without altogether giving up the earlier notion of the Three Estates. Thus *S'B.* 11.2.7 deals with the sacrifice symbolically and mentions what may be gained through such knowledge. It says in this context that *Brahman* is the offerring made to Agni, *Ksattra* the *Upāṁśuyāja* and *Vis* is the latter offering. It then goes on to say that since *Āgneya puroḍāśa*, and *Upāṁśuyāja* take place earlier than *uttra puroḍāśa*, it is only right that *Brahman* and *Ksattra* rest on *Vis* (*brahman ca Ksattram ca viśi pratiṣṭhite*). The same *Brahmana* in the context of *Agnicayana* (6.4.4.) fixes the order in which three animals are to be made to proceed forth and back. In proceeding back the goat comes first, then comes the ass and finally the horse while in proceeding forth the horse comes first, the ass comes next and the goat comes last. A symbolism is then read into this. The horse symbolizes the Ksattriya, the goat the Brahmana while the ass is held to stand for Vaisya and Sudra. Brahmana and Ksattriya act as leaders while the other two *varnas* are held in proper order by them. Hence it is obvious that an originally three Estate context has been moulded to a four *varna* idea. From these two passages, it would be clear that while social leadership was held to vest in the upper two *varnas*, the lower *varnas* were regarded as the economic support of society. It is this idea that is so vividly symbolized in the *Purusasukta*.

A well known text of the *Aitareya Brahmana* (35th *Adhyaya*) seeks to delineate the general characteristics of some *varnas*. The Brahmana is described as "*ādāyyāpāyyāvasāyī yathākāmaprayāpyah*" (35.3). Sayana explains the terms as 'receiving gifts', 'drinking soma', 'eating from others', and 'liable to be turned out at will by others' (Vol. II, p. 881). This description tends to emphasise the dependence of the Brahmana on the Ksattriya since it occurs in a context where it is being suggested that a Brahmana-like son will not be the most suitable for a Ksattriya. It should be remembered, however, that a Brahmana-like (*brāhmaṇa kalpa*) son is less than a Brahmana. A Vaisya-like son is described as "*anyasya balikṛd anyasyādyo yathakāma-jyeyah*". The three terms are explained by Sayana as referring to the 'payment of taxes', 'subordination' and 'lowliness'—'*Karapradāna-parādhīnatvatiraskāryatvākhyā vaiśyaguṇāh*' (Ibid. pp. 882). In the context of a Śūdra-like son, the qualities mentioned are '*anyasya preṣyah Kāmotthāpyo yathākāmavadhyaḥ*'. These are explained by Sayana as 'liable to be ordered about', 'liable to be awakened at any hour', and 'liable to be beaten by the master' (Ibid. loc. cit). The second term actually is the same as used for the *brahmanakalpa* and should be interpreted in the same manner, not as interpreted by Sayana here. In the third term, *Vadhya* refers to 'beating,' not 'slaying' as assumed by some modern authors such as Macdonell and Keith in *Vedic Index* II, p. 256.

It has been surmised in the *Vedic Index* that the upper two *varnas* were closed castes in the later Vedic age but the discussion is vitiated by a constant reliance on post-Vedic evidence. Doubtless, the Brahmanas as priests must have tended to approximate to a professional guild while the Ksattriyas would have included a ruling nobility but we do not know how extensive or rigid these classes had become in the later Vedic age.

The *Viśah* or the popular multitude already comprised a number of occupational groups in the *Ṛgvedasamhita.* The farmers appear to have been the most important of these. The 57th hymn of the 4th *mandala* is specifically devoted to the deities connected with agriculture and ends with the prayer—"May the plough shares be lucky in turning up the field; may the farmers follow the bullocks with luck. May Parjanya shower luck with honey and milk. May *Śunā* and *Śira* bless us."[77] In the Lament of the Gambler, one finds the sterling advice that one ought to engage in agriculture.[78] Cattle-rearing was another important occupation although the assumption that the people in the early Vedic age were mainly pastoralists is without adequate proof. On the other hand, early Vedic society seems to have normally combined farming and cattle rearing as in later times. The word for headman viz. *gopā*, *gopa* etc. came to be used metaphorically for the protector or ruler.

A number of crafts had emerged. We hear of workers in stone and metal, called *karmāra* who images the creator.[79] The smelter or *dhmātṛ* finds a distinct mention.[80] The carpenter called *takṣan* or *taṣṭan* was an important figure and the god *tvaṣṭṛ* was his divine archetype. The chariot-maker was apparently a specialist. Potters and weavers were other professions which go back to that remote age. Stone-grinders find separate mention.[81] Among primitive professions, hunting was important enough for some gods like Rudra to be figured as hunters.

The developed division of labour in early Vedic society naturally implied trade and we find traders as a distinct class, called *vaṇij* normally and *paṇi* in contexts of disapprobation.

Paṇi and Vaṇij in Ṛgs.

The word *Paṇa* occurs several times in the *Ṛg.* generally in the context of Indra's battles. Its interpretation, however, has been the subject of much controversy. Mayrhofer holds Pani to be the name of a class of hostile demons and regards its connection with 'trader' or √*paṇ* to be uncertain. The connection with the name of a foreign people such as the Iranian *parnoi* is held to be equally uncertain.[82] On the other hand, Grassmann holds that *paṇi* is derived from √*paṇ* and meant originally 'a trader, one who would not give without compensation'. Hence it came to mean 'niggardly' and since the 'niggard' did not give to the gods, the word came to mean demon.[83] Roth, Zimmer and Ludwig hold a similar opinion, connecting *Paṇi* with √*paṇ*, to barter. Ludwig thought that "the apparent references to fights with *Paṇis* are to be explained by their having been aboriginal traders who went in caravans—as in Arabia and Northern Africa—prepared to fight, if need be......[84]" Hillebrandt thought that there might have been a reference to a real tribe, the Parnians of Strabo. Along with the Dahae, they were the opponents of Divodāsa who fought them on the Arachosian Haraquiti (Sarasvati).[85] Macdonell and Keith, however, feel that the Panis were simply "non-worshippers of the gods favoured by the singers; the term is wide enough to cover either the aborigines or hostile Aryan tribes, as well as demons.[86]"

If we turn to ancient explanations, we find Yaska stating "*Paṇir vaṇig bhavati paṇih paṇanād vaṇik paṇyaṁ nenekti.*[87]" Sayana naturally accepts this interpretation and yet explains *Paṇi* in *R.* I.32.11 as the demon so named, '*paṇināmako asuro*'. From ancient times thus the meaning of *paṇi* has wavered between 'trader' and 'demon', the two meanings being connected by the idea of 'not giving freely, not sacrificing'. The opposition of meaning between 'bartering' and 'sacrificing' is fundamental. The pious are characterized by the spirit of generous sacrificing while the impious are hard-hearted and niggardly and seek to bargain rather than sacrifice.

While the connection of *Paṇi* with the name of some non-aryan tribe depends on purely speculative assumptions, the derivation of *Paṇi* from the root √*paṇ* has a *prima facie* plausibility. The further derivation of √*paṇ* from *pṛ*. or *spṛ*.[88] is not particularly relevant especially since *paṇ* as 'barter' is already found quite clearly in later Vedic literature.

Turning to the *Ṛgvedasaṁhitā* itself, one may discover forty-seven (47) occurrences of the word *Paṇi* in it viz. 1.32.11;

1.33.3; 1.83.4; 1.93.4; 1.124.4; 1.51.9; 1.180.7; 1.182.3; 1.184.2; 2.24.6; 3.58.2; 4.25.7. 4.51.5; 4.58.4; 5.34.7; 5.61.8; 6.13.3; 6.20.4; 6.33.2; 6.39.9; 6.40.2; 6.44.23; 6.45.31; 6.51.14; 6.53.3, 5,6,7: 6.61.1; 7.6.3; 7.9.2; 7.19.9: 8.26.10, 8.45.14; 8.64.2; 8.66. 10; 8.75.7; 9.22.7; 9.111.2; 10.60.6; 10.67.6; 10.92.3; 10.108.[89]

R. 1.32.11 occurs in a rather well-known hymn to Indra where it is said that the waters were imprisoned by Vrtra as the cows were by Paṇi (*niruddhā āpaḥ paṇineva gāvaḥ*).. Here a distinction is apparently made between *Vṛtra* and *Paṇi.* Although Sayana calls Pani a demon (*asura*) here, the text does not necessarily imply it.

R. 1.33.3 mentions Indra as lord who has control over the cows and who is prayed to be liberal, not to be niggardly (*mā paṇir bhūḥ*). Here Paṇi is used as an adjective. Sayana comments '"*Paṇih mā bhūḥ vyavahārī mā bhūḥ Gavām mūḷyam mā yācasvetyarthaḥ*".

R. 4.83.4 says that the seers Angirases obtained the whole wealth of the Pani, including horses, cows and cattle (*sarvam paṇeḥ samavidanta bhojanam aśvāvantam gomantamā paśuṁ paraḥ*). Sayana calls Pani a demon here also, although the text itself is not definitive.

R. 1.93.4 is addressed to Agni and soma whose prowess in plundering the Pani of his cows is stated to be known (*yad amuṣṇītam avaśam paṇiṁ gāh*). In *R.* 1.124.10 Uṣas is entreated to wake up those who sacrifice and to let the unwaking Paṇis sleep (*Pra bodhayāṣaḥ pṛṇato maghonyabudhyamānāḥ paṇayaḥ sasantu*). Here *pṛṇataḥ* and *paṇayaḥ* stand in clear contrast. Irony would be intended here if *paṇi* were to be itself derived from √pṛ as has been suggested. Here Sayana translates Pani as '*vyayāsahiṣṇavaḥ vaṇijaḥ.*'

R. 1.151.9 is addressed to Mitra and Varuna and declares that Panis have not attained to their divinity or munificence (*na devatyam paṇayo nānaśurmagham*). *R.* 1.180.7 addressed to the Aśvins contrasts the singers engaged in sincere praise with the Paṇi who has hoarded (*vayaṁ ciddhi vām jaritāraḥ satyā vipanyāmahe vi panir hitāvān*). Here again, *pani* is contrasted with *vi* √*pan* and a certain ironical play on words is clearly suggested.

R. 1.182.3 entreats the Aśvins to crush the unsacrificing

person who may be held in esteem and to take away the life of the *Paṇi*. Sayana says '*paṇeh vanighbūtasya*'. *R.* 1.184.2 entreats the Aśvins again to kill the *Paṇis—ut paṇīr hatam*. Here too Sayana explains *Pani* as *Vanij*.

R. 2.24.6 speaks of the treasure of the *Panis*, hidden in a secret place —*nidhim panīṇām paramaṁ guhā hitam*. Sayana explains treasure as referring to the cows. *R.* 3.58 2 addresses the Aśvins to take away the intelligence of the *Paṇi—jarethām asmadvi paṇer manīṣām* In *R.* 4.25.7 Indra is said not to have any friendship with the rich *Pani* and, in fact, to seize his wealth (*na revatā paṇinā sakhyamindrah*). Sayana equates *Paṇi* to 'greedy trader' here.

R. 4.51.3 refers to the sleeping of the *Paṇis* in the dark while the brilliant dawns arise to distribute their gifts (*acitre antaḥ paṇayah sasantu*). Curiously here too Sayana equates the *Panis* with the merchants who do not give.

In *R.* 4.58.4 it is stated that the *Paṇis* hid the 'glowing substance' in the cow in three ways, which the gods discovered (*tridhā hitam paṇibhir guhyamānam gavi devāso ghṛtam anvavindan*). Elsewhere the cow is the treasure of the *Paṇis*, here the treasure is hidden in the cows. Sayana explains *Pani* as *asura* here.

R. 5.34.7 mentions that Indra plunders the wealth of the *Paṇi* and distributes wealth among those who give (*samīṁ paṇerajati bhojanammuṣe*). Here Sayana thinks that *Pani* stands for the greedy trader.

R. 5.61.8 is of uncertain meaning. Sayana interprets *Pani* here as the equivalent of one who praises, i.e. the seer. Griffith, however, interprets differently. "And yet full many a one, unpraised mean niggard, is entitled man.

Only in wergild is he such."

"*Uta ghā nemo astutaḥ pumān iti bruve paṇih. Sa vairadeya itsamaḥ*". Sayana obviously misinterprets *paṇi* and *Vairadeya*. On the alternative interpretation, *paṇi* becomes adjectival.

R. 6.13.3 avers that Agni, the good lord kills Vrtra and seizes the prize from the *Paṇi*—'*vipro vi paṇerbharti vājam*'. Sayana calls *Paṇi* demon here. *R.* 6.20.4 declares that the *Panis* ran away in hundreds from Indra (*śatair apadran paṇaya indrātra*). According to Sayana, they ran away from

Indra's friend Kutsa. In 6.33.2 Indra is said to have laid low the *Panis* with the help of the seers (*Tvam viprebhir vi paṇīraśāyah*). Sayana says *'valasyānucarā asurāh panayaḥ.'* This connects the conflict of Indra with Vrtra and the *Panis* and makes the later mythical. In the same strain 6.40.2 mentions the exploits of Indra in destroying the peak of Vala and contesting the *Paṇis* with words (*Paṇīr vacobhirabhi yodhadindrah*). Similarly 6.44.22 speaks of Soma's victory over the *Pani* with the alliance of Indra—*Indreṇa yujā paṇim astabhāyat*.

On the other hand, *R.* 6.45.31 speaks of the *Panis* in an apparently human way. The sage Bharadvaja praises Bṛbu as the best of the *Panis*, lofty like a mansion on the Ganga—*adhi bṛbuḥ paṇinam varṣiṣṭhe mūrdhannasthāt, uruḥ kakṣo na gāṅgyah.* Sayana recounts an ancient tradition to the effect that Bṛbu was the carpenter of the *Paṇis* and had given gifts to Bharadvaja. He quotes Manu (10.10.7) "*Bharadvājah ksudhārtastu saputro vijane vane, Bahvīrgāḥ pratijagrāha bṛbostakṣṇo mahāyaśāh.*" The hymn itself goes on to praise Brbu as a munificent patron extolled by all the singers—*Bṛbum sahasra-dātamam.*

R. 6.51.14, on the other hand, wants Soma to kill the *Paṇi*, the monster, a veritable wolf—*jahi nyattrinam paṇim vṛko hi saḥ.* *R.*6.53.3 entreats Pūṣan to inspire the niggard to be generous, to soften the heart of even the *Pani* (*paṇeścid vi mradā manah*). Here Pani is held up as the typical niggard. The same hymn goes on to pray for the piercing of the hearts of the *Panis*, for its being marked and made more pliable (Ibid. 6.53.5-7). *R.* 6.61.1 tells us that Sarasvatī blessed the generous Vadhryaśva with Divodāsa but ever eats up the *Pani* (*Yā śaśvantam acakhādavaśam paṇim*). Sāyana regards *Pani* as a niggardly trader here. *R.* 7.6.3 refers to the *Paṇis* as 'unsacrificing, of cruel or indistinct speech, deficient in faith, demons (*dasyūn*)'. Agni is said to destroy them. In *R.* 7.9.2 Agni is said to open up the doors of the *Panis.* In *R.* 7.19.9 as interpreted by Sayana, the seers made even the *Panis* to give.

R. 8.26.10 entreats the Aśvins to kill the *Panis*, Sayana tells us that the *Panis* were the demons who had robbed the

Angirases of their cows (*angirogavām apanetṝn asurān*). In *R.* 8.45.14 *Pani* occurs as an adjective of Indra. Sayana equates '*Pani*' to 'Paṇamāna'. Griffith renders 'to thee as to a trafficker' and explains 'as to one who knows the value of our worship and oblations and will give us something in return.' Here obviously no derogatory sense applies to *Pani.* R. 8.64.2 goes back to the more usual strain and entreats Indra to crush the niggardly *Paṇis*. *R.* 8.66.10 places *Paṇis* by the side of '*bekanāṭas*' who are held by Sayana to have been usurers. The word *bekanāṭa,* occurs only once in Vedic literature and its meaning remains uncertain despite diverse speculative interpretations.[90]

R. 8.75.7 expresses the hope of the Angirases of overcoming the *Pani* with respect to cows with the help of Agni. In *R.* 9.22.7 Soma is said to seize the cows and their produce from the *Panis*. In 9.111.2 the same idea is repeated, Soma being said to have found the wealth of the *Panis*. In 10.60.6 the ungiving *Panis* are similarly asked to be attacked. In 10.67.6 Indra is said to have robbed the *Pani* of his cows. Since the hymn is addressed to Brhaspati, Sayana takes Indra to refer to him here.

In *R.* 10.92.3 Sayana interprets *Pani* as praiseworthy, *Paṇitavya*, and makes it an adjective of Agni. The better interpretation is given by Griffith who interprets '*Baḍasya nīthā vi paṇeśca manmahe*' as 'Yea, we discriminate his and the niggard's ways'.

R. 10.108 is devoted to a dialogue between the *Panis* and Saramā, the divine bitch (*devaśunī*), sent by Indra to track the cows stolen by the *Panis*. Sayana says the *Panis* were the soldiers of Vala and the cattle belonged to Brhaspati, the priest of Indra. We gather that the *Panis* lived in a far off place beyond the river Rasā and scarcely accessible. Presumably a mountain fastness is intended. The hymn does not clearly refer to any stolen cattle. The envoy of Indra is highly aggressive and simply proposes that the *Panis* surrender their cattle and flee. The *Panis* seek to make friends with Saramā but in vain. They also speak of their stone-paved stronghold and their sharp weapons. Saramā mentions Indra, Angirases and Brhaspati as dreaded warriors.

The hymn sheds more light on the military and diplomatic moves of the times than on the identification of the *Panis*. They appear as powerful antagonists of the gods, rich in cattle, dwelling in a distant stronghold, not spoiling for a fight but prepared to fight if necessary.

Reviewing this evidence, we can see that *Pani* is used both to refer to traders and demons and also more generally to convey the sense of one who does not give and sacrifice. Bothling, Roth and Grassmann are basically correct in supposing that the evolution of meaning lies from 'bargaining' to 'trader' to 'one who does not give for nothing' and hence to 'one who is niggardly and does not sacrifice', thence to 'demon'. In *R.* 10.108 we see the *Panis* as fully mythical beings, the demoniac opponents of the gods and seers, closely allied with Vrtra. In *R.* 1.32.011; 6.20.4; 6.40.2 and 6.51.14 the same meaning is clearly evidenced. In the last of these references, the *Pani* is expressly called a demon, *attrin*. On the other hand, when Bṛbu is extolled as the chief of the *Panis* and as a generous donor, the reference is clearly to human beings. Again, when Indra is implored not to be a *Pani*, the reference could not be to a demon but only to the trader. Or, when *Pani* is called man only for wergild, the reference again is plainly to a class of human beings. Again, when Pusan is entreated to soften the hearts of the *Panis* and make them give, the reference would be more easily construed if it were taken to be to niggardly traders rather than to demons.

The ethos of the religion of sacrifice was the opposite of the ethos of bargaining and trading. The seers held the nobility of character to lie in the capacity of giving freely and spontaneously to men as well as gods. Gods gave by nature, men by the goodness of their nature. This ethos naturally led to the deprecation of the mercantile ethos. It is, however. not necessary to assume that the traders belonged to some hostile tribe. The hostile references to them simply reflect the priestly ethos. The hostility is to trading as an attitude, not to the ethnic communities to which the traders belonged. In later times, agriculture is found similarly condemned in some *dharmasutras*. Otherwise, too, deprecatory references to traders and trading are not uncommon in Indian literature even in later times. The assumption, therefore, that the 'Aryan' tribes took to plunder other non-Aryan trading tribes or their caravans is quite unnecessary. The seers do not propose anywhere to fight or plunder the *Panis.* They only entreat the gods to soften their hearts or to punish them. They are also transfigured into demons and appropriately linked with the spirit of Drought and Sterility since they also seem to accumulate wealth at the expense of others and do not use it to any social or religious purpose.

The *Panis* thus appear to have been originally traders within the Vedic community or *viśaḥ.* Although they were much disliked by the priests, there is no need to suppose that they were actually 'demons' or 'non-aryans'. At the same time, it does not seem that 'Pani' was the normal word for trader in the early Vedic age. It was rather a term of obloquy or opprobrium. The usual term in the later Vedic age was Vaṇij and since the term is found to occur in the *Ṛgvedasamhita* also, it is but natural to assume that it had the same meaning in that age too. Yaska, Roth and Grassmann accept the connection of *Paṇi* and *Vaṇij*, though it has been disputed. Mayrhofer seeks to derive *Vaṇij* from *Van* on the analogy of *Uśij* from *Vaś* and discounts the attempts to connect *Vaṇij* with *Paṇi* or *Vasna* or any Dravidian original. This, however, appears to be an uncalled for attempt at subtlety.

In *R.* 1.112.11 we are told that the trader named Dīrghaśravas was blessed by sweet rain by the Aśvins. He was the son of Uśij, described by Sayana as the wife of Dīrghatamas. Sayana tells us that Dīrghaśravas was a seer who had to become a trader during a severe drought. *R.* 5.45.6 appears to refer to the same incident though more obliquely. It is interesting that *Vaṇij* is here given the epithet, *Vanku.* Sayana explains *Vanku* as *Vanagāmī*, which is dubious. The word occurs at 1.114.14 (*rudram......Vaṇkum kavimavase ni hvayāmahe*), 1.51.11 (*indro vaṇkū vaṇkutarādhi tiṣṭhati*), 8.1.11 (*yat tudat surā etaśam vaṇkū vātassya parṇinā*). Vanku thus appears as the adjective of *Vanij*, Rudra and *hari*.

It seems to mean 'twisting', 'moving tortuously' and may be

connected with *vañc* 'to move crookedly[91].' In any case, the sense of 'movement' is certainly implied in *Vaṅku* and is an appropriate characteristic of the *Vaṇij.* We have, therefore, to suppose that the early Vedic trader was given to travelling and wandering.

Trade in the early Vedic age, thus, could not have simply meant barter among the stationary villagefolk, farmers and cowherds. A number of specialised professions including that of the trader had grown up in that age and products were apparently exchanged not merely among local social groups but between localities. It has even been suggested with considerable reason that maritime trade was not unknown.[92] This suggests a more complex situation than that of simple barter. There is definite evidence of buying and selling and of haggling over the price.[93] Cows are definitely mentioned as a standard of exchange value but this could have referred to an ancient age and in any case could hardly have been suitable for the whole range of trade.[94] The mention of *niṣka* in hundreds as part of a royal benefaction could hardly refer to 'necklaces' and it would be reasonable to assume that it signified some kind of measure of value in gold.[95] In the later Vedic age *hiraṇyam śatamānam* refers to gold pieces weighing a hundred *Kṛṣṇalas*[96] and it is not impossible that *hiranya* in the Ṛgvedic *saṃhita* might already have had a similar meaning. It follows thus that by the side of farmers, ranchers and craftsmen, traders too had a stable position in early Vedic society as part of the commonalty or *viśaḥ*.

In the later Vedic age, instead of recognising that the *Viśaḥ* were now constituted by a number of distinct professional and tribal groups, the new theory of four *Varnas* curiously enough seeks to simplify the situation by bifurcating the *Viśaḥ* into just two classes—Vaiśyas and Śūdras. The Vaiśyas were conceived as the commoners with means, the economic mainstay of society; the Sudras as the servitors. This distinction did not exactly correspond to reality for the Sudras were clearly distinct from the slaves and appear to have included not merely some tribal and professional groups but also some agriculturists.[97] Servitude did not reflect their permanent status either occupationally or legally. The notion of their status as if one of servitude tended to become a social attitude towards a larger number of ill-defined social groups, which in course of time expressed itself in a varying assortment of social disabilities.

It is possible that while the *Vaiśyas* represented the ancient *Viśaḥ*, the free men engaged in economic pursuits in the village and traditionally forming part of the village community, the Sudras represented gradually accumulating new groups in the villages who were not wholly or uniformly admitted to the traditional rights and freedom of the village community.[98] Slaves had in ancient times constituted such a group. Although the *dasas* and Sudras were distinct, the former were in some sense regarded as the examplers for the latter. Unlike the *dasas*, the Sudras owned property[99] but possibly they did not have free-hold in the ancient agricultural land of the villages. Like the *dasas*, the Sudras did not avoid personal service. Again, some of the Sudras appear to have been engaged in ritually unclean professions like hunting and scavenging since they were connected with dead animals and 'waste' products.[100] These several factors tended to contribute to the low estimate of the position of the Sudras endorsed by Brahmanical theory. The lowliness of the Sudra was conceived in ritual or moral rather than economic, ethnic or political terms. This is clear when king Jānaśruti Pautrāyaṇa is referred to as Śūdra in *Ch. up.* because he relies on the appeal to baser instincts. Similarly the *A.B.* refers to *Śaudranyāya*, again meaning a mercenary baseness which disregards moral sentiments.

It seems, then, that the origin of the Sudras is neither ethnic nor economic. They were neither the non-aryans, nor slaves, nor landless labourers produced through the expropriation of landed property. They seem to represent the tribals on the outskirts of the villages, partly beginning to settle down. They might clear some forest land and cultivate it.[101] They might work in the fields of the more prosperous farmers or look after their cattle and be paid in terms of a share. They might continue their traditional vocation connected with the forest and its produce. The word Śūdra itself might have been a tribal designation. The Greeks certainly mention a people called Sodrai and the *Mahabharata* speaks of the *śūdrābhīras* suggesting that the former were, like the latter, tribal.[102]

The ritual uncleanness of the Sudra came to be the basic source of his social disabilities. "That is why, as the area of despised or unclean professions or conditions of life gradually expanded in the course of later history, so did the compass of the Śūdra caste. If the origin of the Sudras was ethnic, their disabilities and the rigours in which they lived, would have tended to diminish with time as ethnic conflict abated giving place to an inevitable social acceptance. Actually the condition of the Sudras appears to have declined in the post-Vedic period. This can be understood only by postulating a cultural and ritual origin which gradually became exaggerated and led to untouchability."[103]

The new social theory of the four *Varnas* expanded the traditional notion of society to include the tribal life around the settlements and at the same time freed it from the particularism of tribes and clans by conceiving society as a universal order.[104] The social order later termed *Caturvarnya* thus arose as a solvent of tribal organisation and identity. In this process, however, some of the devices of tribal organisation were taken over into the *Varna* organisation. Such were the rules of endogamy and exogamy.[105] At the same time, the continuation of tribal organisation in some sections, especially among the Sudras, and the emergence of guilds in the crafts or skilled professions, led to the recognition of hereditary groups of a motley character, later called *Jatis*, within the broad framework of *Varnas.*[106]

No taint of untouchability as yet attached to the Sudras in this age. In fact, some *Sutras* and the *Mbh* suggest that the Sudras even acted as cooks.[107] Besides, personal service thought to be the duty of the Sudras necessarily excluded untouchability. The Sudras were counted as an integral part of the social order, a limb of the Great Purusa. This is also clear from an oft quoted Taittiriya Sruti "*Rucaṁ no a ›hi brāhmaṇeṣu, rucaṁ rājasu naskṛdhi rucaṁ viśyeṣu śūdreṣu mayi dhehi rucā rucam.*" (*T.S.* 7.1.1.6). Sudras also figured in the official and political order. "Pālāgala and Rathakāra, Takṣan and Karmāra are included among the Ratnins who were among the most important representatives of the people in the realm."[108] Vatsa and Kavaṣa who were the sons of a Sudra and a *dāsī* are mentioned as having attained to the status of a seer, despite opposition.[109] The mother of the celebrated Vyasa himself belonged to the tribe of fishermen, which shows that the unions of high-class men with low caste women were not unknown, nor did it impose an absolute stigma on their offspring. At the same time, the Sudras were excluded from the active performance of the sacrifices on the ground that they were created from the feet of the Creator.[110] This tendency towards the ritual exclusion of the Śūdra did not go uncontested as is clear from the *Apaśūdra-dhikaranas* of the two *Mimāṁsās*. The Sudra's right to property was admitted but it was said that even though he might own a lot of cattle, he remained outside the sacrifice.[111] This is plainly a theoretical prescription rather than a descriptive rule. When the Sudra is described as under another's order, to be moved at will, to be beaten at will,[112] it is simply a description of the theoretical content of the idea of servitude, not the description of actual legal right. Much less is it a description of any actual social norm.

Thus, although the Sudra was not regarded outside the pale, nor as an untouchable, and although he was free to acquire wealth and office, Brahmanical theory came to consider him ritually unclean and conceived for him a socially servile status. It also imagined the Sudra as a person who placed wealth above everything else, as comes out from the stories of Jānaśruti and Śunahśepa where a Ksattriya and a Brahmana are reviled as acting like a Sudra. This duality in the conception and status of Sudras apparently arises from the fact that they included some guilds of skilled craftsmen on the one hand and primitive tribes following the primitive professions of the hunter etc. on the other. Among the latter, *Cāṇḍāla* and *Paulkasa* are specially mentioned in later Vedic literature as having a despised status.[113] *Cāṇḍālas* apparently took out corpses and acted as hangmen and were required to dwell outside the villages.[114] The *Paulkasas* sold liquor and were similarly despised.[115] These two tribes or professions were the first to be regarded as untouchables.[115a]

The Vaisyas were described as numerous and wealthy and as the mainstay or subsistence of society. Even though the state exploited their resources, these did not get depleted. While the Brahmanas and the Ksattriyas were real classes in terms of social function, position and consciousness, and were included as such in the *Varna* system, all the residual social groups were included in the Vaisyas and Sudras. A number of occupational groups have been listed in later Vedic literature. The priests (*rtvij*) with numerous sub-divisions according to functions, school and family came to top. *Śrotriya* and *sabhāsad* could also have been Brahmanas as *śrotriya* certainly was in later times. Ksattriya naturally came next but did not include all soldiers or officials. Which of the occupations were included among the Vaisyas and which among the Sudras, if such a differentiation was at all carried through, cannot be decided with any certainty. *Ugra* (police officer), *Jīvagrāha* (police officer), *Grāmanī* (village headman), *Kīnāśa* and *Kṛsīvala* (ploughman) *Kusīdī* (usurer), *Bhāgadugh* (tax-collector), *Vaṇij* (merchant) and *Gopāla* (herdsman) were probably included among the Vaisyas. The rest could have been undecided but in later times they were considered Sudras. Skilled professions mentioned are—*Karmāra* (smith), *Kulāla* (potter) *Maṇikāra* (jeweller), *Takṣan* (carpenter), *Jyākāra* (bowmaker) *Dhmātṛ* (smelter), *Peśitṛ*, *Peśaskāra* (carver or engraver) *Kantakīkārī* and *Bidalakārī* (worker in thorns and basket maker), *Rathakāra* (chariot maker), *Vayitr* (weaver), *Hiraṇyakāra* (worker in gold). *Aritṛ* (rower), *Nāvāja* (boatman), *Nāpita*, *Vaptā* (barber), *Rajayitṛ* (dyer), *Malaga* (washerman), *Upalaprakṣin* (grinder at a mill), *Surākāra* (maker of liquor), *Hastipa* (elephant keeper), *Rathin* (charioteer), *Śrapayitṛ*, *Paktṛ* (cook) were also professional groups involving skill. Among primitive professions and tribes, we find mention of *Kaivarta*, *dāśa*, *dhīvara*, *Bainda*, *Maināla*, *Puñjiṣṭha* (fisherman), *Goghāta*, *Govikartana* (butcher of cows), *Pāśin*, *Mārgayu* (Trapper and Tracker), *Śastṛ* (butcher), *Niṣāda* (boatman), *Cāṇḍāla* and *Paulkasa*. Unskilled professions included *Dvārapa*, *Kṣattṛ* (door keeper), *darvāhāra* (wood gatherer), *Pālāgala* (messenger), *Presya* (servant), *Pariskanda* (footman), and *dāvōṛa* (fire ranger). Entertainers included *Āḍambaraghāta* (drummer), *Talava* (musician), *Pāṇighṇa* (hand clapper), *Vaṁśanartin* (acrobat), *Vīṇāvādī* (lute player). To which Varna, *Gaṇaka* and *Nakṣatradarśa* (mathematician and astronomer) belong is not clear. They could have been Brahmanas. Apart from these, there were a large number of other tribes, ancient and regional. Thus Anga, Vanga, Magadha, Andhra and Pundra, were new tribes of the eastern and southern regions. Ancient regional tribes included Gandhari, Kamboja, Paktha etc. These tribes were already forming settlements (*janapadas*) in the later Vedic age.

Later Vedic society was thus actually divided into a number of professional classes, guilds and tribes. The great change which the theory of *Cāturvarnya*, to use a later term, induced was to superimpose on these differences the notion of a unified social order, membership in which became of greater moment than the particularistic notions of economic class or ethnic or regional clan and tribe. *Caturvarnya* cut across any merely economic, ethnic or regional loyalties and helped the creation of a national society even while society was expanding and becoming more differentiated. Thus national and social unification was produced in India by the idea of *dharma* rather than by poltical conquest and legislation. At the same time, the concept of *Varna* imposed a hierarchical order in a distinctive sense explained earlier on the social organism. This hierarchy was not based on conquest or wealth, nor on ethnic or tribal distinctions. It was based on a system of values, which necessarily implies a hierarchy. Spiritual knowledge was deemed the highest value and the real source of authoritative direction and law. Next to it came the power of protecting the social order, i.e. political authority and power. Economic values came at the bottom. The transformation of intellectual and political functionaries into elite hereditary classes was hardly avoidable in those times. In any case, but for these hereditary 'classes', Vedic traditions could hardly have been preserved across troubled millennia.[116]

Although *Varna* (class), *Silpa* (craft) and *Jati* (ethnic or hereditary group) were conceptually distinct, the first of these took precedence over the others as it was based on the abstract notion of social function and aptitude (*karman* and *guna*). Nevertheless, it gradually tended to be interpreted as a hereditary group or 'race'. Thus the tribal rules of maintaining identity by regulating marriage etc., came to be adopted by the *Varnas*. But while the number of *Varnas* was only four, the *Jātis* were actually numerous and the question was bound to be raised—if only four *Varnas* had been originally created, how did so many *Jātis* come about? There was only one possible answer—the *Jātis* have arisen from the intermixture of the *Varnas* and the *Jātis* resulting therefrom. This answer was adopted and the concept of *Varnasamkara* gradually elaborated in the *Dharmasūtras* and the *Smṛtis*. Since the device was totally fictitious, it led to an even greater divergence between social theory and social reality. At the same time, it affected social reality primarily through shaping the social attitude towards it.

REFERANCES

1. *Meaning and Process of Culture*, p. 85.
2. For the role of archaeological records vis-a-vis social history, see my Presidential Address to the Indian Archaeological Society, Dharwar Session, 1978.
3. On *Mitra and Varuna*, cf. K. Chattopadhyaya, *Vedic Religion*, pp. 46 ff. While Varuna protects the law, Indra kills the enemies, *R*. 7.85.3,
4. e.g., *R*. 5. 27.6 : Indra and Agni maintain the high and unaging dominion in the heaven like the sun; *R*. 1. 21. 5-they are the great lords of assembly (tā mahāntā sadaspatī), They lead the five people- *R*. 1.108. 8; 5. 86.2.
5. e.g., *R*. 3.59, 1.136, 1.137 etc.
6. *R* 8 22. 6, 1. 117, 21, *Av*. 10.6. 12, *R*. 1.117.21.
7. *SB* 4. 1. 4.2 as translated by Coomaraswamy *Spiritual Authority and Temporal Power in the Indian Theory of Government*, Indian ed. 1978, pp. 6-7.
8. It has been suggested that the Indo-European Society contained an ancient distinction between the nobles and the commoners-cf. CHA[3] Vol. I, pt. II, p. 863.

   Prof. Dumezil, *L' ideologie Tripartie des Indo Européens*, Brussels, 1958, has suggested an ancient tripartite division of Indo-European society. He has been followed by Benveniste, *Le vocabulaire des institutions indo-europeennes*, Paris, 1969, Eng. tr. 1973, and Renou. See Gonda, *Triads in the Veda*, pp. 125-77.

The mere fact of differentiation leaves its conception obscure. It is also necessary to point out that Dumzil's distinction of 'sovereignty', 'war', and 'growth' totally misses the Indian distinction of *Brahman* and *Ksattra*. Benveniste traces the original meaning of *Brahman* to 'ceremonial form' (*Indo-European Language and Society*, p. 231), but he admits that *Brahman* is a purely Indic word (Ib. p. 232). It is not clear why the Iranian terms should be regarded more faithful to the original picture. The Iranian *pistras* could be as much Iranian as Indian *varnas* Indian. Neither need conform closely to the 'Original' Indo-European' provided the phrase had a definite meaning.

9. CAH[3] I, pt. 1. 1. c.
10. Cf. *Vedic Index* I, pp. 377-78.
11. e.g. *R.* 5.62.1; 6.73.1;
12. Cf. Coomaraswamy, (ed. Lipse), Vol. II: '*Vedic Examplarism*'.
13. Cf. Jayaswal, *Hindu Polity*, Pt. II, p. 35.
14. The divine rulers Mitra and Varuna thus constitute a pair.
15. For the best exposition of this aspect of Vedic thought, see Coomaraswamy, *Spiritual Authority and Temporal Power in the Indian Theory of Government*.
16. Cf. Gonda, op. cit., pp. 143, 151-52.
17. Cf. *Majjhima* : Gopaka moggalana; *Sutta Nip*: Kasibharadvaja.
18. This would answer Gonda's remarks, op. cit., pp. 153-156, Rathakara and Nisada were specialised or distinct groups but neither 'classes' nor separate 'estates'.
19. Cf. *R.* 7.100.4; 7.101.5.
20. *Anna* is the *devata* of *R.* I. 187, *Av*, 6.7; 7.5; 6.142 also refer to the growth of food. While the Ṛgvedic Sukta refers to Soma, the *Av.* 6.142 refers to *Yava-Ucchrayasva bahur bhava svena mahasā yava. Av.* 11.3. refers to *Odana*.
21. Macdonell, *Vedic Mythology*; cf. Bergaigne, *Vedic Religion*, Vol. I. p. 159.
22. Cf. *R.* 1.4.7.6; 1.117.1; On Madhu, see Lüders, *Varuṇa*.
23. Eg., *R.* 9.33.
24. e.g.-*Satapatha*, 1.6.4.5: "*esa vai somo devānām annam—Saihaiva āpaścausadhīśca praviśati*; "Ib. 1.6.4.15 *ad enamadbhya osadhībhyah sambhṛtyāhutibhyo dhi janayati.* Ibid. 16.4.16: *abhiksnam ha vā asyāmusmin loke annam bhavati.*"
25. Cf. BG. 4. which describes the sacrificial cycle as a part of the cosmic cycle "*Yajñād bhavati parjanyah parjanyād annasambhavah*". cf. Bergaigne, op. cit. I. p. 31.
26. See, e.g. *Vedic Mythology*.
27. e.g. *R.* 1.24.7: 'Varuna is called *rajan*; 1.32.15. Indra is called *rajan*; 1.59.3-Agni called *raja* among men.
28. e.g. *R.* 9.65.16; 1.91.5.
29. e.g. *R.* 1.32.15-the king rules over the Carsanis just as the rim encompasses the spokes of the wheel; 1.5-4.7 the king tends the *jana*;
30. e.g. *R.*1.174.1.

31. e.g. *R.* 1.100 lauds Indra marutvan; 1.170.2 speaks of Maruts as the brothers of Indra. See also Macdonell, *Vedic Mythology*.
32. e.g. *R.* 5.59.6-'*te ajyesthā akanisthāsa udbhido madhyamāso mahasā vi vāvrdhuh sujātāso* ...' Their noble birth and equality are asserted.
33. The views expressed in the *Vedic Index* may be contrasted with those in *Hindu Polity*.
34. *R.* 10.173; *Av.* 3.4.2.
35. *Av.* 7.12.
36. e.g. Jayaswal, *Hindu Polity*, Vol. I. p. 18.
37. See J.P. Sharma, *Republics in Ancient India*, pp. 21-22.
38. Cf. *Vedic Index* Vol. II, p. 211, fn. 6.
39. The relationship of mediaeval French monarchy with the Estates may be recalled.
40. Cf. Muir, *Original Sanskrit Texts*, Vol. I. pp. 248-59. Muir concludes "The word *Brahman*. . . appears to have the sense of 'sage', 'poet'; next that of 'officiating priest', and ultimately that of a 'special description of priest' (ibid. p. 258). He does not appreciate the difficulty of placing these semantic variations within a definite *chronological* sequence.
41. *R.* 9.112.3.
42. Cf. Muir, *Original Sanskrit Texts*, Vol. 1, p. 263.
43. Cf. D.D. Kosambi's elaborate attempt to connect the *gotras* with totemic groups.
44. Zimmer, *Altindisches Leben*, pp. 185 ff; Muir, op. cit., Vol. I, Chap. III; *Vedic Index*, Vol. II, pp. 248-42;
45. Ludwig, *Ṛgveda* (tr.) 3.237-43; Nidenberg, ZDMG, 51, pp. 267 ff; *Vedic Index*, Vol. II, pp. 250-52.
46. *Vedic Index* II, p. 251.
47. Muir, op. cit., Vol. II, pp. 293-95.
48. Quoted in *Vedic Age*, p. 222.
49. e.g. in his Naqshi-Rustam Inscription..
50. *The Histories*, Penguin ed. p. 439.
51. See Mayrhofer, *A Concise Etymological Sanskrit Dictionary*, under 'Ari', 'Arya' and 'Aryaman'. It may be noted that Wüst connected 'Arya' with lat. *arare*. Dr. V.S. Pathak traces *Ārya* from *ara* with the original meaning of 'plough'—*Indo-Soviet Joint Seminar at Allahabad*, Feb. 82.
52. *Nirukta*, 6.26.
53. Thus see Sayana ad *R.* 6.22.10; 1.59.2; On *R.* I. 15.8—Skandasvami comments "*Āryān sādhuvṛttān yogaparārthah*'. On *R.* 5.34.6 he equates Ārya to *Svāmī*. On *R.* 34.9 he says "*Āryam uttamam Varnam*", On 10.49.3 "*Āryam pūjyam*". On 8.10.3.1, "*Āryasyottama-varnasya*", On 1.130.8, he says "*āryam araniyam sarvairgantavyam*". Same meaning in 1.157.5 and 10.102.3.
54. *Sakuntala*. Act. I.
55. *Arthashastra*. 3.13.
56. Cf. Rhys Davids, *Pali Dictionary* under '*Arivo*' where the commentator is blamed for not knowing the original racial connotation of the term!.

57. Muir, op. cit. II, p. 359, has sought to collect the Vedic passages supposed to prove the ethnicist interpretation, but they are ambiguous.
58. K. Chattopadhyaya, *Studies*, Vol. I, pp. 206.
59. Sayana—"*Yaśca dāsam varnam śudrādikam yadvā dāsam upaksapayitāram adharam nikrṣṭam asuram guhā guhāyām gudhasthāne narake vākah.*"
60. Sayana explains "*ubhau varnau varanīyāvākārav kāmañca tapaśca pupoṣa.*"
61. Muir, l.c., interprets this to refer to the conflict of Aryans and non-aryans.
62. "*Aryah svāmī yatheccham dāsam dāsakarmānamjanam nayati svavaśam*".
63. Sayana interprets differently, '*svah svātmanāryam preryam jyotih—manave manusyebhyah*".
64. Sayana equates to *karmānuṣṭhānakrt*, *dāsa to karmahīna* and *vrtra* to *upadravra.*
65. Sayaṇa—"*āryā balavadhin Krtāndāsa dāsairasuraih Krtāu vrtrānyu—Upadravān.*"
66. Sayaṇa interprets as pious and impious human enemies.
67. Sayana interprets as in the case of 6.22.10.
68. R. 7.86.7 '*aram dāsona mīdhuṣe karāni*'.
69. K. Chattopadhyaya, *l.c.*
70. Mayrhofer surmises *abhidāsati* to be denominative from *dāsa* op. cit. *dāsa.*
71. With *dāsa* and *dasyu* may be compared Avestan *dah* and *dahyu* and Old Persian *dahyu.* These comparisons have been 'people outside the pale'—Mayrhofer, op. cit. 'dasyu'. But this could be derivative from 'enemy', the human parallel to the 'demons'.
72. *R.*I. 96.5; 1.73.7; 1.92.10; 1.113.2 etc.
73. *R.* 2.12.4; 3.34.9.
74. *Vanna* appears in Pali for colour, appearance, lustre, beauty, expression, social grade or class, kind timbre, praise, reason—*Pali Dictionary.* A well-known passage from *Majjhima* says that among the Greeks there are only two *varnas, Arya* and *dasa.* Here *varna* is simply 'social class'.
75. The *Purusa-sukta* does not use the word *varna* but only names the Brahmanas etc. who together constitute the Man. The *Satapatha,* however, categorically states : *catvāro vai varnāh* (Vol. I, p. 638).
76. See *supra.*
77. *R.* 4.57.8 : "*Śunaṁ nah phālā vi Krṣanta bhūmim Śunam Kīnāśā abhiyantu vāhaih Śunam parjanyo madhunā payobhih Śunāsīrā śunam asmāsu dhattam.*"
78. *R.* 10.34.4 : *Krsim it Krsasva*
79. Ibid. 10.72,2
80. Ibid. 5.95.
81. *Upalapraksinī* Ib. 9-117.3.
82. Mayrhofer, *Worterbuch*, under *Paṇayah..*

83. Grassmann, *Worterbuch* under *Panis*.
84. *Vedic Index*, I. p. 472.
85. Ibid. pp. 472-73.
86. Ibid. p. 472.
87. *Nirukta*. 2.17.
88. Cf. Mayrhofer, *Worterbuch*, under *Panate*.
89. *Vedic Index*, I. p, 473, fn. 20 is not correct in saying that *Panis* occur only once in *mandala* viii.
90. Vide Mayrhofer, op. cit. under Bekanata.
91. Grassmann derives it from Vak and refers to *R.* 7 21. 2—*tvad vavakre rathyo na dhenā.* He translates Vanku as *sich tummelnd.* But he himself derives *vankri* from Vanik and explains the meaning 'rib' as referring to 'bending'. The ribs are 'bent', twisted and thus Vankri would support the meaning suggested above from *Vanku.*
92. *R.* 1. 56. 2 says "*samudraṁ na samcaraṇe saniṣyavah*". Sayana explains, *saniṣyavah* as *Vanijah* and says '*Yathā nāvā samudram adhirohanti*'. The interpretation of *samudra* has been questioned but without much reason. *R.* 7.95.2 speaks of Sarasvati going from the mountain to the sea (*yāti giribhya ā samudrāt*). The *Vedic Index* II, p. 432 admits that the story of Bhujya suggests marine navigation. See *Vedic Age*, p. 400; P. L. Bhargava, *India in the Vedic Age*, pp. 70 ff.
93. *R.* 4.25.9-10 are well-known for mentioning haggling about price or *Vasna* and the sale of Indra for cows., *R.* 8.1.5 uses *śulka* for price *R.* 10.34. 3—"*aśvasyeva jarato vasnyasya*. 7.82.6 "*mahe śulkāya*. . .,,
94. Thus in *R.* 4.25.1 Indra is to be sold for cows. In *R.* 8.1.5, he is not to be sold for a hundred, or thousands or ten thousand. These figures perhaps do not refer to cows but to *niṣkas*.
95. *R.* 1. 126.2—"*Śatam rājño nādhamānasya niṣkān*. . . ."
96. Cf. Dr. Pathak's *Presidential Address* to the *A.I. Numismatic Conference*, June, 1981 on the possible numismatic significance of *Lopāmudrā*.
97. It may be recalled the ancient Ionian society had a four-fold division which included apart from priests and warriors, the farmers, and the artisans (Benvenist, op. cit p. 235). The last would correspond to the Sudras.
98. Cf. R.S. Sharma, *The Sudras in Ancient India*. p. 40, where it is accepted that the Sudras included 'Aryan's' as well as 'non-aryans' and that they emerged from 'external' and internal conflicts leading to dispossession. While the idea of an ethnically mixed (origin) is plausible provided one presupposes the hypothesis of 'Aryan' invasion the hypothesis of dispossession is purely speculative.

Prof. Sharma's position in the first edition of his work is, however, far more critical than that of D.D. Kosambi who declares the Sudras to have been "helots who belonged to the tribe or clan group as a whole in much the same manner as the tribal cattle". (op. cit. p. 86). The Spartan analogy is as baseless as the fiction of 'tribal cattle'. The *Sudras*, in fact, owned cattle in the later Vedic age. See below.

99. Cf. *Tandya* 6.1.11, which assumes that a Sudra might be rich in cattle, also where the Vaisya is connected with cattle—e.g. T.S. 2.5. 10.2, 7.1.1.5; *Tandya* 6.1.10.
100. Such were Nisadas, Candalas and Paulkasas—*Vajasaneyi sam*—30.21, *T:B.* 3.4.171; *Br. Up.* 4.1.22 *T.S.* 4.5.42, *A.B.* 8.11.
101. It may be recalled that the *Arthasastra* 2.1., recommended that in new clearings, rural settlements should have a majority of Sudra cultivators.
102. *Śūdrābhīrān prati dveṣāt yatra naṣṭā sarasvatī.*
103. G.C. Pande in *History of the Panjab.* "Vol. I, "Social and Economic Condition in the Later Vedic Age".
104. Thus the *Purusasukta* conceives the Varnas to be the divisions of the Purusa who is all this and what was and will be. Social philosophy is here grounded in cosmology.
105. This has been commented upon by a number of earlier writers—See Hutton, *Caste in India*. pp. 169 ff; Ibbetson, *Punjab Castes.*
106. Cf. Nesfield *Brief View of the Caste System*, of which the attempt to connect the social status of a caste with the evolutionary stage of its craft is untenable.
107. Cf. Kane, *Hist. of the Dh. S.*, Vol. II, Part I, pp.
108. *History of the Punjab*, Vol I, .*l.c.*
109. Cf. *Vedic Index.*
110. *Tāṇḍya*, 6.1.11.
111. Vide Supra.
112. *Aitareya Sruti* quoted above.
113. Cf. *Ch. up.* 5.10.7.
114. Kane, op. cit. Vol. II, Pt. I. p. 81.
115. Ibid. p. 88.
115a. Cf. my Inaugural Address to the National Seminar on Untouchability held in BHU, March, 1989.
116. Cf. T.S. Eliot, *Notes towards the Definition of Culture* (1972), p. 48.

10

Socio-Historical Order : Post-Vedic

In the early post-Vedic age, the Buddhist and Jaina records show a clear difference between the Brahmanical concept of the *Varnas* and the actual divisions of social reality. The Varna system is recognised as one of hoary antiquity and as part of traditional Brahmanical belief. The rise of the *mahajanapadas* and town-life had, however, led to many changes in the composition of social classes and groups. As a result, the traditional Varna system was thus subjected to much criticism. There was a new independene of thought, ascetic as well as materialistic, and traditional Brahmanical conceptions were assailed in diverse ways.[1]

Fick's admirable analysis of the *Jatakas* reveals that the Brahmanas alone seemed to constitute a caste in the sense of their own theory.[2] It is true that the original *Jatakas* do not survive as narratives and it is the *Jātakaṭṭhavaṇṇanā* of a later date that constitutes the actual source of Fick's analysis. Nevertheless, a good deal of the material in the commentary must derive from the ancient tradition which accompanied the canonical literature into Ceylon. It is, therefore, not without value if used with caution and general support from other and more ancient parts of the canon. It may be noted that the non-mention of Asoka in the canonical literature taken together with Asoka's obvious familiarity with it strongly confirm the pre-Mauryan dating of the canon.[3]

In the age of Buddha, Brahamanahood depended on birth and the Brahmanas were intensely self-conscious and proud. The Brahmanas of the north (Udicya) claimed to be the purest. They functioned as priests and teachers and as counsellors of the kings. They not only studied the sacred literature and ritual in its diverse schools and branches, but also the sciences of astrology, physiognomy and omens and interpreted dreams and signs. They married and ate within their own caste and claimed to be the premier caste. In the north-east, however, it seems that the condition of the Brahmanas was degraded and challenged by the Ksattriyas. The *Vasettha sutta* recounts the complaint of a Brahmana against the rude behaviour of the Sakyas. The Buddha, however, is shown to argue that the Ksattriyas are actually superior because they follow a stricter standard of purity in avoiding inter-caste marriages.[4] The *Bhaddasala Jataka* shows a conflict between two views on inter-caste marriage. The stricter view held by the king of Kosala denied the status of Ksattriya to the offspring of a non-Ksattriya mother but the Bodhisattva recalls the more ancient tradition that the caste of the mother was immaterial.[5]

The conflict among the Ksattriyas and the Brahmanas is apparent in Buddhist and Jain literature. This literature consistently upholds the superiority of the Ksattriyas over the Brahmanas and runs down the latter as greedy and spiritually ignorant. At the same time, the Buddha is stated to delineate the ideal of the true Brahmana whose status is based on conduct, not birth. Such a Brahmana is the spiritual ideal of mankind.[6] It has been argued that the conflict between the Brahmanas and the Ksattriyas went back to the later Vedic Age and that the Upanisads reveal the Brahmanas taking lessons from the Ksattriyas.[7] This, however, appears an exaggeration. Although the Ksattriyas were an educated class not only conscious of their status, but interested in philosophy in an enlightened manner, it would hardly be correct to take the Buddhist and Jain opinions on the relative status of the Ksattriyas and the Brahmanas as reflecting a general social opinion of the times.

It is, however, clear from the Buddhist literature that the Brahmanas were engaged in a number of professions which theory did not normally countenance for them. The *Dasabrahmana Jataka* mentions ten kinds of Brahmanas—*tikicchakasamā, pariçārakasamā, niggāhaka°, khānugghāta°*, *vānijaka°*, *ambatthavessehi samā*, *goghātakasamā*, *samā gopanisadehi*, *luddaka°*, *malamajjana-samā*. These are 'dasa brāhmanajatiyo'.[8] This suggests for the Brahmanas such diverse professions as medicine, service, trade, animal slaughter, hunting, scavenging, etc. The comparisons, however, need not mean the actual adoption of these professions but only the acquiring of their characteristics in personality. Some Brahmanas could have been like hunters or scavengers without actually being hunters or scavengers. Despite exaggeration, however, there is no doubt that the Brahmanas did engage in other professions including agriculture. Some of them had large estates and cultivated them with the help of labourers or leaseholders. Others with smaller holdings cultivated them with the help of their own family. Brahmanas not infrequently acted as the priests and counsellors of the kings and the epics reveal them as teachers in the use of arms. The *Jatakas* also show them occasionally engaged in trade and other professions.[9]

The Ksattriyas sought to ensure the purity of descent and were proud of their position as a ruling class. They are also represented as a highly educated class. The young princes are shown in the *Jatakas* as going to Taksasila and learning the sciences (*silpas*).[10] Apart from the rulers and their scions, it would be natural to suppose that many civil and military officers of the realms were included in the Ksattriyas[11] just as some of them are shown in other vocations in the *Jatakas* and elsewhere.[12] In the republics, the Ksattriyas constituted a numerous ruling aristocracy. The *Arthasastra* distinguishes those who adopted the title of king' (*rājaśabdopajivinaḥ*) and 'those who lived by agriculture, trade and cattle-rearing as well as the use of arms (*vārtāśastropajivinaḥ*)[13]'. The former apparently included the Ksattriyas of the north-eastern republics. We know that among the Sakyas, for example, every one called himself a *raja* and among the Licchavis there are said to have been 7707 different representatives of the ruling families.[14] Agricultural and other labour in these territories was apparently done by people of other castes. In a sense these 'republics' were autonomous federated states of different Ksattriya clans. In the north-west, on the other hand, the Ksattriya clans not merely governed themselves but also looked after the economic and military life of the realm. Here the caste distinctions were apparently much thinner.

As far as the upper castes were concerned, we thus, have a situation which varied according to region. In the north-west, there were numerous martial-cum-agricultural tribes calling themselves Ksattriyas. In the north in Kuru-Pancala region, we have an area of Brahmanical orthodoxy. In the east, we have Ksattriya republics which were specially concerned to emphasise the purity and superiority of its caste and lineage. Brahmanical opinion, on the other hand, held these Ksattriyas in low esteem, a sentiment which was fully reciprocated.

While the 'Vaisya' appears to have been a theoretical concept, the actual classes were of traders and bankers, generally called 'householders' or *Gahapati* in early Buddhist and Jain literature.[15] Apparently the term, despite its extensive denotation, was conventionally used for the moneyed people in the towns. They were the 'householders' par excellence for the Buddhist and Jain mendicants. Possibly, the richer agricultural households in the villages were included but they were not so important in this context.[16]

The rise of a merchant to affluence from poverty through enterprise is illustrated in the *Cullakasetthi Jataka*.[17] The merchants banded together in guilds and organised caravans (*sārtha*).[18] They were led by Eldermen or Jetthakas and a chief or Pramukha. The *seṭthi* was a merchant and banker and also an important official at the court. The wealth of the commercial class finds much exaggerated mention in the Buddhist and Jain literature. Its trade extended even across the seas to Mesopotamia as appears from the *Baveru-jataka*.[19] We know that a part of Alexander's army had returned from India along the coast of the Persian gulf. In fact, Indian trading in this region went back to the Harappan times.

The Sudras as such hardly find mention in this literature. The *Mugapakkha Jataka*[20] speaks of the eighteen guilds. A number of specialised and organised crafts existed and no social stigma attached to many of them. The *Sucijataka* speaks of the wonderful manufacture of a microscopically thin needle by a smith.[21] We hear of *Kammāra-gāma* and of *Vaḍḍhakigāma* and in the cities of *dantakāra-vīthi*.[22]

Below these, however, lay what the *Patimokha-Vibhanga* describes as *hina-silpas* and *hina-jatis*, i.e. despised crafts and ethnic groups. "*Sippaṁ nāma dve sippāni-hīnaṁ ca sippaṁ Ukkatthaṁ ca sippaṁ, Hīnam nāma sippaṁ-nalakārasippaṁ. Kumbha-Kārasippaṁ, Cammakārasippaṁ, Nahāpitasippaṁ, tesu tesu vā pana janapadesu aññātaṁ avaññātam helitaṁ paribhūtaṁ acittīkataṁ. Etaṁ hināṁ nāma sippaṁ Ukkatthaṁ nāma sippaṁ-Muddā, gananā, lekhā, tesu tesu pana janapadesu aññātām anavaññātaṁ, ahelitaṁ aparibhūtaṁ cittīkataṁ-Etaṁ ukkaṭṭhaṁ nāma sippām.*"[23]

The higher crafts relate to trade, banking and accounting. The 'low' crafts are either primitive or unclean such as road-making, potter's art, leather-work, barbers' art etc.

The *hina jatis* are thus enumerated- "*Jāti nāma dve jātiyo-hīnā ca jāti ukkatthā ca jāti. Hīnā nāmā jāti-caṇḍālajāti, veṇajāti, nesādajāti. rathakārajāti, pukkusa jāti. Esā hīnā nāma jāti. Ukkatthā nāma jāti khattiyā jāti, Brāhmaṇa jāti.*"[24]

It is surprising to find the *rathakāra* in this company. A number of *Jatakas* attest to the low condition of the Candalas. While contact between them and the higher castes was not restricted, eating with them or marrying with them was looked down upon as a ritual lapse from the upper class status. Even their sight was sometimes considered a bad omen. They lived in separate villages outside the city and had a distinctive dress, and even 'dialect'.[25] But the Buddhists and Jains often take their side. The Bodhisattva is many times born as a Candala. The Jains represent the monk Heriesabala as condemned by the Brahmanas as a Candala.[26]

The Jains uphold the dogma that no Arahamta, Cakkavatti or Baladeva could be born in a Brahmana family which is equated to *Antakula*, *Panta*°, *Tuccha*°, *Dalidda*°, *Kivina*° and *Bhikkhāga*°. The pure lineages (*visuddha-jāti-kula-vamsas*) are *Uggakula*, *Bhoga*° *Rāiṇṇa*°, *Ikkhāga*° or *Khattiya*.[77] The luxurious life of the nobility meant "food at the time of food, drink at the time of drink, sleep... having bathed being garlanded with ornaments of gold and jewels...... painted with sandal...... enjoying all the pleasures of human life (*māṇuasagāim*, *bhoga-bhogāin bhunjamāṇe*)." Next to the nobility were the Gahavai of whom the *Uvasagadasao* gives a vivid picture.[28] Setthi and Satthavaha are placed besides "*rāīsara-talavaramadambiya-Kodumbiya*".[29] The wealth of the Gāhāvai was divided between *Nihāna* (hoarding), *Vaḍḍhi* (lending), *Pavitthara* (investment of real estate?) and maintaining ranches (*Vayas*). "The last two items suggest the important conclusion that the rich man of town had not yet severed his connections with land." The luxry of the rich merchant was no less than that of the nobleman.

It would seem then that the Vedic Varna system was clearly unreal as far as functional groups were concerned in the age of Buddha. The Varnas constituted a purely social and ritual hierarchy totally unconnected with wealth and occupation. The Varna system was no longer a system of even functional, let alone economic classes. This was the result of a number of historical changes. The Brahmanas appear to have become too numerous to be absorbed wholly in teaching and priestcraft. Similarly, the Ksattriyas were no longer simply a ruling class. As for the Vaisyas and Sudras, they had never constituted homogenous functional classes even in the Vedic age. The occupational diversity of the upper two Varnas must have partly arisen from the growth of town life, trade and industry. The growth of professional armies and administrators must have contributed to the process. The anti-Brahmanical stances of the republican Ksattriyas and ascetic religions in the north-east must also have contributed to the difficulty of the Brahmanas in being secure within their traditional vocations. While the growth of trade made the Vaisyas a more important class, the diversification of crafts and the geographical expansion of settlements added more occupational and tribal groups to the Sudras. While the status of some of the older groups like the Rathakaras declined, the growth of guilds must have in effect raised the social position of many craftsmen.

Buddhist texts distinguish between the concepts of *Varṇa*, *Jāti* and *Śilpa*. *Varna* now corresponds most closely to 'class'. This comes out strikingly in a passage of *Majjhima* where it is said that among the Yonas and Kamobojas there were only two Varnas, freemen (*Ariyo*) and slaves (*dāso*) and that the former could become the latter and *vice versa*.[30] *Jati*, on the other hand, meant a hereditary caste or race. Whereas the original basis of Varna was held to be function or character,

Jati was based on birth and had a wider application than to human castes merely. That castes are not species, was pointed out by the Buddhists as a criticism of their hereditary character. *Silpas* were crafts but formed the basis of occupational groups. The hierarchy of high and low pervaded all these three kinds of groups—*Varna*, *Jati* and *Silpa*. The hierarchy was essentially as conceived in the Brahmanical Varna system except that the relative position of the Brahmanas and the Ksattriyas was disputed in favour of the Ksattriyas in the republican north-east. The Buddhists and the Jains criticised the hereditary character of the hierarchy but accepted the notion of a hierarchy based on merit or excellence. They further agreed that while moral excellence was available to all, those who possessed spiritual knowledge or exercised political authority constituted the social elite. Thus non-hereditary Brahmanas and Sramanas would be the highest elite, and the ruling aristocracy would come next. Buddhist and Jain views, however, had little effect on the prevailing hierarchy. Brahmanas remained hereditary. The Ksattriyas did not become the top class in general social estimation. The Vaisyas, despite their patronage of the heterodox movements, remained in their traditional place. The only change in the social structure was the emergence of a new class of mendicants outside the caste system.

It is difficult to connect the rise and spread of Sramanism with the development of urban life or the break-up of 'clan' republics though townsmen and clansmen doubtless contributed to the Sramanic following. The Sramanas and their patrons were drawn from almost all sections of society—Ksattriya clansmen and learned Brahmanas, rich merchants and affluent craftsmen, poor slaves and servants, outcastes, criminals and prostitutes.[31] One cannot, therefore, think of Sramanism as having any specific class affiliation. Nor do we know whether any specific historical situations helped the growth of that attitude of disenchantment with life which underlies Sramanism. Its propounders, unlike the Hebrew prophets, certainly did not appeal to any historical situations or experience but only to the impermanence, bondage and unhappiness of life. These are perennial and universal features of human experience, not the feautres of histcrically conditioned social experience. It is, of course, possible that a certain social tradition may so mis-educate a people as to prevent them from discerning the Noble Truth of Suffering, a situation to which the modern age bears the most eloquent testimony. In the case of the age of Buddha, it is obvious, that the ancient Vedic tradition with its robust optimism had somehow declined in its social effectiveness. Perhaps the faith and discipline which that tradition required had been gradually undermined by the growth of abstraction and doubt, wealth and luxury, arbitrary authority and servility. In this sense, the spread of the Sramanic tradition may have been aided by the impact of the growth of civilization on the ancient cultural and social traditions of the Vedic age. This does not, however, affect the fact that Sramanism as a spiritual tradition must be held to date from an immemorial age. As is generally known, the social impact of Sramanism was not revolutionary. It challenged the supremacy of the Brahmanas and their hereditary position and disregarded all caste distinctions within the monastic fold. Nevertheless, the doctrine of Karman which it upheld so strenuously seemed to morally reconcile the individual to the social injustice of his situation. If Brahmanical thought had sought to justify the social order in terms of divine creation, Sramanic thought tended to think of it as the result of human activity and propensities but it held the individual's present situation to be determined by his own past actions. It sought the individual's psychic transcendence of social reality rather than its social transformation through historic action.

The value of the *Mahābhārata* as a source of social testimony is as undoubted as is the difficulty of locating it in time. Modern historians have no doubt that the *Mbh* is not the unitary work of a single author but has resulted from the agglomeration of heterogenous material over a long time. Thus Winternitz claiming to speak on behalf of critical historians of literature declares "The *Mahābhārata* as a whole is a literary monster.[32]" The different parts of this conglomeration are held to be widely separated in time and to range from the 4th century B.C. to the 4th century A.D.[33] The termini rest on the one hand on the mention of the Yavanas in the *Mbh* and on the other, on the mention of the *Śatasāhasrī saṁhitā* in records of the Gupta age. This view of Winternitz has been lifted as such and incorporated in the *Age of Imperial Unity*,[34] where, however, it has been added that the battle of Mahābhārata was a historical event datable between 1400 B.C. and 1000 B.C. and that the original epic probably goes back to the Brahmana period.[35] A recent re-assessment of the problem in the light of the growth of archaeological information does not seem to lead to any fresh consensus.[36]

The disunity and heterogeneity of the *Mahābhārata* have been over-emphasized by scholars whose sense of critical history exceeds the acuity of their literary and philosophical perception. It may suffice to mention that Sukhthankar, the greatest *Mahābhārata* scholar of our times, came out of a long critical travail to believe at last in the meaningful unity of the *Mahābhārata*. Doubtless episodes and verses have been added and embroidered and *ākhyānas* and *Upākhyānas* have been interpolated and thus the size of the epic has grown. Nevertheless, the continental unity of the work has never been lost and was always clearly perceived by ancient literary critics.

The reference to the Yavanas does not mean a date posterior to the invasion of Alexander since the Yavanas were known earlier in the north-west of India.[37] Similarly a marginal acquaintance with Buddhism may not mean anything more than up-dating touches of the 5th century B.C. or later. On the other hand, the frequency of un-Paninean usages, and the marginal role of urban sophistication for the greater part suggest the early *Mahājanapada* age as the time when the epic was composed. If the original epic was composed not long after the end of the Vedic age on the basis of heroic legends and ballads but in moral retrospect, its expansion through the interpolation of other bardic tales and the systematic expansion of philosophic material, could be put during the *mahajanapada* and the early Imperial Ages c. 700 B.C.—300 B.C., that is from the age of Janaka to that of the *Arthaśāstra*. Such a view has been condemned as 'violating "every known principle of historical criticism" (CHI, Vol. I, p. 261). This would be true only if fashionable opinions were to be identified with principles. There is no reason to suppose that the original epic was heroic in the Greek sense and hence bereft of religious, philosophical and *smṛti* material. Anandavardhana saw the essence of the epic in *Śāntarasa* which depends on the feeling of resignation and spiritual discernment.[38] Sri Aurobindo has emphasized its vigorous intellectual note[39] while Sukthankar has pointed out the central place of the *Gita* in the epic.[40] Thus while it is likely that religious, philosophical and legal material in the epic was elaborated in course of time, the whole of it need not be held to be an extraneous and inconsistent later addition.

From the point of view of social history, the epic contains relatively earlier and later material ranging over the later Vedic and early post-Vedic ages coming down to the age of Buddha. As Hopkins has remarked "It is true that our verdict as to which is early and which is late must in a measure be based upon purely a priori assumptions; while it should, where this is possible, certainly be dependent upon an intimate acquaintance with the literature preceding and following the epic, for many of the threads of our poem are older than its present literary form".[41]

From his study of the position of the ruling class in the *Mahābhārata*, Hopkins[42] concludes that in practice the Kṣattriyas must have enjoyed a position superior to that of the Brahmanas because the former represented the power of the state while the latter were without organisation and dependent on the former.[43] This argument, however, is of too general a nature and goes far beyond the epics. It is true again that the Brahmanas have never been organised as a church while the ruling class or caste would naturally have the control of the state apparatus. This does not, however, mean that the social power, position and esteem of the Brahmanas was lower than that of the Ksattriyas who had political power. It was, in fact, the unique feature and achievement of the Varna system not only to place spiritual power above the temporal but to so educate public opinion that the Brahmanas did not need to organise and struggle for their position. But what they claimed was social eminence, not political power. That the former did not depend on the latter is the unique feature of Varna society as distinguished from class society as known elsewhere.[44] In the *Mbh* itself, the standard opinion expressed is that Brahman and Ksattra constitute two mutually cooperating estates where the former is the more eminent but the latter is more powerful, physically and politically. The power of the Brahmana lies in his possession of a sacred and magical lore and his title to respect lies in his high moral character and austerities. It would be rash for a king to disregard the Brahmana for fear of magical and moral retribution.[46]

If we consider the instances in the epic where a conflict of Brahmana and Ksattriya emerges on special occasions, this would become clear. The story of Paraśurāma's destruction of the Ksattriyas is doubtless a Bhargava invention arising perhaps from some maltreatment of their class by the Haihaya rulers,[47] a kind of imaginative redressal, but it does not establish either a general conflict nor does it lead to the presumption of a normal tendency on the part of the rulers to treat Brahmanas as inferior. The conflict of Drupada and Drona[48] or of Śarmiṣṭhā and Devayānī[49] are other instances of a similar kind. In both of these instances, the Brahmana is sought to be slighted as poor and dependent but ultimately gets the upper hand by virtue of his special knowledge and position as teacher or magic-working priest. *Mahābhārata* undoubtedly shows kings and warriors of an imperious temper who brook no displeasure or disobedience. At the same time, it shows priests, sages and ascetics who are accustomed to be sought after and listened to with the highest respect. To argue that the picture of the kings is true of the original epic but that the picture of the Brahmanas belongs to a later stratum of it, is really to beg the question.

The Ksattriyas included the kings, their kinsmen, high officials, king's companions and warriors. They are clearly enough not merely a class of rulers but a class of warriors and fighters. They are distinguished from the common people by their weapons, equipment and training. As the incident of the war for the cows in the Araṇyaparvan shows, the cowherds and other ranchers of king Virāṭa are no match for the Kuru warriors.[50]

The king, in fact, suggests in the story at an earlier point that arms may be given to the Pandavas disguised as non-Ksattriyas.[51] This shows that while fighting was not confined to the Ksttriyas, the latter constituted a superior class of professionals. And yet sometimes high military positions were held by non-Ksattriya warriors. For example, Kīcaka, the commander of Virāṭa's forces, has been called a Sūta.[52] Niṣādas, Śabaras, Mlecchas and others too are recognised as warriors.

It has also to be remembered that both in the north-east and the north-west Ksattriyas still existed as ancient classes who still claimed ancient lineage and traditional rulership. In fact, even in later times when the ancient class had long ceased to exist, the claims continued to persist. It is, however, worth noting that the *Mbh.* itself raises the problem of the failure of constituted and hereditary monarchy and of resultant anarchy. It goes on to say that if order is secured even by a non-Ksattriya ruler, he is to be respected.[53] This goes a long way to sanctify political revolutions and actual authority and apparently reflects the situation that gradually emerged in the Imperial Age. A high ethical code was laid down for both kings and warriors. Dying in the battle was a high honour for the warrior and personal loyalty to the prince or leader was enjoined upon him. The ransom for his capture was estimated at 1000 paṇas.[54] Soldiers fought on foot, on chariots, on horseback and on elephants. They fought with bows and arrows, swords and spears. At one place there is a discussion about whether the bow or the sword is the chief weapon. The decision is given in favour of the sword. When not fighting, the warriors indulged in eating and drinking, gambling and hunting.

Like the *Dasabrahmana Jataka*, the *Santiparvan* speaks of several varieties of Brahmanas. The *brahmasama* Brahmanas were educated and possessed scriptual learning. Those who belonged to the priestly tradition into learned teacher and kept to their distinctive functions, are described as *devasama*. Those who served the kings as their *purohita*, minister (*mantrin*), envoy (*duta*) or counsellor (*arthanusasaka*) are described as *ksatrasama*, 'akin to the Ksattriyas', those who rode elephants, horses, or chariots or followed on foot were the *vaisyasamas*. Those who had no proper lineage or conduct were the *sudrasamas*. It is recommended that those who were not *srotriyas*, nor tended the sacred fires, should be subjected to taxation and forced labour. Brahmanas serving in the temples or as astrologers are severely condemned as Brahmana-candāla. Under straitened circumstances, the king is permitted to gather taxes from the Brahmanas except from those who are *Brahmasama* or *Devasama*. The king is declared to be the master of the wealth of all non-Brahmanas as well as of those Brahmanas who do not perform their duties. If a learned Brahmana finds no means of livelihood in a kingdom, the king is to blame. But if finding livelihood, the Brahmana acts unlawfully, he should be turned out of the kingdom.[55] The Vaiśyas are divided into three classes-ranchers (*gopālas*, living in *ghoṣas*)[56] farmers and traders.[57] They constituted the producing classes on whom the economic burden of the state rested.[58] The craftsmen and artisans were organised in guilds.[59] The *Mbh.* describes the 'people' as 'townsmen and countrymen', *paura* and *jānapada*, as a non-descript mass led by the Brahmanas (*Brāhmaṇapramukhāh*).[60] In the villages, they were led by the *grāmaṇis* who represented them for official purposes. The people or *paura-janapada* also appear to have acted collectively as the 'constituents' (*prakrtayaḥ*) of the state on occasions like the coronation of the king and took an active part in the questions of succession.[61] Otherwise the *Mbh.* is largely silent about the 'people'. Unlike the *jatakas*, there are no heroes or their tales drawn from the people or the lower classes in the *Mbh.* nor do the towns really figure except as political centres. In this respect, the *Mbh.* represents a much more archaic social landscape than the *Jatakas* or other Buddhist literature. The *Mbh.* represents a more rural and aristocratic society.

The Sudras represented a servile class and were said to be devoid of rights of property or personal independence.[62] This, however, is not wholly in consonance with the evidence of the epic itself. Vidura, was counted a Sudra and yet respected as a man of wisdom. The Sudras were again recommended to be members of the king's council.[63] There is plainly much revision in the theoretical and legal portions of the epic. This revision appears contemporaneous with that of the *Manusmrti* and probably belongs to the Sunga age.

Primitive and frontier tribes are called *dasyus*.[64] Sabaras and Nisadas are examples of these.[65] So are the foreign tribes or *mlecchas*. The *candalas* lived in the margin of society and food belonging to them was held to be unfit for eating by the higher castes. They lived in their own settlements called *pakkaṇas* and in the story of Visvamitra stealing a piece of dog's meat from the house of a *candala*, we have a vivid description of a *candala pakkana*.[66]

For the greater part, the epic describes a society divided into the four *varnas* with the Brahmanas and the Ksattriyas constituting the top. There is a clear division into high and low *varnas*. The Vaisyas apparently constitute the mass of the people and the Sudras are conceived as servile. In the earlier portions of the epic miscegenation as *anuloma* marriage between the Varnas is not uncommon[67] but at other places the fear of *Varna-samkara* or of *adharottara* is expressed forcefully.[68] This is in line with the *Manusmrti*, though briefer and milder. Here again the epic seems to span a period of several centuries during which the *Varna*-system of the Vedic age was gradually riddled with the rise of numerous *jatis* based on functional specialization and the expansion of geographical horizons bringing new regional, ethnic and tribal groups within the ken of orthodox society. The age of the Mahajanapadas and the first Magadha empire apparently constitutes the period of this social transformation. Valmiki's Ramayana must clearly have been famous before Asvaghosa.[69] On the other hand, its composition could not be older than the age of the Mahajanapadas.[70] On the whole, then, the age of the *Rāmāyana* would tend to coincide with that of the *Mahābhārata*[71] with an important difference in terms of the geographical area which is chiefly reflected in them. There is also an obvious difference in terms of the styles and attitudes of the original authors.

In comparison with the *Mahābhārata*, the *Ramāyana* shows greater familiarity with a more sophisticated urban culture as well as a more primitive forest world. Other evidence also suggests that between 600 B.C. and 300 B.C. the development of urban life was greater and more rapid in north-eastern India than in the north-west.[72] The Deccan, on the other hand, had vast forests with numerous primitive tribes.

The ideal picture of the society divided into the *Varnas*

is naturally similar to that in the *Mbh.* but the *Rāmāyana* does not concentrate so much on the Ksattriyas as a ruling and military class divided into many classes as on a few ancient Ksattriya families ruling with habitual assurance over the people of the town and the country. The heroes of the *Rāmayāna* are more gentle and moral, less 'primitive' and impassioned than those of the *Mahābhārata*. This could be due to a difference in the predilections of the authors or to a difference in the area or epoch of civilisation. What we have here is a difference in the character and manners of the aristocracy. The *Rāmāyana* represents a more settled political order, a greater respect for law and customs, and a gentler social ethics. The *Mahābhārata* shows its heroes in a state of turmoil and questioning. It portrays a 'time of troubles'. The relationship of the Brahmanas and Ksattriyas is alluded to in the episode of Visvamitra in the usual manner, viz., the Ksattriyas have physical might but the Brahmanas have spiritual might.[73] The sages engaged in austerities represent the top of the Brahmanas. The *purohita* speaks on behalf of the assembled people. We hear of ministers but their caste is not clear.[74] We hear of a Brahmana engaged in farming.[75]

The urban population is much more clearly detailed in the *Rāmāyana* than in the *Mahābhārata* and this brings it nearer the *Jatakas* than the *Mahābhārata*. The guilds are a leading constituent of the people.[76] The city includes traders and craftsmen of various descriptions. The craftsmen or *śilpivarga* are detailed as—

atha bhūmi-pradeśajñāḥ sūtrakarma-viśāradāh.
sva-karmā-bhiratāh śūrāh khanakā yantrakāstathā.
karmāntakāḥ sthapatayaḥ puruṣā yantrakovidāḥ
tathā vardhakayaścaiva mārgiṇo vrksa-takṣakāḥ
sūpakārāḥ sudhākārāḥ vaṁśacarmakṛtastathā.[77]

We have here water diviners, architects, diggers, irrigation experts, paid labourers, carpenters, machine-makers, wood-cutters, cooks, masons, workers in cane and leather. Elsewhere we hear of jewellers (*manikāra*), potters, armourers, weavers, workers with the saw, those who pierced gems, polishers and glazers. ivory workers, perfumers, maker of liquor, tailors, dyers, actors and fishermen. Many of these were organised in guilds.[78]

People of the villages, ranches and tribal settlement were led by the headmen or *mahattaras*. The lowly sections of society were constituted by such tribals as the *candalas* and *niṣādas*.[79] *Nisadas* apparently had their own autonomous tribal settlements such as of Guha at Srngaverapura.[80] Guha is called a *Niṣādasthapati*, a phrase much discussed in the *sūtras*.

In the search for the actual social classes as distinct from the theoretical castes in the early historical times, the evidence of Megasthenese must be deemed as the most important. His description of the seven 'classes' in India is surely not one of the conventional caste system but of something which may be presumed more real.[81] The philosophers (*philosophoi, sophistai*) were the first in rank but the smallest in number. They were employed as priests by private persons and the king gathered them at the gates at the beginning of the new year and they made observations about improving the crops and the cattle or promoting public interests. They were immune from labour and taxation but lived an ascetic life. Apparently, the class included the Brahmanas as well as the Sramanas, or rather, the priests, diviners and wise men. Megasthenese has clearly put Brahmanas and Sramanas in one class although the former constituted a caste and the latter lay outside the caste system. Their similarity lay in their claims to wisdom and in the social esteem given to them. The rise of the Sramanas, drawn from all the castes, into a class parallel to the Brahmanas, as remarked earlier, was a major social change to which Buddhism contributed. The second class consisted of the husbandmen (*georgai-karsaka*)[82] "who form the bulk of the population, and are in disposition most mild and gentle. They are exempted from military service and cultivate their lands undisturbed by fear."[83] From the fact that the armies did not disturb the peaceful cultivators, Megasthenese seems to have wrongly concluded that the cultivators were wholly distinct from soldiers as a caste. The huge armies of the Nanda-Maurya age suggest that the soldiers must have been recruited widely. Nor does Megasthenese appear correct in saying that all land belonged to the king. He seems to have confused the tax payable to the king with rent.[84]

The third caste consisted of herdsmen and hunters,[85] who alone were allowed to hunt and to keep cattle, and to sell draught animals or let them out on hire. "In return for clearing the land of wild beasts and fowls they receive an allowance of grain from the king. They lead a wandering life and live under tents." This seems to confuse two quite different classes, the herdsmen and hunters. In the orthodox caste

Sanchi: Stupa No. 1 : Worship of *Triratna* under the *Pipal* tree, 1st century B.C.

system, the *gopālas* in *ghoṣas* have a higher status than the hunters in the *pallīs*. What this compounding of classes suggests is that some of the nomadic hunting groups also kept cattle and that it was not always easy to distinguish between the village ranchers and the tribals on the margin.

"The fourth class consists of those who work at trades, of those who lend wares, and of those who are employed in bodily labour.[86] Some of these pay tribute, and render to the state certain prescribed services. But the armour-makers and ship-builders receive wages and victuals from the king, for whom alone they work." Here, again, traders and craftsmen are joined together in one class whereas they are separated in the caste system. This may be explained because they were organized in similar guilds. In fact, the second, third and fourth classes sub-divide the third and fourth castes which originally constituted the single mass of people.

"The fifth class consists of fighting men who, when not engaged in active service, pass their time in idleness and drinking. They are maintained at the king's expense......"[87] Here again, we have a functional class which would be a sub-class of the Ksattriya caste and yet overlap with other castes contributing to the army. "The sixth class consists of the overseers, to whom is assigned the duty of watching all that goes on, and making reports secretly to the king. Some are entrusted with the inspection of the city, and others with that of the army."[88] They are said to have employed courtesans as their agents. The sixth class apparently refers to the civil officials or bureaucracy and would be another sub-class of the ancient Ksattriyas again overlapping the Vaisyas.

The seventh class consisted of the counsellors and assessors of the king.[89] "To them belong the highest posts of the government, the Tribunals of justice, and the general administration of public affiairs." This class was numerically the smallest but the most highly respected socially. The highest officials, civil as well as military, were drawn from this class.

In this description of the 'castes' by Megasthenes, we may notice that Brahmanas and Sramanas are joined together, the Ksattriyas have simply become a professional soldiery, the Vaisyas are divided into three distinct classes—farmers, traders and herdsmen, and of the Sudras there is no distinct mention except as included under artisans and hunters. On the other hand, officials and ministers, constitute purely functional classes drawn from all the upper castes. The seven 'classes' of Megasthenese, thus, sometimes join and sometimes split up the four *varnas*. Philosophers and wise men, officials and soldiers, farmers, merchants and craftsmen, herdsmen and hunters, these apparently constituted the real system of classes in the fourth century B.C. We can notice from this that the Brahmanas have been paralleled by the Sramanas and the second and third *varnas* subdivided into occupational classes. Just as the Brahmanas have been paralleled by a class of Sramanas of mixed caste origin, the old Ksattriyas have been paralleled by the growth of professional administrative and military classes. The description of Megasthenes also shows that the Sudras could hardly be distinguished from an inconspicuous class of servitors except as tribal groups. Slaves were apparently even more inconspicuous.

According to Megasthenes "No one is allowed to marry outside his own caste, or to exchange the profession or trade for another, or to follow more than one business. An exception is made in favour of the philosopher, who for his virtue is allowed this privilege." This is in line with the formal rules of caste theory and most probably is based not on the observation of reality but on what was held in theory. Megasthenes' 'caste' thus would on the whole resemble *jatis*, rather than *varnas*.

As already mentioned, the theory of Four *Varnas* had to reconcile itself with the actual diversity of the occupational, ethnic and social groups which had acquired the status of *jatis*. The orthodox theory explained the origin of the *jatis* from the miscegenation of the *varnas* (*varnasankara*). Where the father came from a higher caste and the mother from a lower one, the union was called *anuloma*. When the mother belonged to the higher caste, it was dubbed *pratiloma*. The progeny of *anuloma* marriages was looked upon either as equivalent in status to the father's caste or as of the mother's caste of intermediate status. The progeny of *pratiloma* marriages was condemned as of low status. Since these explanations were theoretically contrived, the fitting of the *jatis* to their supposed *anuloma* and *pratiloma* origins could only reflect the actual status of *jati* and the degree of orthodoxy in the *sastrakara*. The actual origin of the *jatis* was diverse, their explanations in terms of the idea of *varnasankara* largely contrived. What the theory of *varna-sankara* achieved was to keep alive the idea and hierarchy of the *varna*system in and through a growing welter of *jatis*. It is in the *sutras* that the first systematic account of *varnasankara* transforming the *varna*-system into a *varna*-cum-*jati* system is to be found.

Apastamba[90] ignores *anuloma* and *pratiloma* marriages and mentions *Candala, Paulkasa* and *Vaina* only.[91] But Gautama who is older[92] mentions a number of *anuloma* and *pratiloma* castes. He says, '*anulomānantaraikāntara dvyantarāsu jātāh savarṇāmbaṣṭhogra-niṣāda-dausmantapāra- śavāḥ*' — (1.4.14). This gives a list of six *anuloma* castes. The six *pratilomas* are "*pratilomāstu sūta-māgadhā-yogavakrta-vaidehaka-cāṇḍālāh.*" (1.4.15). Gautama also quotes the opinion of some mentioning a few more names—*mūrdhāvasikta, dhīvara, pulkasa, bhrjja-kantha, mahisya yavana* and *karana* (Ibid. 17). Gautama also holds the view that the continuation of *anuloma* and *pratiloma* marriages among the *varnas* or the *jatis* will lead in the seventh or fifth generation to an ascent or descent in the status of the progeny.[93] These rules thus visualize intermarriages among the castes and a mobility in their status. The inclusion of the Yavanas in this list is of some interest. Baudhayana additionally mentions *Rathakara, Vaina* and *Kukkuta.*[94] The first two were ancient and well-known, the third is little known. *Utkarsa* and *apakarsa* are admitted but the *jatis* arising from *varnasankara* are all declared *vrātyas* (Ibid-1.16.15).

The *Dharmasūtras* roughly covering the period from *c.* 500 B.C. to *c.* 200 B.C.[95] tend to be more archaic than the times to which they actually belonged. This was partly due to their attempt to codify ancient traditions, partly due to their moral bias. As some of the *Dharmasūtras* were apparently composed in the Deccan,[96] they would naturally tend to appeal to the more ancient traditions which the pioneers brought with them from the north. Thus, although more or less contemporaneous with the epics and the Jatakas, the *Dharmasutras* present a more archaic social picture.

Nevertheless, the very attempt at the codification of laws and customs arose from contemporary need. Ancient traditions apparently were in danger of being forgotten or disregarded. Conflicts in them needed to be resolved and new problems needed explicit attention. Apastamba is thus quite categorical in stating that social conduct had reached an age of transgression and one could not expect any seer to be born in such an age.[97] For socio-ethical guidance, one must now appeal to the *Aryas* and presume that there were ancient texts which once must have provided authority to their usage, even though such texts were no longer extant.[98] *Arya* in this context has the sense of the elite respected for its learning and character. The commentator renders it by *visista.*[99] Elsewhere *arya* in the *Sutras* is equivalent to the *dvija* and is contrasted with the Sudra and the outcaste. The reading of a racial sense in *arya*, as done by Hopkins, really begs the question for it rests on regarding the Sudras as a distinct race.[100]

The Sudras are doubtless placed low in the hierarchy but they are not outcastes. They are allowed to cook in the households of the upper castes,[101] and even their gifts are acceptable in times of emergency.[102] The Candala and Paulkasa were, as in more ancient times, treated as out-castes. A well-known *sutra* of Panini—*śūdrāṇāṁ cāṇiravasitānām*—makes them a sub-class of the Sudras such that their eating vessels were considered unpurifiable.[103]

The growth of *jātis*, as stated above, necessitated the theory of *varṇasankara* and here the *Sutras* were attempting to adapt the old theory to the newer reality. The principles of *utkarṣa* and *apakarsa* not only recognized intermediate and overlapping social classes or *jatis*, but also gave sanction to social mobility. This 'sanction' could only be a recognition of an existing reality. Such *jatis* as *Niṣādas*, *Pāraśavas*, *Ugras*, *Sūtas*, *Māgadhas* and *Vaidehakas* have obviously diverse origins, tribal and functional. Placing them within the *varna* gradations and assigning them a fictitious origin in terms of the *sankara* must have required considerable exercise of ingenuity.

With respect to function also, the *Sutras* cannot help noticing that the ksattriyas as the king required a separate treatment. The various *varnas*, again, required to be sanctioned the occupations of other *varnas* in times of emergency and this theory of emergency or *apaddharma* could only mean that in point of fact unfavourable social condition had forced many to abandon their traditional occupations. Emergency thus presumes an 'age of transgression', a slow but sure process of social change. The *Arthasastra* reflects a truly national society under an informal government where town and country both receive their due importance. Vedic tradition is recognized to be the source of the *Varnasramadharma.* It is clearly recognized that the two principal functions of the Ksattriyas are the 'use of arms' and the protection of the people.[104] Kautilya holds that the army should principally consist of the Ksattriyas.[105] He disapproves of Brahmana soldiers even though he quotes an earlier opinion which favoured them. It is also admitted that an army consisting of Vaisyas and Sudras may also have much strength.[106] We also hear of *Śreṇībala* and *Āṭavikabala*.[107] Apparently organized but mercenary bands of soldiers in the countryside and the forests were a noticeable feature of the times. The force with which Candragupta Maurya himself rose to power may have been similar. The destruction of the ancient Ksattriya clans and kingdoms from Ajatasatru to Mahapadma Nanda and Alexander must have been responsible for these bands of adventures. The regular soldiery was hereditary as well as hired.

It is clear from the *Arthasastra* that the officials did not necessarily belong to the Ksattriyas or the Brahmanas. After discussing several views, Kautilya concludes about the *Amātyas* that 'the worth of a person should be assessed on the basis of his work'.[108] He would like the *Mantrin* to be of 'noble birth' (*abhijata*)[109] but that need not mean anything more than an exclusion of those who could be called 'base born'. The *Purohita*, however, was obviously to be a learned Brahmana.[110] It is obvious that in an empire like that of the Mauryas who did not boast of ancient and orthodox Ksattriya lineage, administration was sought to be placed in the hands of a class of persons chosen for their efficiency and loyalty to the king. The *Arthasastra* makes it clear that the occupations of the Vaisyas and the Sudras over-lapped. The

Vaisyas engaged in 'farming, cattle rearing, and trade,' the Sudras in "service, *varta*, crafts and minstrelsy'. Now *vārtā* is defined as *kṛṣi-pāśupālye vanijyā ca*'.[111] Again, while the strength of the country (*janapada*) is said to lie in its farmers, the king is advised to people the newly established villages largely by Sudra farmers.[112] It seems then that a significant section of the agriculturists belonged to the Sudra caste. The rest must have been Vaisyas with a sprinkling of Brahmanas and Ksattriyas enjoying rural estates obtained from royal benefaction. Some of the Brahmana cultivators would also be poor inasmuch as among them primogeniture did not obtain and with the original estate fragmented among numerous children, its dwindling into insignificance would be inevitable. Grant of land is mentioned for the priests, learned teachers and Vedic scholars and, on different conditions, to royal officers, central as well as local.[113] Craftsmen and traders in the village also engaged in farming.[114]

According to the *Arthasastra*, the children of a Brahmana or Ksattriya from a wife belonging to the immediately lower *varna* belong to the father's caste but when the wife comes from a caste not immediately lower, the children belong to mixed castes. The following list of mixed castes is given—*Ambastha*, *Niṣāda*, *Pāraśava*, *Ugra*, *Ayogava*, *Ksattṛ*, *Cāṇḍāla*, *Māgadha*,, *Vaidehaka*, *Sūta Kukkuta*, *Pulkasa*, *Vaina*, *Kuśīlava* and *Śvapāka*. This list is almost identical to that found in the *Dharmasutras*. But Kautilya distinguishes the Pauranika *suta* and *magadha* as different and says that *Rathakara* is merely a functional Vaisya class.[115] While the *jatis* in the *Arthasastra* correspond to those in the *Dharmasutras*, a large number of functional classes are mentioned in the former. Thus apart from Sudras, the *Arthasastra* distinguishes the slaves (*dasas*) and the wage-earners (*karmakara*).[116] Mere wage-earners, again, are distinguished from salaried employees (*bhṛtyas*) or hired workers (*bhṛtaka*).[117] *Kāru* and *Silpin* are mentioned together suggesting that they were not quite the same.[118] We hear of washermen (*rajaka*), porters (*bhārika*), weavers (*tunnavāya*), goldsmiths (*suvanakāra*), physicians (*bhisaj*), actors (*kusīlava*), accountants (*sankhyāyaka*), writers (*lekhaka*), musicians (*tūrya-kāras*), stone-diggers (*saila-khanaka*), etc. It is thus obvious that the growth of urban life had led to the emergence of a large number of new types of workers and functionaries and not all of these were yet formally recognized as *jatis*. *Varṇa*, *jati*, and *śilpa* were not in perfect accord and attempts were still under way to devise a complex and comprehensive system embracing them all.

It is Manu who gives a detailed description of the castes and their 'mixture', showing thereby that the ancient *Varna* system had been completely overgrown by *jatis*. Occupational, regional, tribal and ethnic groups were emerging within the social ken in an age in which the vast Magadha empire had considerably enlarged the frontiers of national society. *Manusmṛti* has been interpreted to hold that children from a mother belonging to the immediately lower caste are similar to the caste of the father but a little lower since the fault of the mother taints them (10.6).[119] A few verses later, Manu clearly declares the *anantara-jāta* as lower than the *savarna-jātas*, equating them with the *dvyekāntara-jātas* (10.10; 10.14).[120] This probably represented a later opinion or a stricter one. We have already seen how the *Bhaddasala jataka* attests to the controversy about the role of the mother in determining the status of the progeny. The *pratiloma* progeny is described as *bāhya* and *hīnā* by Manu (10.28.31).

"Manu refers to six *anuloma*, six *pratiloma* and twenty doubly mixed castes." He also refers to numerous classes and regional peoples and races as *vratyas*. Some Ksattriyas have become *vratyas* through the neglect of sacrament and Brahmanas (10.43). These include *Paundrakas*, *Codra*, *Dravida*, *Kamboja*, *Yavana*, *Saka*, *Parada*, *Pahlava*, *Cina*, *Kirata*, *Darada*, *Khasa* and *Licchavi* (10.44). These regional and ethnic groups have been called degraded Ksattriyas apparently because they were known to be ruling somewhere or the other during the Sunga period.[121]

While in the most of the *Smrti* works, the *jatis* are mere names, Manu and Usanâs give some helpful description also. According to Manu *Sairindhra* is servile though not a slave. He acts as a trapper and is also skilled in hair-dressing, toilet etc.[122] Maitreya rings the morning bells.[123] *Margava* who is called *Kaivarta* in Aryavarta (and also *dāsa*, *dāśa* rather) lives by plying boats.[124] All these three are the progeny of *Ayogava* women who wear the clothes of dead bodies and eat the leavings of others.[125] *Kārāvara* is a tanner (*carmakāra*). He is said to be descended from *Nisada* and *Vaidehi* who is the progeny of Vaisya and Brahmana. Since the *Nisadas* were hunters and *Vaidehas* degraded traders, the occupation of the tanner is given a suitable origin. *Andhra* and *Meda* lived outside the village.[126] *Pandusopaka* lived by working on and trading bamboos. *Sopakas* lived as hangmen. *Antyāvasāyin* lived on the cremation ground.[127] The *sutas* acted as grooms and charioteers. *Ambasthas* were physicians *Vaidehakas* looked after the king's women. *Magadhas* engaged in trade. *Nisadas* were fishermen, *Ayogavas* were carpenters; *Meda*, *Andhra*, *Cuncu* and *Madhu* hunted wild beasts. *Ksattr*, *Ugra* and *Pukkasa* hunted and trapped animals living in holes. *Dhigvanas* lived by producing and selling leather goods. *Venas* played on musical instruments. These lived in or near the cremation grounds.[128] *Candalas* and *Svapakas* lived outside the village. If they ate from a vessel, it could not be used by a person of the upper castes even after cleaning. Their wealth consisted of dogs and assess. clothes of the dead, broken pots and iron ornaments. They were expected to lead to nomadic life. They were not to enter the village or the city at night. During the day they could move in the habitations with royal permits. They were to take out the dead bodies which had no one to look after them. They were to act as hangmen under orders and could take away the clothes and belongings of the corpses.[129]

Manu accepts the doctrines of *jātyutkarsa* and *jātyapakarsa* and expresses himself in favour of the view that the father is of greater moment in determining the castes of the progeny than the mother.[130] The upper castes are allowed to take up the professions of the lower castes in times of need and the Sudras allowed to live by crafts and service.[131] This only confirms the fact that the people of the different *Varnas* actually included diverse occupational groups. Caste and class thus became quite disparate. Political changes altered the composition of the ruling class and economic necessity forced the ancient Ksattriyas and dispossesed aristocrats as well as the Brahmanas to take up agriculture and trade also as means of livelihood. The Vaisyas were becoming identified more and more as traders.

The sudras now included many 'out-castes' with whom dining was prohibited as regular social contact. The distinction between *niravasita* and *aniravasita* Sudra went back to an ancient period since Panini draws the distinction, as noted above. Patanjali says that *niravasita* does not mean excluded from Aryavarta, for *Sakas* and *Yavanas* were so excluded but were *aniravasita*. Nor does it mean excluded from towns and villages (*grāmo ghoṣo nagaraṁ saṁvāha iti*) because *Candalas* and *Mrtapas* were not excluded from them.[132] Nor does it mean excluded from Vedic ritual because *Takṣan* and *Ayaskāra*, *Rajaka* and *Tantuvāya* were so excluded but were *aniravasita*. Hence *niravasita* meant those after whose eating the vessels could not be 'purified'. This class included Cāṇḍāla and *Mṛtapa*. Thus Patanjali mentions six classes of *aniravasita śūdras—Śaka, Yavana, Takṣan, Ayasakāra, Rajaka* and *Tantuvāya*, and two classes of *niravasitas—Cāṇḍāla* and *Mrtapa*. It is, worth noticing that while Patanjali counts *Śakas* and *Yavanas* as Śūdras, Manu treats them as *vrātya* Ksattriyas originally who have become reduced to the status of the Śūdras. The number of out-castes seems to have increased. Apart from *Cāṇḍāla*, *Mṛtapa* and *Paulakasa*, we have *Andhra* and *Meda* in the same category.

Yājñavalkya follows Manu in the theory of *Sankara* as well as *jātyutkarsa* and *jātyapakarṣa*.[133] Interestingly enough, he also adds a new clause which visualizes change in caste status by continued adoption of the profession of a lower or higher caste.[134] How far the practical implications of this rule were accepted, is difficult to say. It was apparently meant as a device for discouraging continued departure from the scheme of professions as prescribed for the *varnas* and takes for granted a situation where such departure must have been dangerously common.

From the contradictory description of the *jatis* in the *smrti* texts, it seems that many of the *jatis* only represented traditional names and not contemporary realities. Thus the *Ambasthas*, one of the principal *anuloma* castes, are made out to be physicians by Manu[135] but 'agriculturist, *āgneya-vartaka, dhyajaviśrāvaka* or soldier' by Uśanas.[136] Kane identifies them with the Baidyas of Bengal.[137] Actually they might have been an old tribe which the Greeks described as *Abastanes*. Having been important once in the days of Panini and the invasion of Alexander, they might have continued only as tribal stragglers in diverse professions.[138] Hence the divergent descriptions. *Ayogava* is similarly another of the ancient and basic *anuloma* castes. Manu makes him a carpenter, Usanas a weaver or brazier.[139] Still later texts make him an actor or mason or white-washer. The *Tattirīya Brāhmaṇa* speaks of "*akrayāyāgūm*.[140] *Ayāgu* was thus connected with sale and trade, some ancient trading group, which in course of time seems to have been engaged in a variety of professions. *Ugra*, again, was originally a royal official, perhaps a police official but Manu makes him a low hunter. Uśanas and some others recall him as the officer of the king.[141] *Karaṇa* was similarly a royal official but of a clerical rather than a military kind like the Ugra. About the *Kukkuṭas*, it would be reasonable to suppose that they were poultry farmers of some kind. Manu calls the Māgadha a trader but he was probably a bard. *Mahisya* and *Mūrdhāvasikta* remain enigmatic. *Vaidehaka* is similarly attributed quite disparate occupations by Manu and Usanas.[142]

As noted above *Auśanasasaṁhitā* refers to the *Kāyasthas* and to *Pañcarātra* and thus probably belongs to the Gupta period. It appears to be referred to by Kulluka and *Mitākṣarā*[143] and appears to have had a reputation as an authority on the mixed castes. While it reiterates the traditional names of mixed castes, it also mentions a large number of occupational castes. Among the former, it lists *sūta*, *rathakāra*, *māgadha*, *caṇḍāla*, *śvapaca*, *ayogava*, *pulinda*, *pukkusa*, *ambaṣṭha*, *pārasava*, *niṣāda*, *ugra*, and *vaidehika*. Among the latter it mentions *tantuvāya* (-*Ayogava*), *kaṁsyopajīva* (-*Avogava*) *carmakāraka* (-*Venuka*), *tailapiṣṭaka-jivi* (-*Cakri*), *rajaka*, *rañjaka*, *nartaka*, *gāyaka*, *pācaka*, *nāpita*, *bhiṣaj tāmropajīvin*, *sunika*, *udhandhaka*, *maṇikāra*, *śuṇḍika*, *sūcaka*, *takṣaka*, *matsyabandhaka* and *Kāyasthas*. These occuptional groups are not new, except for the *Kāyasthas*, but the attempt to make them into sub-castes within the scheme of *varṇas* through *saṇkara*, carries forward the attempt which had already more or less reached a final stage with Manu.

The *Samhita* makes an interesting distinction between

saccūdra and *asaccūdra*, a distinction which continued in late post-Gupta times.[144] The 'good Sudras' are distinguished by their devoted service to the upper castes and by their performance of *Pākayajñas*. It also seems to be implied that the *Pañcarātra* and similar sects found adherents among the lower castes also.

The *Parāśara Smṛti* shows an attempt to regulate the contact with the Śūdras. The *Cāṇḍālas* are untouchables. Among the Śūdras, however, slaves, barbers, cowherds, dependents and family friends and cultivators in one's fields are *bhojyānna*.[145] Fa-hien's celebrated description of the Middle Kingdom confirms the segregation of the *candalas*. "These live away from other people, and when they approach a city or market, they beat a piece of wood, in order to distinguish themselves. Then people know who they are and avoid coming into contact with them."[146] "Only the Candalas go hunting and deal in flesh."[147] Although the *candalas* existed from ancient times and were despised, the Greeks did not notice such marked segregation. Even Patañjali does not place them outside villages or cities. But later *smṛtis* do so. Fa-hien also says "In this country they do not keep pigs or fowls, there are no dealings in cattle, not butchers' shops or distilleries in their market-places."[148] As the *smṛitis* testify, all the groups connected with these and similar professions were classed as low and gradually placed under varying degrees of segregation.

Bṛhaspati recommends that the king should have his counsellors only from among the upper castes, preferably Brahmanas. He should avoid the Sudras in any case.[149] This repeated prohibition seems to imply that the Sudras could be visualized as possible ministers. Saka and Kusana or Buddhist rulers may have appointed Sudra counsellors and thus earned the ire of the Brahmanas as the Nandas and the Mauryas had.

Among the occupations allowed to the Vaisyas, Bṛhaspati specifically includes money-lending or *kusīda* and for the Sudra he permits all crafts and all trade.[150] Even during times of distress, the Brahmana is forbidden to take on a Sudra's duty and similarly the Sudra is prohibited to adopt the special functions of the Brahmana.[151]

Brhaspati defines a craftsman or *śilpin* as one who is proficient in art (*kalābhijña*) and fashions works from gold, *kupya*, threads, wood, stone or leather.[152] Wage-earners and slaves are sharply distinguished. The former, called *Bhṛtaka* as in the *Arthasastra*, are divided into three classes—*uttama*, *madhyama* and *adhama*. Soilders are placed in the first class, farmers in the second and porters in the third.[153] Brhaspati regards the slave as regularly performing 'unclean' work for his masters.[154] This departs from the more enlightened prescription of the *Arthaśāstra*.

The distinction between *sat-śūdra* and *asat-śūdra* is implied by Bṛhaspati.[155] It is also notable that the general untouchability of the Sudra seems to be implied.[156] This would imply a clear distinction between the sudras and the *dasas* since the latter were expected to render personal and domestic service. In the *sutras*, *dasa* and sudra seem much nearer. Later they appear to diverge more and more. The service to be rendered by the Sudra became largely communal and the Sudras came to comprise a number of sub-castes engaged in rendering such services to the community as were considered unclean and low while the *dasas* were essentially personal servitors. The variety of the *dasas* seems to have increased. Thus Nārada mentions fifteen kinds of *dasas* instead of the seven kinds which Manu mentions.[157]

Kātyāyana rules that the Brahmana should not be made a *dasa* and in the case of the other three castes, slavery should not run counter to the hierarchy of the *varnas*.[158] This rule is not to be found in this explicit formulation earlier although it is implicit in the spirit of the orthodox *varna* system. Kātyāyana also distinguishes *jati* from such groups as *naigama*, *pūga*, *śreṇī*, *gaṇa*, *vrāta*, *pāṣaṇḍa*, *gulma* and *saṇgha*. These latter are essentially functional groups while *jati* is based on birth or rather miscegenation within the *varna* system.[159] *Naigama* is an association of townsmen, *pūga* of traders, *vrāta* of armed men, *pāṣaṇḍa* of mendicants, *gaṇa* of Brahmanas, *sangha* of Buddhists and Jainas, *gulma* of outcastes. In fact, the general notion of a class as a collectivity with some criterion seems to be reached and such classes are called *varga*.[160] We, thus, have three kinds of social groups—*varna* which gives hierarchy, *jati* which subsumes deviations within the *varna*-system and *varga* including diverse functional associations placed under varying degrees of segregation.

Yuan Chwang's account confirms Fa-hien's. He says "Butchers, fishermen, public performers, executioners, and scavengers have their habitations marked by a distinguishing sign. They are forced to live outside the city and they sneak along on the left when going about in the hamlets."[161]

In the post-Gupta period while the difference between the upper three castes tended to decrease, the Sudra caste came to have a wide and residual compass especially as the craft guilds were finally merged into it as sub-castes, and at the same time the outcastes or *antyajas* too tended to become more numerous. Alberuni says that the Ksattriyas are not much lower than the Brahmanas and that there is no very great distance between the Vaisyas and the Sudras. "Much, however, as these classes differ from each other, they live together in the same towns and villages, mixed together in the same house and lodgings."[162] "After the Sudra follow the people called *Antyaja*, who render various kinds of services, who are not reckoned amongst any caste, but only as members of a certain craft or profession. There are eight classes of them, who freely intermarry with each other, except the fuller, shoemaker, and weaver, for no others would condescend to have anything to do with them. These eight guilds are the fuller, shoe-maker, juggler, the basket and shield maker, the sailor, fisherman, the hunter of wild animals and of birds, and the weaver." These outcastes lived outside the villages and towns. Even lower than these are *Hadi*, *Doma*, *Candala* and *Badhatau* who "are not reckoned amongst any caste or guild. They are occupied with dirty work, like the cleaning of villages and other services". They were considered as "one sole class and distinguished only by their occupations. In fact, they are considered like illegitimate children". "Among these the Hadi are the highest. The Doma came next. They play on the lute and sing. "The still lower classes practise as a trade killing and the inflicting of judicial punishment. The worst of all are the Badhatau, who not only devour the flesh of dead animals, but even of dogs and other beasts."

With Al-beruni's account of *Antyajas* may be compared their lists from the later *Smṛti* texts—"*Rajakaścarmakāraśca naṭo buruṃḍa eva ca kaivarta-meda-bhillāśca saptaite cāntyajāhsmṛtāḥ.*" "*Caṇḍālah śvapachah kṣattā sūto vaidehakastathā Māgadhāyogavau caiva sahaite 'ntyāvasāyinah.*" "*Carmakāro bhaṭo bhinno rajakaḥ puskaro naṭah Virāṭo medacāṇḍālau dāśah śvapaca kolikāḥ. etentyajāḥ samākhyātāḥ ye cānye ca gavāśanāḥ esāṁ saṁbhāṣaṇāt snānam Darśanād arkavīkṣaṇam.*"[163]

These texts mix up the two categories which Alberuni has distinguished. Only the third list clearly includes the weavers while the second list is full of traditional and uncertain names. Some of these are known to have enjoyed a much higher status in the Kusana-Satavahana and Gupta periods. The guilds of bamboo-workers and braziers, of weavers and oil-men, are known from inscription to have been prosperous, respected, cultured and important in civic matters. Brahmanical opinion tended to condemn these and other craft guilds from the later Vedic period itself and with time, this condemnation became more and more pronounced. So long the guilds were economically important and its members were not merely skilled but educated and participated in civic affairs, Brahmanical opinion could have been of but little significance Gradually, however, the guilds sank into mere sub-castes, and then naturally the long-standing brahmanical opinion overtook them and condemned them to the status of depressed castes (*hīnajātis*). Thus Vīra-mitrodaya states:

"*Śreṇyo rajakādyaṣṭādaśa hīnajātayaḥ.*"[164]

The Brahmanical criterion of social evaluation tended to be consistently anti-economic and deprecatory of physical labour. Now economic development required the combination of knowledge with labour and capital. The brahmanical view tended to separate these and devalue labour in particular. Th separation of head and hand proved a most unfortunate circumstance. Similarly the imposition of a servile status on an ever-increasing section of the population tended to destroy the very source of the strength of Indian society in ancient times, which had been essentially a society of freemen—

Aryas—contrasted with other societies such as the Greeks where slavery was so important.

References

1. Cf. my *Sramana Tradition*, pp. 52ff.
2. R. Fick, *The Social Organisation in North-East India in Buddha's Time* (tr. S.K. Maitra).
3. Cf. My *Studies in the Origins of Buddhism*. The use of the *Jatakas* by Dr. T.W. Rhys Davids and Mrs. Rhys Davids may be contrasted with the critical opinions of Kosambi and Basham. The portrayal of some of the *Jatakas* at Bharhut and Sanchi shows that they must have existed as a recognized body of Buddhist literature before the second century B.C. The date when the present *Jatakatthavannana* was written down is not of great consequence since it is admittedly based on earlier traditions. A reference to Ceylon or a *couple* to Suvannabhumi are compatible with the tradition which places the writing down of the canon and the original commentaries in the time of Vaṭṭagāmaṇi. When, therefore, Winternitz says that "much of the prose assuredly belongs to the Christian era", (Winternitz, *Hist. of Ind. Lit.* Vol. II, p. 120), he does not, as far as the substantive question is concerned, speak with adequate reason which even scepticism requires. Similarly when Prof. Basham says that the "*Jatakas* and the commentaries must be rejected out of hand "(Foreword Wagle's *Society at the time of the Buddha*) for an account of society in the Buddha's day, he appears to exaggerate the unreliability of the *Jatakas*. Unlike Buddhist dogmatics, the structure of Indian society moved very slowly indeed. Consequently 'early' and 'late' do not have the same meaning in different developmental contexts. We can easily distinguish between Buddhist ideas in the first and the third centuries B.C. but it will be a virtually impossible task to distinguish the structure of Indian society in the age of Buddha from that in the age of Asoka. Nor indeed does the slow rise of towns or the emergence of long distance trade in a few luxury goods constitute, *a priori*, any economic 'revolution' leading to significant changes in social structure. The so-called Urban Revolution can only be called a misnomer. The growth of town life was a gradual process and could have affected but a small part of the population.

   Thus despite the possibility of the *Jataka* Comy. containing post-Asokan material, it does not cease to be of value for the general societal history of the period extending from the Mahajanapadas to the first Magadha empire. A more serious difficulty besetting the use of the *Jatakas* in this context is their fictional, conventional and idealizing character. This has, unfortunately, been lost sight of generally and requires extreme caution.

4. *Majjhima*. The sutta occurs in *Suttanipaṭa* also.
5. *Jataka* no. 465, *Jatakas*, IV, 153-7.
6. Cf. *Vasalasutta or Aggika Bharadvāja Sutta*
7. Cf. Muir, *Original Sanskrit Texts*.
8. Cf. A. III, 224ff (PTS) : Five kinds of Brāhmanas viz., *brāhmasamā, deva, mariyāda*; *sambhinnamaryādā, brāhmanacaṇḍāla*.
9. Cf. *Kasibharadvāja sutta* in *Suttanipāta*, also *Samyutta*; the Brahmana minister Vassakāra is mentioned in D. 16. *Phandana Jutaka* mentions a Brahmana carpenter. Cf. *Culladhanuggahajatak*, *Gopaka moggalāna moggalāna sutta* (*Majjhima*).
10. Cf. DPPN, Vol. I, p. 982.

    It is curious that Taksasila is not mentioned in the *suttas*. It certainly lay far from the sphere of Buddha's activities which were confined to the north-east.
11. Cf. *Kurudhammajataka* : *Rājā mātā mahesi ca Uparājā Purohito Rajjuko Sārathī setthī dono dovārikotatha Ganika tekādaśajanā Kurudhamme patitthitā*. This certainly includes diverse castes. *Purohita* was a Brahmana, *Setthi* a Vaisya.
12. Cf. *Majjhima* : occupations befitting the dignity of a Kulaputta were *muddā, gananā, sankhāna, Kasi, Banijja, Gorakkhā, issattha*, service as a *rajaporisa* (P.T.S. ed. I. p. 85). Kulaputta here apparently does not refer to the Ksattriyas alone.
13. *Arthasastra*, 11. 1.
14. Cf, *Jatakas* I, 504; III, l. The licchavi ruling class included *raja, uparaja, senapati* and *bhandagarika* (*Jataka*, III. l).
15. Cf. Fick, op. cit. p. 252, *Vinaya* speaks of kings, officers, Brahmins and gahapatis-*rājā vā rājabhogyo vā brāhaman o vā gahapatiko vā* (Ib. p. 152).
16. Fick includes the lower land-owning class among the *Gahapatis*, identifying the higher land-owning class with the Khattiyas (op. cit. p. 253). This does not appear to be correct for *setthis* like Anathapindika owned villages.
17. *Jataka* no. 4, *Jatakas* Vol. I, 114-23.
18. Fick, op. cit. pp. 272ff.
19. *Jataka* no. 339, *Jatakas*, III. 126ff.
20. *Jatakas*, VI. 1-30. Cf. Majumdar. *Corporate Life in Ancient India* on the guilds.
21. *Jataka*, III, 281-6.
22. *Pacittiyam*, p. 11.
23. *Pacittiyam*, p. 11.
24. Ibid., pp. 10-11. For a similar distinction of high and low among the Jainas, cf. J.C. Jain, *Life in Ancient India*, p. 141.
25. This may well be a piece of fiction on the part of the *Jataka* commentator. cf. *Citta sambhuta Jataka*, which refers to *Candala-bhasa*, *Jatakas*, IV. 391.
26. *Uttarajjhayana, adhyayana*, XII.
27. *Kalpasutra* (1977), pp. 32-34.

28. *Uvasagadasu*, see *Angasuttāni*, Vol. III, pp. 397-98.
29. *Uvasagadasa*, ed. PL Vaidya, d. 5. *Angasuttāni*.
30. *Assalayana sutta.* It may be noted that Asoka's RE V and XII mention *Yonas* along with the *Kambojas* on the frontiers of his empire.
31. A large number of Buddha's Sakyan kinsmen had joined the Sangha. Ananda and Anuruddha were Sakyas. So had many learned Brahmanas. Sāriputta himself had been a Brahmana. So were Mahā-kaccāna, Mahākassapa and others. Mahāmoggalāna's mother was a Brahmana, his father, a *gahapati*. Anāthapiṇḍika was a devoted upāsaka. Uppalavaṇṇā was a setthi's daughter. Subhaddrā and Upāli had been barbers. Angulimāla had been a robber, Ambapāli and Addhakāsī hetaerae. Sāti was a fisherman's son. Khujjutara had been a slave of queen Sāmāvatī. Isidatta was the son of a caravan guide—See Malalasekara's *DPPN*, 2 vols.
32. *History of Indian Literature*, Vol. I, p. 326.
33. Ibid. p. 465.
34. *Age of Imperial Unity*, p. 251.
35. Ibid. pp. 251-52.
36. S.P. Gupta and Ramchandran (ed.) *Mahabharata : Mythor Reality*, (1976).
37. 'Yavana' seems to refer to Ionians and a much earlier phase of Greek history than the rise of Macedon. Panini (1.4.41) refers to 'Yavana'. *Majjhima nikaya* refers to Yona. This together with Asoka's reference to Yonas as a border settlement supports that there was a pre-Alexandrian Greek colony in the extreme north-west of India. It may be recalled that the inhabitants of Nysa claimed to be Yavanas cf. CHI Vol. I. 354.
38. *Dhvanyāloka*.
39. *Kalidasa*.
40. *The Meaning of Mahābhārata*.
41. Op. cit. p. 15 Cf. Iravati Karve, *Yuganta*.
42. Hopkins, *Social and Military Position of the Ruling Caste in Ancient India*.
43. *C.H I.* Vol. I, p. 266. Hopkins concludes "Thus, while the priestly law-book says that the priest is the norm of the world', the epic says' the king is the norm of the world." (l.c).
44. Cf. Hopkins, op. cit., pp. 45-106.
45. For Hopkins, the social superiority of the Brahmanas was a product of later times. He believes that the earlier position of the Brahmana was due to the influence he exercised where as a Purohita he was a member of the king's council l.c.).
46. Cf. Mbh., Vol. I, p. 80, 147ff.
47. Cf. Sukhthankar,
48. *Mbh.* I. p.174.
49. I bid., I. p. 110-11.
50. *Mbh.* I. p. 836.

51. Ibid., I. p. 832, *Kanka-ballava-gopālā yudhyeyuriti me buddhih.*"
52. Ibid., I. pp. 894ff.
53. Ibid., III. p. 2094 : *Apāre yo bhavet pāram aplave yah plavo bhavet| śūdro vā yadi vāpyanyah sarvathā mānamarhati.* Also cf. Ibid., p. 2163 which relates how Kāpavya, a *niṣāda* and *dasyu*, rises to respectable rulership.
54. Cf. Hopkins, op. cit.
55. *Mbh.* III. pp. 2090-91.
56. *Mbh.* I. p. 836.
57. Ibid., III. p. 2214.
58. Ibid., p. 241-42.
59. Cf. Hopkins, op. cit., pp. 25-26.
60. *Mbh.* I. pp. 119-20.
61. *Mbh.* I. p. 116.
62. Ibid., III. p. 2103.
63. e.g. Ibid., III, p. 2074.
64. Ekalavya was the son of a Niṣāda chief. Ibid., p. 178. The ungrateful Gautama had gone to a Sabara settlement—ibid., III. pp. 2213.
65. Ibid., III. 2180.
66. Ibid., I., p. 43 mentions a Brahmana with a Niṣāda as wife. Parāsara has a son by and Śantanu married Matsyagandḥa or Satyavati, a fisherman's daughter—ibid. I. pp. 80-143. Yayāti's marriage—to Sarmistha is *pratiloma.*
67. Ibid., p. 110. Vidura and Kaksivata had sudra mothers and Brahmana fathers, I, p. 148ff. Pandu and Dhrtarastra had a Brahmana fathers and Ksattriya mother I. p. 150-51.
68. *Varanasankara—Mbh.* III. 2038f; *Adharottara, Mbh.* I. p.117.
69. This is ensured by their stylistic comparison. Kalidasa proclaims Valmiki as a master and his date, contrary to the usually accepted opinion, could well be earlier than that of Asvaghosa.
70. This is shown by the basic geographical data as well as the urban picture.
71. Cf. Winternitz, op. cit., Vol. I. p. 500ff. where the *Ramayana* is placed between the 3rd century B.C. and the 2nd century A.D. One fails to see the logic behind the hypothesis of the 3rd century B.C. especially when Winternitz believes that the *Ramayana* shows no contact with the Greeks.
72. The *Ramayana* too speaks of miscegenation. Ibid., p. 2:2. The famous instance of Sambuka is an example of 'disorder'.
73. *Ramayana* pp. 92-95.
74. Ibid p. 130 (verse 44) speaks of *amātyās*,. Ibid., p. 131 (verse 1) speaks of mantrin.
75. Ibid., p. 195.
76. Ibid.., p. 194, 280.
77. Ibid., p, 281.
78. Ibid., p. 285,

79. Ibid., pp. 97-98.
80. Ibid., p. 226.
81. McCrindle, *Ancient India as Described by Megasthenese and Arrian* pp. 38ff; Cf. *C.H.I.* Vol. I, pp. 409-11.
82. Cf. *CHI* Vol. I, p. 477, fn 3,
83. McCrindle, op. cit., p. 39.
84. It is true that Megasthenese is quite categorical in asserting that "all India is the property of the Crown, and no private person is permitted to own land." He further says that the peasants are required to pay, in addition to the land tribute, a fourth part of the produce of the soil. This apparently corresponds to *bhāga* since Asoka lowered it to 1/8th in case of the Lumbini village, apparently reducing the tax by half. Did *bali* then, correspond to land tribute ?
85. Thomas suggests the following equivalents, *boukoloi, poimenes, n mes, theretai-gopāla, śvaganin, vāgika, mārgāyuka—CHI.* Vol. I, p. 477.
86 *tekhnitai, demiourgoi, kapelioi-kāru, śilpin, vaidehaka*—Thomas—*loc. cit.*,
87. *Stratiotai, polemiotai—bhaṭa*, Thomas, *loc. cit.*
88. *episkopoi ephoroi—prativedaka, adhyakṣa sattrin*, Thomas, op. cit.
89. *Symboloi, synedroi—mantrin, amātya, mahāmātra*, Thomas, op. cit
90. Buhler places him between 5th century B.C. and 3rd century B.C. Vol. II, p. XLIII. *Apastamba* is also placed in the Deccan.
91. *Apostamba*, II. 1.26. Birth in the low castes is attributed to sins of the previous life : Ibid., II. 5. 11.10-11.
92. Bühler, op cit.
93. *Gautama*, 1.4.18-19. Gautama, however, goes on to condemn the *pratilomas* as ineligible for Vedic rites—Ibid. 1.4.20. Even the *anulomas* born of a sudra woman are similarly condemned—Ibid. 1.4.21.
64. *Baudhāynna*, 1.16-17.
95. Bühler, *Sacred Laws* pl. I, Vol. II, *Introduction*; Kane, *Hist. Dh.s'* Vol. I. pp. 844.
96. Apastamba and Baudhayana have been placed in the Deccan. So has been the Grammarian Katyayana.
97. *Apastamba*, I. 25.4.6.
98. Ibid. I. 4.12.10.
99. Haradatta on *Apastamba*, I. 4.12.6.
100. Cf. *C.H.I.* Vol. I, p. 240.
101. *Apastamba*, II. 2.3.4.
102. Ibid. I. 6.18.4. One may recall the *Ch. upa.*
103. Patanjali, *Lahābāhya*, Vol. II, p. 850.
104. Kangle (ed), *Arthasastra*, Part I, p. 5.
105. Ibid. p. 164.
106. Ibid. p. 221.
107. Ibid. 220.
108. Ibid. p. 10.

109. Ibid. p. 10.
110. Ibid. p. 11.
111. Ibid. p. 5.
112. Ibid. p. 32.
113. Ibid. p. 32.
114. Ibid. "*grāma-bhrtaka-Vaidehakā vā Krseyuh*".
115. Ibid. pp. 106-07.
116. Ibid. pp. 117-18.
117. Ibid. p. 119, 157.
118. Ibid. p. 134.
119. The occurrence of the word *ānulomyena* in the previous verse suggests that all *anuloma* progeny would have the caste of the father but this seems to be contradicted by '*tulyāsu*' in the same verse. Both Kulluka and Medhatithi seek to connect *ānulomyenà* with the next verse. Perhaps we should explain 10.5 as "*sarua-varṇese tulyāsu-ānulomyena* (ea) .*sambhūetāh* "and then explain 10.6 as *mātṛdosa-vigarhitānpitṛ sadṛsān eva*".
   This then would be the *vidhi* referred to in the first line of 10.7 while the second line would refer to the succeeding verses. As it is, Medhatithi is constrained to observe that 10.7 is redundant.
120. This seems to contradict 10.7 where *anantarajāta* and *dvyekāntara-jāta* are sharply distinguished.
121. Medhatithi says this verse has the effect of showing that the peoples whom the *Mbh.* mentions as Ksattriyas had ceased to be so.
122. *Manu* 10.32.
123. Ibid. 10.33.
124. Ibid. 10.34.
125. Ibid. 10.35.
126. Ibid. 10.36.
127. Ibid. 10. 37-39.
128. Ibid. 10.47-50.
129. Ibid. 10. 51-56.
130. Ibid. 10.64. ff. *Manu.* 10.65. roundly declares that by this process Brahmana become Sudra and vice versa. This is then elaborately questioned and partly denied—Ib. 10-66-67. The controversy over *bija* and *ksetra* in Ib. 10.69-72 is reminiscent of the *Jatakas*, see above.
131. Ibid. 10.81 ff.
132. *Mahabhasya*, Vol. II, p. 850.
133. *Yajnavalkya* (Bombay, 1914), pp. 25-27.
134. *vyatyaye karmanām sāmyam*" Ib. p. 27. *Mitākṣarā* elaborates it and says that if one continues the occupation of a lower caste even when there is no distress and this goes on for several generations, the rule of *jātyapakarṣa* applies, but it is silent on *jātyautkarṣa* through *karmavyatyaya.* In fact, 'purva-*vaccādharottaram*' in the text *prima facie* comments with what proceeds, i.e. *utkarṣa* and *apakarṣa.*
135. *Manu*, 10.47.

136. *Auśanasa Saṁhitā*, vv. 31-32 in *Smṛti Sandarbha* Vol. III. From the reference to *Kaysatha*, Usanas could not be earlier than the Gupta period. cf. Kane, Vol. pp. 110-16.
137. Kane. op. cit., Vol. pp. I, p. 72.
138. Cf. *C.H.I.* Vol. p. 376.
139. *Smrtisandarbha* Vol. II, p. 1545, V. 13.
140. *Tai-Br.* Vol. II. p. 957.
141. *Usanas*, op. cit., p. 1548, V. 41-"*nrpasya dandaharah syāt*. . . . ."
142. *Usanas*, op. cit. p. 1546. Wher *Vaidehikas* are herdsmen. Cf. Kane, op. cit., Vol. II, pl. I p. 96.
143. Kane, *Hist. of Dharma*, Vol. I, p. 115.
144. *Smrtisandarbha* Vol. III, pp. 1548-49. Cf. Yadav, B.N.S., *Society and Culture*, pp. 38ff for the diversity of social and occupational group which gradually came to be included among the *sūdras*.
145. *Paraśara smrtī*, 11.22-25.
146. *Travels* (tr. gils), p. 21.
147. Ibid. *l.c.*
148. Ibid. *l.c.*
149. *Brhaspati smrti*, pp. 12-13, verses 72-75.
150. Ibid. p. 304, vv. 528-30 "*Śūdrasya divijaśuśrūṣā sarvaśilpāni cāpyatha Vikrayaḥ sarvapaṇyānāṁ śūdradharma udāhṛtaḥ.*
151. Ibid. p. 71.
152. Ibid. p. 135. *Silpa* is also called *Vijnana*, Ibid. p. 142, v. 7.
153. Ibid. p. 142, vv. 11-12.
154. Ibid. p. 143.
155. Ibid. p. 171, v. 13.
156. Ibid. p. 383, vv. 74-75, p. 385, v. 86.
157. Cf. Kane, op. cit., Vol. II, pt I, pp. 184-85.
158, *Katyayana-mata-sangraha*, by N.C. Bondyopadhyaya, p. 52.
159. Ibid. p. 55.
cāturvarnyasya yā sūtirasājātyādi sambhavā.
tasyadharmaḥ samuddiṣṭaḥ jātiḥ sāparikiritītā.
160. Ibid. "*samūharthāścha ye cānye vargākhyāste Bṛhaspatih.*"
161. Watters, Vol. I, p. 147.
162. Sachau, *Alberuni's India*, Vol.I, p. 101.
163. Vide Kane, *Hist. of the Dharma*, Vol. II, pt. I, p. 70 fn. 170 and 171, p. 171, fn. 173.
164. *Viramitrodaya*, Kane curiously says "This shows that these low castes had risen in social status in the medieval ages by their organisation and wealth." (op. cit. p. 70).

11

Political Order and Ideas

Historical Development :

Traditionally political authority has been held in high esteem in India. The state was expected to provide security against internal disorder and external invasions, maintain the external conditions of virtue, promote the happiness and welfare of the people and patronize learning and culture. To protect the people, the state was required to wield force in accordance with Law. By regulating social behaviour, it was to hinder the hindrances to the pursuit of virtue. It was to promote public prosperity through a wise policy of taxation, public works, charitable works, assistance to economic activities and organising economic enterprise. It was to promote culture by maintaining and rewarding learned men and scholars, poets, authors and artists. The fabric of culture, thus, depended on the state at three levels—at the level of security, at the level of general prosperity, and at the level of direct patronage. Till the end of the Mauryan period, the state was generally successful in its tasks but in the post-Mauryan period, it failed to meet the challenge of foreign invasions though it continued to follow an enlightened economic and cultural policy till the Gupta period. In the post-Gupta period, the political order is now increasingly held to have become relatively more oppressive in the socio-economic sphere and it had certainly become more anarchic, though it continued to patronise culture till its overthrow by foreign invaders.

According to the commonly accepted opinion about Vedic polity, the people were then divided into clans or tribes called *Janas*. Five *Janas* are commonly mentioned *Puru*, *Anu*, *Yadu*, *Tṛtsu* and *Druhyu* are examples of *Janas*. Similarly, we hear of the *Bharatas* or the *Bhārata Jana*. It may be mentioned that the most ancient commentarial tradition regarded the names as simply names of men.[1] Sayana occasionally follows this, at other times following the epic tradition which makes these simply as names of ruling families or Ksattriya dynasties. It is possible that ancient tribes, calling themselves simply as human collectivities, came to survive in later times as simply ruling clans or families. It is, however, not clear as to where exactly the early Vedic period belongs in this process of evolution. The prevalence of agriculture certainly rules out a nomadic tribal polity for the period. By the later Vedic times, we might assume that *Puru* etc., were simply ancient ruling families because the *Janapadas* which were formed at this time do not correspond to these ancient names. Later Vedic Janapadas suggest clans like *Sivi*, *Kuru* or *Pañcāla*. The continuity between clan and family may be seen in the history of mediaeval Rajput *gots* like Sisodia etc. of Rajasthan.

Again, general opinion holds that the Vedic *Janas* were ruled by kings with the help of *Sabhā* and *Samiti*. Several scholars, most prominently Jayaswal, have argued that Vedic kingship was elective.[2] Some other scholars have sought to amend this by arguing that the election might have been simply selection or approval. One recent author has sought to reconstruct the diversity and developmental stages of Vedic polity, arguing that Vedic literature evidences monarchy as well as aristocratic republics.[3] This is not impossible in view of what we know of later times but the republican form was conceivably of later origin than the popular monarchy since the early Vedic pantheon seems to be organized as a monarchy rather than as a republic.

Samiti appears to have been the larger body, a gathering of the clans or of all the people, while *Sabhā* might have consisted of the companions of the king or the elders. The resolution of the *Sabhā*, expressing the opinion of many, was held inviolable and its connection with the dispensation of justice is clear in the later Vedic age. The two are called the 'twin daughters of Prajāpati'. It is clear that although the

Vedic king was the leader in war, the final judge and the representative of the people and thus invested with authority which made him an earthly parallel to Indra and Varuna, the divine rulers, he was no autocrat. He was the leader of a free people and responsible to their assemblies and councils. The responsible character of the king did not mean that he was to pander to the whims of the common people or was continuously required to obtain a favourable vote in the assembly. The *Samiti* could meet occasionally to elect a king or decide on war, while the *Sabhā* was more a body of councillors and assessors. The leadership and authority of the king were undisputed. His responsibility was primarily to Law, not to mere men and opinions. Law (*vrata*, *dharman*) was not the mere fiat of one man or many men. Law was revealed and traditional and echoed in the sense of equity in the community. The king was expected to conform to high ideals and tradition. The body of priests was the custodian of the revealed law but the people in their assemblies voiced the traditional mores. Governance was a matter of high moment and the role of the people in it was neither that of passivity nor of detailed interference. The priests and the people were interpreters of an order of which the king was the chief custodian and executive. The early Vedic king was a hero, the companion and patron of seers whose immortal hymns commemorate the names of some of their patrons. The priest declared the revealed law but did not rule. The king accepted the law and strove to enforce it. The priest and the king worked in coordinate independence and constituted a unique hierarchy.

In the later Vedic age, we find divergent tendencies. While the principle of heredity replaced that of election in the monarchical states, some states appear to have developed as republics. At the same time, within the monarchies the notion of approval by the people did not die out. The *Ratnins* remained as the representatives of the people. They included persons from the household of the king, his administrative officials, representatives of the villages of the estates. The king sought to become superior to others and to attain an imperial status not merely by war but by ritual. The kinsmen of the king formed an aristocracy which, as the epics depict, was engaged in fighting, hunting, drinking and gambling. The lure of power brought the aristocracy into not merely internecine conflicts such as reflected in *Mbh.*, but also in conflict with the Brahmanas, which is illustrated by the legends of the *Haihayas* and the *Yādavas*. The notion of the exploitation of the Vaiśyas and the Sudras probably arose within this unrestricted aristocratic ethos.

The kings themselves sometimes turned away from the pursuit of war to that of philosophy. This represented the other side of the aristocratic ethos. The idea of the philosopher king or sage-king (*rājarṣi*) who combines in himself wisdom as well as power was an alternative to the hierarchial principle of two powers. In the nature of the case, the idea remained a rare ideal. On the other hand, the imperial ideal and the sacrifices designed to help the king to realize it became a permanent part of the Hindu political tradition, and this made the priest a ritual assistant to the king. A class of bards recounted the exploits of the kings and sought to preserve their names and genealogies. This bardic tradition came to constitute history and antiquity (*Itihāsa Purāṇa*). Some modern scholars have argued that there was a conflict between the kings and the priests. Conflicts there must have been between kings and priests and so much is attested by ancient texts. But one can hardly speak of any organized, continued or general conflict. In fact, neither of the two castes had an organization which could ensure such a conflict.

Samiti still functioned in the later Vedic age as a reference in the *Chāndogya* suggests. *Sabhā* continued as the king's court. The administration of the state depended on the regular collection of taxes called *Bhāga* and *Bali*. Tax collectors were permanent officials called *bhāgadugha*. The army had its own regular commander called *Senānī*. The king was kept informed by couriers designated *Pālāgala*. The household was under the chamberlain or *Kṣattā*. *Ugras* were armed members of the king's retinue acting as policemen. The villages largely governed themselves under their headmen called *grāmaṇī*. Where the realm was large enough to have provinces, the king appointed a kinsman of his to the office of the governor.

The 'imperial' and internecine conflicts and wars of the later Vedic kings as recounted in the bardic tradition may sound unreal but their interest in philosophy and patronage to philosophers started a greater tradition. Kings like Aśvapati of Kekaya, Pravāhaṇa Jaivali of Pañcāla, Jānaśruti Pautrāyaṇa, Ajātaśatru of Kāśi and Janaka of Videha are avid teachers or students of *Brahmavidyā* in the *Upaniṣads*. *Dharma* was the King of Kings.[4] It was revealed to and proclaimed by the Brahman while Ksattriya maintained it. The two constituted the twin pillars of Vedic polity. The 'sacred marriage' of spiritual authority and temporal power ensured a law-abiding government which in turn ensured public safety and a just order.[5] This pristine order was corrupted towards the end of the Vedic age by the growth of aristocratic pride and priestly cupidity. Traditionally the *Mahābhārata* battle destroyed the flower of ancient chivalry and thus began the Kali Age.[6]

From the sixth century B.C., we see an intense conflict between monarchies and between monarchies and republics. Behind this conflict lay the phenomenon of a declining and effete aristocracy, in the republics as well as the monarchies. These Ksattriyas, proud of their ancient lineage. engaged in duelling and fighting, romancing, hunting and gambling, remind one of European mediaeval chivalry. They fought according to a code, and honour was dearer to them than life or victory. They lost ground increasingly to new parvenu princes who captured power with the help of mercenary and professional soldiery and councillors who followed the new science of politics concerned with the realities of power rather than conventional tradition. The rise of cities and commercial wealth certainly made the hiring of soldiers and officials possible. Upstart adventurers with hired assistants ultimately succeeded in destroying the traditional aristocracy, which reminds one of the rise of the New Monarchy in the 15th century in Europe at the expense of traditional chivalry.

Bimbisara, Prasenajit and Udayana are historical examples of the heroic and aristocratic rulers, chivalrous and generous, virtuous and romantic. Ajātaśatru, though not an upstart by birth, is said to have acted like a bastard and certainly followed the principles of the new Realpolitik. He destroyed the old aristocratic republic of the Licchavis. Vidūḍabha was treated like a bastard and reacting like one wreaked vengeance on the republican Śākyas, a kind of cruel nemesis for their pride of caste. Mahāpadma Nanda and Candragupta Maurya whom the *Purāṇas* dub as Śūdras and base-born finally eliminated the ancient Ksattriya ruling families and not only rescued the country from endemic anarchy but also created a state capable of resisting the invasions of powerful states beyond the Indian frontier. For a time, India became politically and militarily respected and enjoyed political security and peace. The age of the rise and fall of the First Magadha Empire remains the real classical age of India when her basic philosophies and sciences, institutions and ideals were formulated in the *sūtras* and in the original and now largely lost *saṁhitās* and similar works. The creative age of Indian political science lies entirely in this period The Greeks were favourably impressed by the Maurya empire and described the people as truthful and just, law-abiding. and loyal, free and brave. The period of the *sūtras* saw the emergence of the two distinct conceptions of *rājadharma* and *daṇḍanīti.* The former looked upon governance as the performance of a socially given and codified duty by a ruler for whom the problem of acquiring and maintaining power did not arise. *Nīti* on the other hand, concentrated on governance as the acquisition and exercise of power. Since popular contentment was a source of strength for the ruler, *Nīti* oriented itself towards the conception of a welfare state, which is best illustrated by the *Arthaśāstra.*

Vast and orderly, the Maurya empire was no despotism. By necessity and choice, life was largely autonomous in the country-side. Taxation was mild, crime infrequent. But the state supervised affairs indefatigably. It had an efficient intelligence and courier service and insisted on detailed records and periodical inspections. There was a regular bureaucracy and departmental organization where officials were often organized into supervisory boards. Councils discussed affairs at the local as well as the central level. Provinces were placed under princes of the royal blood. Villages were looked after by the elders and royal officers called *Gopa* and *Sthānika*. Towns were governed by a body of municipal officers. Civic regulation about sanitation and cleanliness, markets and traffic was quite strict. The state looked after the cleaning of the forests, the needs of irrigation, and the requirements of widows, orphans and destitutes. Life was kept in regular order without too much interference. The state was strong and enlightened but not despotic. The people enjoyed security and prosperity along with freedom.

From about the middle of the second century B.C., there is a dramatic change of scene. The country is now repeatedly overrun by foreign invaders—Bactrians, Scythians, Parthians and Kusanas. Following the Hellenistic, Roman and Chinese traditions brought into country by these Central Asian invaders, the character of the monarchy began to change. Kings now claimed divinity and assumed high sounding titles raising them above their fellowmen. A new ruling class came into existence and began to share administrative and economic power with the rulers. The traditional system of social classes was badly shaken and distorted and the *Smṛtikāras* felt the social order threatened. They invoked the notion of social miscegenation or *varṇasaṅkara* as the determining phenomenon of the day. A new emphasis on rigidity and orthodoxy was the reaction to the current mixture and multiplication of social groups. The position of women suffered under the conditions of insecurity and the impact of male-dominated invading groups. The age of marriage was lowered and consequentially restrictions placed on women's opportunities of Vedic study. The *Vedas* were preserved ever more jealously from the ineligible classes. At the same time, a more anthromorphic religion arose to meet the need of the foreigners recruited to Indian culture. Anthropomorphic deities and images acquired importance and so did the notion of the saving grace of God. Mahayanic Buddhism and Puranic Hinduism both exhibited these tendencies fully.

Two factors, however, checked this mounting wave of Central Asian influences. The cultural vitality of the people captivated the conquerors who were quickly and wholly Indianized. Economic prosperity continued to grow on account of the new contacts with other countries. Thus political anarchy was compensated by economic and cultural expansion and a new refinement of urban civilization. The rise of polished literature, patronized by kings and merchants, of rational philosophical systems and of science abreast of international standards attested to this phase of progress in civilization. All these tendencies reached their culmination in the Gupta period.

The Gupta empire was essentially an empire of Āryāvarta which left out the Uttarāpatha and Dakṣiṇāpatha. The trans-Indus region tended to move out of the Indian into the Iranian and Central Asian spheres of influence. The decline of political power, thus, had the direct consequence of contracting the boundaries of Indian society. The Gupta emperors claimed the majesty of the divine *lokapālas*. They were themselves educated and accomplished and patronized learned men, saints, poets and artists. It is the brilliance of the poets and artists of the age which has made the Gupta period memorable. New temples and monasteries were built and art reached a distinctive refinement of style. The prosperity of the age is attested by its abundant gold coinage. Fa-hien speaks of the mildness of the rule, of the small incidence of crime and light punishments. There is ample evidence of religious toleration and of the growth of science and learning. Tradition remembered the age of Vikramāditya as a golden age.

From the middle of the fifth century, the danger of invasions from the north-west loomed large again and the cultural fabric created under a century of peace stood threatened. For a time, the empire was able to withstand the danger successfully by adopting a vigorous policy of frontier defence. It was still able to produce some heroic rulers and warriors. The end of the century, however, saw a reversal of fortunes. The struggle for succession made the empire ineffective and the Hūṇas appeared like a terrible scourge. A wave of destruction swept through the empire and a great age passed.

Although the post-Gupta age saw many brilliant courts and powerful dynastic empires, the extent, stability and prosperity of the Gupta age were not recovered. Dynastic wars were frequent and a new aristrocracy claiming to stem from Rajput clans came on the scene. It has been suggested that these clans owed their origin to the impact of the Hūṇas or of the aboriginal tribes in central India and Rajasthan. While this remains a surmise, there is no doubt of the emergence of new ruling groups which sought to legitimize themselves as Ksattriya clans.[7] The character of the monarchy tended to change as a result. The kinsmen of the ruler or the clan as such began to claim special rights and the practice of assigning revenues to officials in lieu of services coupled with the growth of nobles and conquered rulers as vassals of the king created a near-feudal system. Sovereignty came to be regarded as a privilege arising from the circumstances of birth and closely connected with the right of collecting taxes over an area and exercising police functions in it. While in theory sovereignty remained impartible and was quite distinct from property or land-owning, in practice a good deal of confusion was bound to arise. The most important consequences of this system were the increase of burden on cultivators and traders by the multiplication of imposts and tolls and the decrease in the cohesion of the army. The army of the king largely came to consist of the levies brought by his vassals. These soilders owed their loyalty to the vassals primarily and the vassals had only a personal bond with the ruler. The 'dynastic armies', thus were very fragile and instable in structure. Defeats and victories were decided by single battles as if wars were nothing but personal combats. The political structure ceased to be a deep-rooted and stable structure in which the people participated. It became a system of many small princedoms owing temporary allegiance to the precarious power of a suzerain.[8] It became just a dynastic matter at the top. In course of time, the top came to be managed by rulers of foreign origin who refused to be converted as in the Scythian period. The state informed by a wholly different political tradition, thus, came to be hostile or at best indifferent to the traditional social and cultural order.

The Character of the State

The state was expected to promote public 'good and happiness' (*hitasukha*) through the adoption of a policy ultimately backed by force (*daṇḍa*) but in accordance with Right (*dharma*). Although the ends which the state ultimately promoted, formed part of the general scheme of human ends (*puruṣārtha*) as conceived in the social system, the direct objectives of its policy were defined as *dharma* and *artha*. *Dharma* stands in a manner reminiscent of Plato for justice as well as for the social allocation of roles and duties. *Rāja-dharma* as political obligation is part of *dharma* in the wider sense and is constituted by the duty of conforming to and supporting the traditionally conceived socio-ethical order. *Artha* stands for interests and utilities, for power and goods. Although objectively seen, the contents of *dharma* and *artha* would seem to overlap, their distinction arises from the way in which each is given to us. *Dharma* is transcendently given. It cannot be apprehended by mere instinct, perception or reason. *Artha*, on the other hand, is what is desired directly or indirectly. For example, one may fight to protect oneself or to gain glory. One would then be pursuing *artha*. On the other hand, one may give up one's life or fight out of a sense of duty, which would be part of *dharma*. *Dharma* as the Law is primarily revealed but practically known through tradition, especially the sacred tradition (*Trayī*). *Artha* comprising economic and administrative affairs is known through the imperial sciences of *Vārtā* and *Daṇḍanīti*. The belief in *dharma* as a perennial moral order to be followed in practice tended to orient the traditional political system towards stability and conservatism especially since *dharma* was believed to be ultimately accessible through revelation and its details authoritatively formulated in the *smṛtis*. Thus formally there could be neither doubt nor question about the content or validity of the system of *dharma*. Learned Brahmanas and their councils (*pariṣad*) constituted an authentic source of decisions about the interpretation of *dharma*. The legislative activity of the ruler was required to be wholly subordinated to the code of *dharma* thus formulated and interpreted. The state, thus, was checked from attempting to play a 'progressive' or 'revolutionary' role. 'Revolution' was, therefore, conceived to be synonymous with either anarchy or the re-establishment of order after anarchy. In fact, the prevalent view was that the order of *dharma* is periodically undermined and then resuscitated. History shows a tendency, not towards progress, but towards the decline of virtue, though in the long run it follows a cyclical pattern.

Originally, however, in the Vedic period, the idea of *ṛta* or *dharma* was more the idea of a general divine or 'natural' law rather than a formulated code. For long the attempts to decode *Ṛta* were only in terms of ritual symbolism which was added to diverse social ceremonies. In due course, these were themselves codified and conceptual explanations added. This process of the codification and interpretation of the *dharma* went on slowly for millennia and in its course did include not only the elaboration but also the modification of laws. Consequently, despite the conservative orientation of the ancient political system, the socio-legal system which it sought to maintain, underwent a slow change through a process of adaptive interpretation. Nevertheless by the early mediaeval period, the *smṛti* tradition came to exercise sometimes an almost paralysing and cruel grip on the political functioning. The Yadavas of Devagiri or the Senas of Bengal are examples of this.

It is true that there were some thinkers who denied the reality of any transcendent or revealed order. They tended to be materialistic and hedonistic and exalted the king as the sole source of law and justice. The school of thought was hostile to brahmanical orthodoxy and did influence some sections of political thought which tended to look upon religion and morality as merely conventions to be taken note of by the ruler. This Lokāyata positivism tended to encourage the non-metaphysical tendency of the *Arthaśāstra* and also its characteristic amoral or 'Machiavellian' doctrine of *raison d'etat*. This tended to produce a conflict between the *Dharmaśāstra* and the *Arthaśāstra* in which the latter was ultimately wiped out as a rational theory leaving behind only the ideas of expediency and customary.

The brahmanical tradition of *dharma* was opposed by the Sramanic tradition which sought to hark back to the original idea of *dharma* as an imponderable and universal moral law which was to be apprehended not in terms of ritual symbolism but by one's own purified intuition. Such an appeal to one's own self (*paccattam*) and the disregard of established orthodoxy constituted a tradition of moral and social reform to which belonged not only Buddha and Mahavira but many later saints from time to time. The spiritual authority of these reformers enabled them to create new communities, especially religious, but they did not essay the more difficult task of radically altering the traditional social order. By and large, Buddhist and Jaina rulers remained conservative in their social policy. Asoka was undoubtedly an exception but there was none to emulate him conspicuously. It should, however, be remembered that Asoka like Buddha appealed to the universal and essential idea of *dhamma* as the standard by which current distortions or natural deviations may be judged and corrected. This was not formally disputable within the tradition and hence the authority of the ruler to act in accordance with the idea of reform also could not be disputed. The really disputable thing was the claim of brahmanical orthodoxy to have the monopoly of interpreting the *dharma*. That is why Manu following Asoka lays all the stress on the position of the Brahmanas who were at the very time giving the lie to Manu by assuming royal authority through engineering a political revolution.

The peaceful co-existence of rival interpretations of *dharma* made the state catholic and tolerant, a feature which has attracted wide attention. The freedom of opinion and worship were rarely challenged and the philosophical and religious literature of ancient India, which is full of diversities, bears eloquent testimony to this freedom as do the copious records of benefactions unhampered by sectarian consideration.

If the brahmanical privilege provided too narrow a base for the understanding of *dharma*, the appeal to personal intuition would appear to have been too variable. Under the circumstances, it is not surprising that the actual rules evolved by each locality, community and corporation were treated as valid laws for them to the extent they were consonant with morality. Actually operative laws must have depended far more on this free creativity and variability of 'local' tradition than on the supposedly Procrustean bed of canonical law.

This leads us to what may be called the free or 'democratic' ethos of the ancient polity. Despite western deprecation, a host of Indian historians proved during the national movement that democratic institutions were a real and significant part of the ancient political tradition. Elective kingship, popular assemblies, and republican constitutions were known in the Vedic and early post-Vedic times. In classical polity too, royal power was not absolute but limited in a variety of ways. The king was required to keep the people pleased and to ascertain their opinions through their assemblies and leaders. Councils existed at all levels. Procedures of debate and voting were well developed, although consensus was the ideal usually striven after. The consent and judgment of the elders were generally sought. Corporate bodies of diverse kinds existed, villages and towns, guilds and castes being the most important. They had their own councils and leaders. Their traditions were respected and this ensured their autonomy.

Nor was this democratic ethos, this spirit of governance by consultation and consensus, a mere looseness of grip; for administrative mechanisms adequate to the governance of vast territorial empires had been successfully devised. This democratic spirit was essentially the spirit of autonomy (*svarājya*), of respect for law which was not the fiat of any man however high but a just norm discoverable by the wise leaders of any corporate group. It did not give any concession to the spirit of license (*Kāmakāra*) but only recognized the right of a community to discover and follow its corporate law and tradition. The success of democratic institutions in contemporary India certainly tends to disprove the contention of those who regarded such reconstructions as merely patriotic fabrications. The tradition of democratically managing social affairs through village and caste *pancayats* did, in fact, survive long centuries of militaristic and feudal misrule. This democratic ethos, however, was based on the traditional solidarity of the community, not the rights of the individual. The whole of our contemporary emphasis on individualism and rights has a wholly modern western origin. The whole conception of man as a social animal whose rational being is exhausted by social roles and relations and of society as a system of competing individuals and classes is alien to the Indian tradition for which man is a spiritual being characterized by moral reason, individual identity being inseparable from social roles, and classes being essentially co-operative.

Since social being is not an externally given reality, the nature and meaning of social or political institutions cannot be comprehended simply by noticing their formal features. It is only in terms of the interpretation put on them by the social psyche for which they primarily exist, that they can be adequately understood. Thus the transportation of western political forms to India does not ensure any real transference of the institutions concerned. For this reason, it is necessary to relate politcal institutions to their underlying moral ideas and the general social and cultural milieu. It will be short-sighted, indeed, to assume that the western political tradition has been appropriated in India simply by institutional imitation and class-room teaching. The examination of political reality in India necessarily passes into the historical examination of its tradition. Now what is perennially important about the ancient political tradition is its philosophy, not the ephemeral laws and forms it threw up from time to time.

According to the *Arthaśāstra*, Ānvīksikī or Philosophy illumines all the sciences (*vidyās*). This recognition should be pondered over by those modern critics who accuse the ancient Indian political tradition of being unphilosophical. As a matter of fact, they fail to see that knowledge was conceived as a hierarchy of sciences in ancient India. *Nītiśāstra* being concerned with the strategy of managing empirical behaviour, could not itself be philosophical but it presupposed philosophy. Philosophy was basically metaphysical and cosmological. As rational reflection over revealed knowledge, it came next to *trayī*, though in its methodological aspect as the logic of statements (*nyāya*) and imperatives (*mīmāṁsā*) it took precedence in the order of principles and training. As *adhyātma-vidyā*, of course, it depended on the *āgama* and showed that the understanding of man (anthropology) can only be reached through cosmology (*brahmavidyā*). Since the macrocosm (*brahmāṇḍa*) and the microcosm (*piṇḍa*) were held to be in correspondence, it was believed that the empirical order of human behaviour (*vyavahāra* or *adhibhūtam*) is to be understood in terms of inner psycho-ethical phenomena (*abhidhar-*

mataḥ, adhyatmam) which can be understood only in terms of their cosmic ground or ultimate value (*paramārthataḥ*), *Trayī* and *Ānvīkṣikī*, thus, are superior in the hierarchy of knowledge to *Vārtā* and *Daṇḍanīti*. The former are concerned with foundational and intelligible principles while the latter deal with empirical and behavioural realities which they seek to control, something entirely different from philosophical reflection moving towards vision (*theoria*) and inner freedom. Nevertheless, since the whole of social life is based on the manner in which the self and the non-self are mutually related in consciousness proper philosophical understanding tends to influence social attitudes, values and modes of action. Philosophy as faith helps right action which in turn helps the rise of wisdom. The content of faith insofar as it includes the norms of action and the corresponding institutions of practical life, though adumbrated in *Trayī*, is formulated in the *Dharmaśāstra* which, again, is presupposed more proximately by the *Arthaśāstra*. The political tradition of ancient India is thus not confined to *Daṇḍanīti* or *Arthaśāstra* but is extended over all the four *vidyās* mentioned by Kautilya. It includes by implication political philosophy as well as political science.

Basic Philosophy

The essential idea of the ancient political tradition of India may be said to have lain in the conception of an appropriate union of two principles viz., wisdom and power. In the Vedic age, this idea was imaged as the dual deity Mitrā-Varuna and was sought to be institutionalized as the twin offices of Purohita and Rājanya, Brahman and Kṣattra. The *Varna* system provided a social expression and safeguard to this idea by placing the Brahmana above the Ksattriya as the authoritative exponent of traditional sacred wisdom but reserving the exercise of power as a privilege for the Ksattriya. In the post-Vedic age, the basic ideal came to be understood in due course as the unity of *Dharma* and *Nīti*. *Dharma* stood for justice as such and for the traditionally conceived social order. What has been called Natural Law in the West is possibly the best equivalent of *Dharma*. *Nīti*, on the other hand, was conceived as Policy or the system of means employed in the exercise of power. *Dharma* was codified and interpreted by the Brahmanas. *Nīti* was basically Kṣattra-vidyā, the prudence of the ruler and his administrative counsellors and assistants. The separation and co-ordination of the Brahmana and the Ksattriya were thus again brought into play, but, unfortunately, this no longer served as an effective practical device because the *Varnas* had become hereditary and their functions had ceased to be uniquely characteristic.

Within *Dharma* and *Nīti* severally also an inner duality was sought to be harmonized. *Dharma* included *sādhāraṇa dharma* as well as *varṇāśrama-dharma*, general morality as well as specifically codified and institutionalized social ethics. The perception of *Dharma* thus required moral intuition as well as access to tradition. Only in terms of a wisdom which was at once pure in its intuition and well informed in its preception of social content could *Dharma* be adequately apprehended and interpreted. Similarly *Nīti* comprised a basic quality of intelligence and force, which is implicit in the very phrase *daṇḍanīti*. Just as in the case of *Dharma*, emphasis was to be placed on its conventional rather than rational side, similarly in the case of *Nīti*, emphasis was placed on prudence and expedience rather than on force or the will which is its psychic source. Indeed Kalidasa expresses scorn at the idea of mere *nīti* as sheer cowardice, mere bravery as sheer barbarism. "*Kātaryaṁ Kevalā nītiḥ Śauryaṁ śvāpadaceṣṭitam*". (*Raghu*, 17.47).[9]

Right governance thus requires the regulation of force by intelligent policy and of policy by moral reason. Only those who have a pure character and high wisdom can act as lawgivers. Only those who respect the law and are at the same time gifted with prudence and determination can act as rulers. The former can only be obtained within a living tradition of moral and spiritual wisdom. Rulers of the right kind can only be obtained through right education "*Vinayo rājyamūlaṁ*" (*Arthaśāstra*). The union of disinterested wisdom with effective power in society can result only from a mode of education which teaches individuals self-government within. To restrain the senses and subordinate the mind to higher reason, this is the path of self-government or spiritual education called *Yoga* and vividly described in the *Kaṭhopanisad* and the *Gīta*. Without it, there cannot be produced any *Brahmarṣi* or *Rājarṣi* or *Dhārmika Cakravartin*, nor any 'sacred marriage' of *Brahman* and *Ksattra*. Unless philosophy as the search of wisdom is well established as the most valued activity in a society, the possibility of its being well-governed does not arise. At the same time, virtue in the original sense, as *vīrya*, must also be cultivated. That is why *Brahmacarya*, 'the tending of Brahman', is held to confer both wisdom and manly prowess.

Unfortunately the ancient *Varnas* were corrupted into hereditary castes, the ancient formulations of *dharma* and *niti* became converted into systems of conventions, the ancient institution of *Brahmacarya* simply fell into disuse, and philosophy became otherworldly. As a result, Indian polity was perverted from its high moral purpose into a petty game of self-seeking; a situation in which rulers and politicians cannot possibly stake their all in the event of a serious foreign invasion.

References

1. *Nighaṇtu*, 2.3. includes them among twentyfive *'manusya namani'*. Yaska mentions several interpretations of "*Gandharvāḥ pitaro devā asurā raksāṁsītyeke Catvāro Varnā niṣādah Pancamah ityaupamanyavāḥ*" (*Nirukta*, 3.8). Some modern linguists have suggested that *panca* originally may also have had the sense of 'all'.
2. *Hindu Polity*.
3. J.P. Sharma, *Republics in Ancient India*.
4. *Br. Up.* quotd supra.
5. Coomarswami, *Spiritual Authority and Temporal Power*.
6. Modern scholarship regards it as an age of progress based on the introduction of iron.
7. Cf. B.D. Chattopadhyaya, *IHR*. Vol III. No. 1, pp. 59ff.
8. Cf. D.C. Sircar, *The Emperor and Subordinate Rulers*.
9. This refernce was pointed out to me by my friend Dr. S.C. Pande of the Deptt. of Sanskrit, University of Allahabad.

Selected Bibliography

I. Original Texts and Translations

(a) *Vedic*

Aitareyabrāhmaṇa, 2 Vols., Pune, 1930.

Atharvavedasaṁhitā, Aundh, V.S. 1995.

Īśādidaśopaniṣadaḥ with Śaṅkara's commentary, Vāṇīvilāsa Series, Kashi.

Nirukta, 2 Vols., Bombay, 1921.

Ṛgvedasaṁhitā with Sāyaṇa's commentary, 4 Vols., Pune, 1933.

Ṛgvedasaṁhitā with commentaries, ed. Vishwabandhu, 8 Vols., Hoshiarpur, 1965-66.

Śatapathabrāhmaṇa, 2 Vols., Kashi, V.S. 1994.

Taittirīyabrāhamaṇa, 3 Vols., Pune, 1934.

Taittirīyasaṁhitā, 8 Vols., Pune, 1901.

Taṇḍyamahābrāhmaṇa, Varanasi, 1936.

Vājasaneyisaṁhitā, Bombay, 1929.

Vedic Word Concordance, 16 Vols., Hoshiarpur.

Geldner (tr.), *Der Ṛgveda*, 4 Vols., Harvard University Press, 1951-57.

Grassmann, *Wörterbuch zum Ṛgveda*, Leipzig, 1873.

Griffith, R.T.H., (tr.), *Hymns of the Ṛgveda*, 2 Vols., Chowkhamba Sanskrit Series, (C.S.S.), Varanasi.

Lüdwig (tr.), *Ṛgveda*.

(b) *Buddhist and Jain*

Ācārāṅgasūtra and Sūtrakṛtāṅga with Śīlāṅka's commentary, Delhi, 1978.

Aṅgasuttāni, 3 Vols., ed. Muni Nathmal, Ladnu, V.S. 2031.

Aṅgavijjā, Vol. I, ed., Muni Punya Vijay, Prakrit Text Series, Varanasi, 1957.

Bhagavatī Viyāhapannatti, with Abhayadeva's commentary, Bombay, 1918-21.

Catuḥśataka by Āryadeva. ed. H.P. Śāstrī, Calcutta, 1914.

Dasa-veyāliya, Calcutta, V.S. 2020.

Divyāvadāna, Cambridge, 1886.

Jaina Sūtras, tr. Jacobi, S.B.E., Vols. 22 and 45.

Jātakaṭṭhavaṇṇanā, ed. Fausböll.

L'Abhidharmakośa de Vasubandhu, Louvain, 1923-29.

Mahāvastu Avadāna, 3 Vols., Calcutta, 1963-68.

Milindapañha, ed. Trenckner, 1928.

Pāli Tripiṭaka, 40 Vols., Nalanda ed.

Samantapāsādikā, Nava Nalanda Mahavihara, Patna.

Thāṇam, Ladnu, V.S. 2033.

Uttarajjhayaṇam, Jamnagar, 1938.

Vajrasūcī, ed. & tr. S.K. Makhopadhyaya, 2nd ed., Shantineketan, 1960.

II. Dharmasutras, Arthaśāstra & Itihāsa-purāṇa

Agnipurāṇa, C.S.S., Varanasi, 1966.

Āpastamba Dharmasūtra, ed. A.C. Shastri & A.R. Shastri, Banaras, 1932.

Arthaśāstra, 3 Vols., ed. & tr. R.P. Kangle, Bombay University.

Arthaśāstra, 3 Vols., ed. & ann. Gaṇapati Śāstrī, Trivandrum.

Arthaśāstra, ann. Rājeśvara Śāstrī Drāviḍa.

Arthaśāstra with Bhaṭṭasvāmin's commentary, Patna, 1926.

Baudhāyana Dharmasūtra, C.S.S., Varanasi, 1972.

Bhāgavatapurāṇa, pub. by Krishna Shankar Śāstrī, Varanasi, 1965.

Bṛhaspatismṛti, Reconstructed by K.V.R. Aiyangar, G.O.S., Baroda, 1941.

Devalasmṛti, collected in *Smṛtīnām Samuccayaḥ*, ed. V.G. Apte, Ānandāśrama Sanskrit Series (A.S.S.), Poona, 1929.

Gautama Dharmasūtra, Ānandāśrama ed., 1910.
Kāmandakīya Nītisāra, ed. T. Gaṇapati Śāstrī, Trivandrum Sanskrit Series (T.S.S.), 1912.
Kṛṣiparāśara, ed. & tr. G.P. Majumdar & S.C. Banerji, Calcutta, 1900.
Laghuvarhannīti of Hemacandra, Ahmedabad.
Mahābhārata, 4 vols, B.O.R.I., Pune, 1971.
Mahābhārata, Critical ed. in several vols., B.O.R.I., Poona.
Manusmṛti with the commentary of Kullūka, C.S.S., Varanasi, 1975.
Manusmṛti with the commentary of Medhātithi, Calcutta, 1932-39.
Mārkaṇḍeyapurāṇa, Venkateshvar Press, Bombay.
Matsyapurāṇa, Venkateshvar Press, Bombay.
Mīmāṁsāsūtras with *Śabara-bhāṣya*, A.S.S., Poona.
Nāradasmṛti, ed. J. Jolly, B.I. 1876.
Nītivākyāmṛta of Somadeva, ed. by Pandit Pannalal Soni, Bombay, V.S. 1939.
Parāśarasmṛti, Venkateshwar Press, Bombay, 1958.
Rāmāyaṇa, ed. Vasudeva Sharma, Bombay, 1930.
Rāmāyaṇa in 10 vols. with Hindi tr., Allahabad, 1958.
Rājataraṅgiṇī of Kalhaṇa, 2 vols., ed. & tr. M.A. Stein, *Delhi*, 1961.
Ślokavārtika of Kumārila, Varanasi, 1978.
Smṛti-candrikā of Devaṇṇa Bhaṭṭa, ed. L. Srinivasacharya, Mysore. 1914.
Śukranītisāra, ed. B.D. Basu, Prayag, 1914.
Vaśiṣṭha Dharmasūtra, ed. A. Führer, Bombay, 1916.
Vāyupurāṇa, Venkateshvar Press, Bombay.
Viṣṇudharmottarapurāṇa, Venkateshwar Press, Bombay.
Viṣṇupurāṇa, Gita Press, Gorakhpur.
Yājñavalkyasmṛti with the commentary of Vijñāneśvara, C.S.S., Varanasi, 1967.

III. Kavya

Abhijñānaśākuntalam of Kālidāsa, Nirṇayasāgara Press, (N.S.P.) Bombay.
Bhāsanāṭakacakram, Pune.

Caturbhāṇi, ed. Motichandra, Banaras.
Gāthāsaptaśatī of Hāla, N.S.P., Bombay.
Harṣacaritam of Bāṇa, N.S.P., Bombay.
Kathāsaritsāgara of Somadeva, N.S.P., Bombay, 1930.
Kāvyamīmāṁsā of Rājaśekhara, Baroda, 1934.
Kumārasambhavam of Kālidāsa, N.S.P., Bombay.
Mālatīmādhavam of Bhavbhūti, N.S.P., Bombay.
Mālavikāgnimitram of Kālidāsa, Bombay, 1950.
Mṛcchakaṭikam of Śūdraka, Bombay, 1908.
Mudrārākṣasam of Viśākhadatta, Bombay, 1980.
Naiṣadhīyacarita of Śri-Harṣa, N.S.P., Bombay, 1933.
Nāṭyaśāstram of Bharata with *Abhinava-bhāratī*, G.O.S. Baroda.
Raghuvaṁśa of Kālidāsa, N.S.P., Bombay.
Ratnāvalī of Harṣa, Madras, 1935.
Śiśupālavadham of Māgha, Venkateshvar Press, Bombay.
Uttararāmacaritam of Bhavabhūti, N.S.P., Bombay.
Yaśastilaka Campū, ed. Pt. Śivadatta, Bombay, 1916.

IV. Miscellaneous

Āin-i-Akbarī of Abū'l Fazl, tr. by H.S. Jarrett, B.I., Calcutta.
Ātmatattvaviveka of Udayana, C.S.S., Varanasi.
Bṛhatsamhitā of Varāhamihira with Utpala's commentary, 2 Vols., ed. A.V. Tripathi, Varanasi, 1968.
Kāmasūtra of Vātsyāyana with Jayamaṅgalā commentary, ed. D.L. Goswami, Benares, 1929,
Kāśikā, ed. A.S. Phadake, Benares, 1931.
Kāśikāvṛttiḥ, 6 Vols,, ed D.D. Shastri & K.P. Shukla, Varanasi, 1965-67.
Mahābhāṣya, ed. F. Kielhorn, Poona, 1962.
Mahābhaṣya, Rohtak, 1963.
Mānasāra, ed. P.K. Acharya, Oxford University Press, 1935.
Pañcadaśī, N.S.P., Bombay, 1935.
Praśastapādabhāṣya with *Nyāyakandalī*.
Sāṅgayogadarśana, C.S.S,, Benares.
Vedāntasūtras with *Śāṅkarabhāṣya*

V. Foreign Accounts

Arrian, *History of Alexander and Indica*, tr. Itiff Robson, E., London, New York, 1833.

Beal, S., *Buddhist Records of the Western World*, tr., 2 Vols., London, 1906.

—*Life of Hiuen Tsang* by the Shaman Hwui-li, London, 1911.

Giles, H.A., *The Travels of Fa-Hien or Record of Buddhistic Kingdoms*, Cambridge, 1923.

Herodotus, *History*, (Eng. tr.) Penguin.

Legge, J.H., *Record of the Buddhistic Kingdoms*, being an account of the Chinese monk Fa-hien's travels, Oxford, 1886.

Mc Crindle, J.W., *Ancient India as described by Megasthenese and Arrian*, (Eng. tr.) Calcutta, 1960.

—*Ancient India as Described in Classical Literature*, Westminster, 1901.

—*The Invasion of India by Alexander the Great, as Described by Arrian, Q Curtius, Diodoros, Plutarch and Justin*, New ed. Westminster, 1896.

– *Periplus of the Erythraean Sea*, ed. & tr. Schoff, W.H., New York, London, Bombay, Calcutta, 1912.

Pliny, *Natural History*, tr. Rockhem, H. & others, London, Cambridge Mass., 1942-61.

Ptolemy, *Geography*, ed. & tr. Sterenson, E.I., New York, 1932.

Strabo, *Geography*, tr. Jones, H.L , London, New York, 1917-32.

Takakusu, J.A., *Record of Buddhistic Religion as practised in India and the Malay Archipelago* by I-tsing, Oxford, 1896.

Watters, T., *On Yuan Chwang's Travels in India*, ed. by Rhys Davids, T.W. & Bushell, S.W., 2 Vols, London, 1904, 1905.

VI. Archaeological, Epigraphic and Numismatic

Allan, J., *Catalogue of the Coins of Ancient India in the British Museum*, London, 1936.

—*Catalogue of the Coins of the Gupta Dynasties and of Śaśāṅka, King of Gauḍa* (in the British Museum), London, 1914.

Altekar, A.S., *The Gupta Gold Coins in the Bayana Hoard*, Bombay, 1954.

—*The Coinage of Gupta Empire*, Varanasi, 1957.

Barua, B.M., *Old Brahmi inscriptions* in the Udayigiri and Khaṇḍagiri Caves, Calcutta, 1929.

Cunningham, A., *Coins of Ancient India*, London, 1891.

Fleet, J.P., *Corpus Inscriptionum Indicarum*, (*C.I.I.*) Vol. III, Inscriptions of the Early Gupta Kings, London, 1888.

Gardner, P., *The Coins of the Greek and Scythic Kings of Bactria and India*, London, 1886.

Hultzsch, E., *C.I.I.*, Vol. I., Inscriptions of Aśoka, London, 1925.

Konow, Sten, *C.I.I.*, Vol. II, pt. I, Kharoṣṭhī Inscriptions with the exceptions of those of Aśoka, London, 1929.

Lüders, H., *C.I I.*, Vol. I, pt. II.

C.I I., Vol. II, Bharhut Inscriptions, Ootacamund 1963.

Marshall, J., *Mohenjodaro and the Indus Civilization*, 3 Vols., Delhi, 1973.

—*Taxila*, 3 Vols., Cambridge, 1951.

Marshall, J., Foucher, A., & Majumdar, N.G., *The Monuments of Sāñchī*, 3 Vols , Bhopal.

Mirashi, V.V., *C.I.I.*, Vol. IV, pts., I & II, Inscriptions of Kalchuri-Chedi Era, Ootacamund, 1955.

C.I.I., Vol. V., Inscriptions of the Vākāṭakas, Ootacamund, 1963.

Pandey, R.B., *Aśoka Ke Abhilekha*, Varanasi, V.S. 2022.

Rao, S.R., *Lothal and the Indus Civilization*, London, 1973.

Rapson, E.J., *A Catalogue of the Indian Coins in the British Museum, Coins of the Andhra Dynasty, the Western Kṣtrapas. etc.*, London, 1967 (reprint).

Sharma, G.R., *Excavations at Kauśāmbī 1957-59*, Allahabad, 1960.

Sinha, K.K., *Excavations at Śrāvastī*, 1959.

Sircar, D.C., *Select Inscriptions; Bearing on Indian History and Civilization*, Vol. I, University of Calcutta, 1965.

Smith, V.A., *Catalogue of Coins in the Indian Museum, Calcutta*, Vol. I., Oxford. 1906.

Wheeler, Sir Mortimer, *The Indus Civilization*, Cambridge University Press, 3rd ed., 1968.

Whitehead, R.B., *Catalogue of Coins in the Punjab Museum, Lahore*, Oxford, 1914.

—*Indo-Greek Coins*, Vol. I, Vāranasi, 1971.

Modern Works

Adhya, G.L., *Early Indian Economics*, Bombay, 1966

Agrawal, V.S., *Mārkaṇḍeya Purāṇa—Eka Sāṁskritika Adhyayana*, Allahabad, 1961

—*Matsya Purāṇa—A Study*, Varanasi, 1963

—*Pāṇini Kālīna Bhāratavarṣa*, Patna, V.S. 2012

Aiyangar, K.V.R., *Aspects of Ancient Indian Economic Thought*, Benares. 1934

Ali, S.M., *The Geography of the Purāṇas*, New Delhi, 1966

Allchins, B & R., *The Birth of Indian Civilization*, Middlesex, 1968

Altekar, A.S., *Raṣṭrakūṭas and Their Times*, Poona, 1967

Beni Prasad, *The State in Ancient India*, Allahabad, 1923

—*Theory of Government in Ancient India*, Allahabad, 1968

Benveniste, *Indo-European Language and Society*.

Bhandarker, D.R., *Carmichael Lectures on Ancient Indian Numismatics*, Calcutta, 1921

Bhattacharya, S.C., *Some Aspects of Indian Society*, Calcutta, 1978

Bose, A.N., *Social and Rural Economy of Northern India*, 2 Vols , 1961, 1945

Chandrasekhar, S., *Hungry People and Empty Lands*, Baroda, 1952

Chattopadhyaya, K., *Studies in Vedic and Indo-Iranian Religion & Literature*, Vols. I & II ed. Misra, V.N., Varanasi, 1976.

—*Vedic Religion*, Varanasi, 1975

Chattopadhyaya, S., *Achaemenids and India*, New Delhi, 1974

Chaudhuri, S.B., *Ethnic Settlements in Ancient India*, 1955

Coulburn, R., 'Feudalism, Brahmanism and the Intrusion of Islam upon Indian History' in *Comparative Studies in Society and History*, Vol. X., 1967.

Cunningham. A., *Ancient Geography of India*, *London*, 1971

Coomaraswamy, A.K., *Selected Papers*, ed. Lipsey, 3 Vols.

—*Spiritual Authority and Temporal Power in the Indian Theory of Government*, New Delhi, 1978

Dange, S.A., *India from Primitive Communism to Slavery*, Bombay, 1951

Delbruck, *Indogermaniesche Verwandtschaft-Verhaltnisse*, 1890

Dube, S.N., *Cross Currents in Early Buddhism*, New Delhi, 1980.

Dumezil, *L'ideologie Tripartie des Indo-Europeans*, Brussels, 1958

Elliot H.M. & Dowson, J., *Early Arab Geographers*, pub. Sushil Gupta.

Fairservis, *The Roots of Ancient India*, Chicago, 1975

Felix Gilbert & Stephen R. Graubard, (ed.) *Historical Studies Today*.

Fick, R., *Social Organization in North-East India*, tr. from the German by S. Maitra, Calcutta, 1920.

Foucher, *La Geographieancienne du Gandhara*, BEFEO, 90.

Fung, Yu-Lan, *A History of Chinese Philosophy*, 1937

Gibbon, E., *Decline and Fall of the Roman Empire*, 5th ed., London, 1912

Ghoshal, U.N., *A History of Indian Political Thought*, Oxford 1959

Ghurye, G.S., *Vedic India*, Bombay, 1979

Gonda, J. *Triads in the Veda*.

Gopal, L., *Aspects of History of Agriculture in Ancient India*, Varanasi, 1980
—*The Economic Life of Northern India*, Delhi, 1965
—*The Sukranīti*, Varanasi, 1978
Heeren, *Asiatic Nations.*
Hegel, *Encyclopadia der philosophischen Wissenschaften in Grundrisse*, Hamburg, 1969
Hopkins, E.W., *Social and Military Position of the Ruling Caste in Ancient India*, Varanasi, 2nd reprint, 1972
Jain, J.C., *Life in Ancient India as Depicted in the Jain Canons*, Bombay, 1947
Jayaswal, K.P., *Hindu Polity*, 3rd ed., 1955
Kane, P.V., *History of Dharmaśāstra*, 5 Vols., B.O.R.I., Poona, 1930-62
Karve, I., *Yugānta* (Hindi tr.).
Keith, A.B , *Religion and Philosophy of the Veda and the Upaniṣads*, 2 Vols., 1925
Kosambi, D.D., *The Culture and Civilization of Ancient India*, Delhi, 1977, reprint.
Law, N.N., *Studies in Indian History and Culture*, 1925
Levi, *Pour L'historie du Rāmāyaṇa.*
Lüders, H., *Varuṇa*, 2 Vols., Göttingen, 1951, 1959
Macdonell, A.A., *Vedic Mythology*, Strassburg, 1897
Macdonell, A.A., & Keith, A.B., *Vedic Index of Names and Subjects*, 2 Vols., Delhi, 1967
Mahalingam, T.V., *Readings in South Indian History*, ed. R.S. Ramchandran, New Delhi, 1977
Maitland (tr.) *Gieke' Political Theories of the Middle Ages*
Majumdar, R.C., *Corporate Life in Ancient India*, Calcutta, 1922
Malalsekar, G.D., *Dictionary of Pali Proper Names*, 2 Vols., London, 1960
Malthus, *An Essay on Population*, Everyman's Library ed.
Manfred Mayrhoffer, *Concise Etymological Sanskrit Dictionary*, Medalberg, 1956
Marc Bloch, *Feudal Society*, 1967, reprint
Marx, K., *Capital*, tr. Moore and Aveling, Allen & Unwin, 1949

Misra, G.S.P., *Age of the Vinaya*, Delhi, 1972

Moreland, *India at the Death of Akbar*, London, 1920

Motichandra, *Sārthavāha*, Patna, 1963

Muir, J., *Original Sanskrit Texts*, 5 Vols. New Delhi, 1976, reprint

Mukerjee, Sandhya, *Some Aspects of Social Life in Ancient India*, Allahabad, 1976

Mukerji, R.K., *Aśoka Inscriptions: A Commentary*, Allahabad, 1942

Negi, J.S., *Some Indological Studies*, Vol. I, Allahabad, 1966

Pande. G.C., *Studies in the Origins of Buddhism*, Allahabad, 1957; 3rd ed. Delhi, 1983

—*Śramaṇism and Its Impact on Indian Culture*, L.D. Institute, Ahmedabad

—*The Meaning and Process of Culture*, Agra, 1972

—*Aspects of Jain Political Thought*, Rajasthan Prakrit Bharati, Jaipur, 1983

Pant, A.D. Introduction to Beni Prasad's *Theory of Government in Ancient India*, Allahabad, 1968

Philips, C.F. (ed.) *Historians of India, Pakistan and Ceylon*, Oxford University Press, London, 1967, reprint

Pirenne, M., *History of Europe from the Invasions to the Sixteenth Century*

Possehl, G.L. (ed.), *Ancient Cities of the Indus*, New Delhi, 1972

Pran Nath, *Economic Condition in Ancient India*, Allahabad, 1980, reprint.

Rai, G.K., *Involuntary Labour in Ancient India*, Allahabad, 1981

Rapson, E.J. (ed.) *Cambridge History of India*, Vol. I, Delhi, 1955

Raychaudhuri, H.C. *Studies in the Antiquities of India*, Calcutta, 1960

— *Political History of Ancient India*, Calcutta, 1950

Roy, U.N., *Prāchīna Bhārata Men Nagara Tathā Nagara-Jivana*, Allahabad, 1965

Russel, E.J., *World Population and World Food Supplies*, London, 1954

Rhys Davids, T.W., *Buddhist India*, Delhi, 1971
Rhys Davids & Stede, W., *Pāli-English Dictionary*, P.T.S., London, 1921
Sachau, E.C., *Alberuni's India*, Vol. I, London, 1910
Sethana, K.D., *Karpāsa in Prehistoric India*, New Delhi, 1981
Singh, Baljit, *Population and Food Planning in India*, Bombay, 1947
Singh, M.R., *A Critical Study of the Geographical Data in the Early Purāṇas*, Calcutta, 1972
Shah, K.T., *Ancient Foundations of Economics in India*, Bombay, 1954
Sharma, G.R., *Reh Inscription of Menander and the Indo-Greek Invasion of the Ganga-Valley*, Allahabad, 1980
Sharma, J.P., *Republics in Ancient India*, Leiden, 1968
Sharma, R.S , *Indian Feudalism*, 2nd ed., Delhi, 1980
—*Śūdras in Ancient India*, 2nd ed. Delhi, 1980
Sircar, D.C., *The Emperor and Subordinate Rulers*, Santiniketan, 1982
—(ed.), *Land System and Feudalism in Ancient India*, University of Calcutta, 1966
Smith, V.A., *Early History of India*, 4th ed., Oxford, 1924
Spate, O.H.K., & Hearmonth, A.T.A., *India and Pakistan*, *London*, 1960, reprint
Stein, Burton S. *Peasant State and Society in Medieval South India*, Delhi, 1980
Subbarao, B., *The Personality of India*, Baroda, 1958
Sukthankar, *On the Meaning of the Mahābhārata*, Asiatic Society, 1957
Tarn, W.W., *The Greeks in Bactria and India*, Cambridge, 1951
Tara Chand, *History of the Freedom Movement*, Vol. I
Tod, J., *Annals and Antiquities of Rajasthan*, ed. W. Crooke, 3 Vols., Delhi, 1971, reprint
Toynbee, A., *A Study of History*, London, 1960
Trevelyan, G.M. *Illustrated English Social History*.
Wadia, D.N., *Geology of India*, New Delhi, 1976, reprint
Wagle, N., *Society at the Time of Buddha*, Bombay, 1961

Warmington, E.H., *The Commerce between the Roman Empire and India*, Cambridge, 1928

Wilson, J.A., *The Culture of Ancient Egypt*, Phoenix Books.

Winternitz, M., *History of Indian Literature*, 3 Vols., Delhi

Yadava, B.N.S., *Society and Culture in Northern India in the Twelfth Century*, Allahabad, 1973

Zimmer, H., *Altindisches Leben*, Berlin, 1879

Index